# CREATIVE ARTS PHD COMPASS



*Creative Arts PhD Compass: Essential Insights from Practice to Wellbeing* equips creative arts doctoral candidates with the knowledge and frameworks to navigate their PhD with confidence and clarity, fostering genuine research independence at every stage.

Organised around 11 decalogues, each comprising ten key principles, the book guides scholars through both fully written and creative artefact theses. It can be read sequentially or used as a reference, with individual decalogues consulted as needed. Rather than prescribing universal rules, it offers decision-making frameworks and contextually informed principles that reflect the lived reality of doctoral study, encompassing its technical, practical, existential, emotional, ethical, and intellectual dimensions. The book's structure allows readers to engage with each stage before reaching it, anticipating challenges rather than encountering them unprepared. Extensive suggested reading lists direct scholars to resources suited to their own focus and circumstances.

This book is for anyone considering or currently undertaking a creative arts PhD and is especially valuable for practitioners coming to academic research for the first time. It accompanies the scholar from the decision to enrol through to completion, preparing them for the requirements, challenges, and complexities unique to creative arts doctoral study.

**Sarah Stollman** holds a PhD from the School of Media, Creative Arts and Social Inquiry at Curtin University in Perth, Australia, and lectures in media arts at the University of Technology Sydney. Originally from the United States, Stollman has practised as a production designer, artist, and educator, with research interests spanning doctoral education, screen production, and creative arts inquiry.

# CREATIVE ARTS PHD COMPASS

## Essential Insights from Practice to Wellbeing

*Sarah Stollman*

Routledge
Taylor & Francis Group
LONDON AND NEW YORK

Designed cover image: Circle of care, oil on canvas, illustration by Sarah Stollman

First published 2027
by Routledge
4 Park Square, Milton Park, Abingdon, Oxon OX14 4RN

and by Routledge
605 Third Avenue, New York, NY 10158

*Routledge is an imprint of the Taylor & Francis Group, an informa business*



*British Library Cataloguing-in-Publication Data*
A catalogue record for this book is available from the British Library

ISBN: 978-1-032-95306-9 (hbk)
ISBN: 978-1-032-95307-6 (pbk)
ISBN: 978-1-003-58420-9 (ebk)

DOI: 10.4324/9781003584209

Typeset in Times New Roman
by SPi Technologies India Pvt Ltd (Straive)

# CONTENTS

# FIGURES

# PREFACE

> research is a mysterious adventure that inspires passion and holds many surprises.
>
> Umberto Eco, *How to Write a Thesis*

This book originated from a simple idea: "Ten things I wish I knew before I did my PhD". This remains my shorthand description when people ask about the book. It evolved from notes I kept as a sidebar while researching my own PhD. As I write this book, I sit wondering: how did I end up in doctoral study? What fortuitous moment enabled me to fall into a PhD?

This sort of serendipity had happened before. Having studied and initially worked as an architect, I found myself in New York, not feeling that architecture was my true place. A friend of a friend introduced me to filmmaking and to production design. I had found my place, working in the late 1980s with directors Hal Hartley, Todd Haynes, Kelly Reichardt, David O. Russell, and John Waters. But again, circumstances intervened. I got married, and we moved to Australia. The relationship didn't work out, but I had fallen in love again, this time with a country (and a New Zealander). I stayed.

My growing family paused my practice, leading me towards teaching. First production design and then running a master's degree in filmmaking. While breaking down the various elements of production design for my lectures, my discoveries surprised me. The range of research for a designer can be as broad as your imagination. Areas span from academic-like research of a specific time period to observational research, such as watching people at a mall. A story can be about anything, and your visual interpretation can take you anywhere; thus, research across a career can include everything. I realised how much I love research; it is my favourite part of the job.

While teaching, a screen studies colleague asked me to research the cinematic mode of magical realism to see if any design conventions recur among these films, and if so, could I put together a lecture. I watched a lot of films; the visual approaches had similarities, props reappeared, and repetition in their characteristics was undeniable. I also discovered a magical quality in these objects. I made lists, endless lists. Someone casually suggested I turn the lists into a thesis, and that was it; I fell into doctoral study.

Given my work as a filmmaker, many asked me why I didn't create a work as part of my thesis. Until teaching, I never articulated why I was compelled to meticulously choose an object's qualities or how I communicated their characteristics. But after watching films with this in mind, including my own, I had to answer these questions. I began to understand my own work, but I wanted to explore further. In analysing a range of work by others, I might find answers connected to particular filmmakers, cinematic modes, or contexts that wouldn't have been clear by focusing on my own creative practice. There was another reason that perhaps I didn't admit at the time. I took on the challenge to prove that I, too, could be "academic". Or perhaps I was merely fulfilling my father's Yiddish sing-song refrain about me, *harter beyn*, loosely translated as "dog with a bone".

In the original edition of *How to Write a Thesis*, Umberto Eco recounts a story of his own serendipitous moment during the writing of his thesis.[1] Wandering through a market, hoping to find something to break through a year-long "interpretive stumbling block", he discovered a book written by a little-known author, abbot Vallet. Eco describes this slim book as the "key" that solved his theoretical impasse.[2] In a subsequent edition, he relates how a reviewer doubted the authenticity of his abbot Vallet story, so Eco invited him home to have a look at the book in question.[3] When they opened the book to the page of significance, marked in red, he discovered that Vallet had not made the point cited in his thesis. In fact, it was Eco who made the critical intellectual connection, clearly stimulated by something on that page. He confesses: "I had produced the magic key on my own" (Eco [1977] 2015, xxvi).

## Notes

1 Eco's seminal guide was aimed at students enrolled in the Italian *Laurea* in the humanities. At the time of Eco's writing, this undergraduate degree was considered terminal and required a substantial thesis. However, his advice is equally relevant to postgraduate theses.
2 This story is told in section 4.2.4 "Academic Humility" of Eco's book ([1977] 2015, 142–144).
3 Eco'' 1985 introduction tells this story, which appears in the 2015 English translation. See Eco ([1977] 2015, xxiii–xxvi).

## Reference

Eco, Umberto. (1977) 2015. *How to Write a Thesis*. Translated by Caterina Mongiat Farina and Geoff Farina. MIT Press.

# ACKNOWLEDGEMENTS

I would like to acknowledge and pay my respects to the Elders past, present, and emerging of the Gumbaynggirr people of the Gumbaynggirr nation, the land on which I now reside, which makes up part of the expansive ground that nourishes the first storytellers of this continent, Australia.

***

Thank you to Taylor and Francis, and to my editors, Adam Woods and Georgia Thompson, for their immediate support and encouraging feedback.

Special thanks to Prof. Laura P. Hartman, Professor *Emerita*, DePaul University and Executive Director, The School of Choice, Haiti, for her incomparable editing of this book. She contributed many hours towards giving *CAPC* its spine, considered every word, and was my "human AI".

Many Thanks to Alison Page, descendant of the Dharawal and Yuin people, Professor of Practice in the School of Architecture at University of Technology Sydney, designer, filmmaker, and storyteller for her invaluable feedback on the First Nations material of this book.

Thanks also to my PhD supervisor, Dr. Antonio Traverso, Adjunct Senior Research Fellow; School of Media, Creative Arts and Social Inquiry at Curtin University in Perth, for his constant encouragement and care during my own thesis. Gratitude to Martin, Uma, Louis, and Clara for their love and support, and to my librarian mother and urban planner father for unknowingly developing my love of research.

# INTRODUCTION

My background, my PhD topic, and this book are all grounded in the creative arts; though I initially conceived it as a general guide for doctoral students, I ultimately narrowed the focus to academic research specifically within the field. When I started my thesis research, as a practitioner, I didn't know what questions to ask, and I had considerable ground to cover. Many of the thesis and research resources I encountered were valuable, but they often felt overwhelming and didn't provide a clear introduction to embarking on a PhD. Therefore, my objective was to write a book organised into accessible lists that are easy to use and revisit. This book offers principles and decision-making approaches, not universal rules. Where institutional practices vary, the goal is to equip you to ask informed questions, recognise appropriate boundaries, and make thoughtful decisions within your own context, rather than to provide a single correct procedure. For significant procedural decisions, always check with your university and supervisor.[1]

Rather than outlining every chapter in detail here, I let the concise titles indicate each area of inquiry. Each decalogue (chapter) opens with its own brief contents summary. Some themes recur across decalogues, but each approaches them from a different angle or for a distinct purpose. It is the nature of doctoral research to return to earlier concerns as understanding develops. This is why the book might discuss writing in terms of grammar in one decalogue, process in another, and inspiration in a third.

*Creative Arts PhD Compass* (*CAPC*) treats the PhD process not only as a technical (or practical) one, but also as an existential, emotional, ethical, and intellectual one. The decalogues, therefore, move intentionally from the external structures of this process towards your internal experience. Early decalogues focus on framing, systems, and academic requirements of your thesis, while later decalogues turn increasingly towards practice, identity, emotion, and relational dynamics.[2] This progression reflects the lived reality of doctoral study: before intuition or emotion can become useful

DOI: 10.4324/9781003584209-1

research resources, you must understand the structures within which you are working. Only then can internal experience become a valid research resource rather than a source of confusion or vulnerability.

In this introduction, I trace the origins of *CAPC*, define key terms, describe the thesis forms covered in this book, and suggest how readers might use it most effectively.

## Decalogues of things

After a career as a filmmaker and a production designer, followed by years as a screen production educator, my transition into a PhD programme was profound. I had much to learn in academia. As questions, tasks, and academic practices kept arising, I found myself thinking: "If I had known about this from the beginning, I might have been more aware, more focused, more prepared, less stressed, and wasted less time". Perhaps I wouldn't have been ready to absorb so much information, but I would have liked to have been given the opportunity. The "things" gathered in this book range from practical to theoretical, from philosophical to emotional; all may be encountered during your PhD journey.

A close friend of mine, a professor of business and law, objected to my use of the word *thing* to denote the categories in this book. She has always believed that a more precise term can be found. I accept her argument in many contexts, but I retain the word here for three reasons. First, its very imprecision suits the PhD process effectively. Ideas such as topic, methodology, and argument often begin as indistinct, unfixed, or obscure formations that slowly become embodied into a single, tangible, and significantly precise "thing".

Second, the etymology of the word *thing* illuminates the research process in a suggestive manner. The word derives from the Old English *þing*, meaning "assembly" or "meeting", not simply "that which exists" or "inanimate object". The Gothic term for "time" derives from a word meaning "assembly" or "gathering", a semantic layering that quietly binds the temporal to the spatial (Klein [1971] 2003, 761). Bruno Latour builds on this history when he describes a thing as both an object and "a *gathering*" (2004, 158; emphasis in original). This book covers an assembly of ideas gathered at a particular stage of doctoral work.

My third reason for retaining the word *thing* is more personal. My own thesis argued that cinematic objects hold a magical quality, enabling them to actively motivate character and story.[3] Through this research, I moved from the world of production design into a broader conceptual world of things. My film-based thesis became interdisciplinary, incorporating thing theory, phenomenology, and sensory theory. Unsurprisingly, "things" remained central in the notes I kept for future ideas, including those that eventually became this book.

I have chosen to use the term decalogue from the Greek phrase *hoi deka logoi* ("ten words"), most often associated with The Ten Commandments.[4] I borrow it here to convey structure, as others have before me, including filmmakers Krzysztof Kieślowski for his ten-part series *Dekalog* (1988/2016) and Jan Švankmajer for his own list of artistic principles ([1999] 2008). In *CAPC*, the word signals a recurring form: ten ideas, ten reflections, and ten practices. The book ultimately includes eleven such decalogues, the final one devoted to well being, a fitting reminder that one's research inevitably expands beyond its boundaries and is only possible as long as one is capable of conducting it.

My choice of decalogue pairs with another Greek-derived term central to this book: exegesis, meaning explanation. Brad Haseman suggests that exegesis, if understood simply through its association with textual analysis, might be taken to mean "an explanation or interpretation of the creative or artistic work" (2007, 262).[5] That definition risks reducing the written component of an academic thesis that includes an element of practice to a reiteration of what the work is articulating. Instead, Haseman returns to the Greek roots, *ex-* (out of, from) and *hēgeisthai* (to lead, to guide), to suggest a more active function. The exegesis not only interprets but also leads and guides (262). In this sense, the exegesis accompanies the creative work through the research process rather than merely analysing it after completion.

Together, these terms reflect a deliberate attempt to build conceptual coherence into this book's terminology.

## Defining artefact

The term *artefact*, meaning a "thing" made or manipulated by a human being, is sufficiently comprehensive to encompass existing and future creative art forms. In the context of doctoral research, Linda Candy and Ernest Edmonds establish that this term may refer to a physical object, a time-based work such as a film, or an interactive or performative work whose impact depends on audience engagement (2011, 123). Tara Brabazon similarly uses the word "artifact" broadly (2020b).[6] In doctoral contexts, she stresses that it is the research, not the artwork alone, that is being assessed (78). Using this terminology, the distinction between art produced as part of academic research and independent artistic practice is built into the word itself.

I therefore use the term *artefact* to refer specifically to artistic works that raise ideas, test questions, and present findings to the academic research community. It is not work produced solely as an expression, or for the advancement of an individual artistic practice outside a formal research framework. Artists and designers do conduct research within their practice, though, unlike work created within a thesis, that work is not typically organised around a formally articulated research question or scholarly argument.

## Defining creative artefact

I use the practice-inclusive term, *creative artefact*, to designate theses comprised of a creative work and an exegesis. This phrase is broad enough to describe art as a mode of research without prematurely designating the originating basis: research question, practice, outcome, or other.

This general mode of PhD has a range of forms and names. Many scholars default to the term practice-based; however, this term carries a specific meaning. For example, Candy explains that "[i]f a creative artefact is the *basis* of the contribution to knowledge, the research is practice-*based*" (2006, 1; emphasis in original). In that usage, the research is about practice.

Many terms describing practice-inclusive research trace back to Christopher Frayling's influential distinction between research *into, through*, and *for* art and design, as discussed in his article, "Research in Art and Design" (1993, 5). The first preposition refers to a written analysis of existing works. The second focuses on technique, innovation, and process. The third is research that culminates in an artistic work: the ideas are "*embodied in the artefact*" (5; emphasis in original). *CAPC* categorises all three approaches as belonging within creative arts research, while the latter two sit more specifically within creative artefact research.

Other terms, often used interchangeably, carry distinct but nuanced meanings. The most commonly used, practice-based (as described) and practice-led (the practice generates research questions and methods), are often used interchangeably. Some terms are shaped by geography, some by discipline, and some by the specific role practice plays in the research. Appendix A provides a chart of key creative artefact research terms, their orientations, and principal sources. This mode of doctoral work is continually developing, and I am certain there are more terms not included in the chart.

## Creative arts PhD and creative artefact PhD

Although this book focuses on the "creative arts PhD", many aspects explored may be relevant to doctoral study more broadly. Here, creative arts research encompasses both written creative arts research projects (a fully written thesis) and practice-inclusive projects that combine creative work with an exegesis. When I use the term "creative arts PhD", I refer broadly to doctoral research in the creative arts. When I refer to a written thesis, I mean a fully written doctoral thesis in the creative arts, typically supported by images, as opposed to a thesis that includes a creative artefact.

A "creative artefact PhD" comprises an artefact and an exegesis. The exegesis sits alongside the creative artefact, providing critical context and scholarly analysis; each component informs the other. The artefact itself may serve as a driver, process, outcome, or some combination of these within the research process.[7]

In a limited sense, a creative artefact PhD may be compared with laboratory work, fieldwork, or innovation components in science-based or medicine-based research, insofar as making becomes part of the investigative process.[8] Helga Nowotny observes that the arts and sciences are closer in character than institutionalised notions suggest, because both are driven by curiosity and imagination (2011, xviii). Creative work is guided by an intention: the eventual result emerges only through the experimentation process itself. This unfolding is similarly characteristic of all doctoral study, which reveals the final argument only through the research process.

In short, while the creative arts PhD situates theory at its core, the creative artefact PhD situates both theory and artistic work (that is created within the research, not pre-existing) in parallel relation as inquiry and outcome. This book addresses creative arts research in all its forms, whether fully written analytical research or practice-inclusive research with an artefact integrated within the research process or presented as its outcome.[9]

## How to navigate Creative Arts PhD Compass

This book aims to help you determine whether pursuing a creative arts PhD is the right path for you at this point in your professional or academic career. Beyond this initial purpose, it offers two further and equally significant functions.

First, *CAPC* acts as a companion throughout your PhD journey: clarifying terminology, reminding you to stay organised, and offering guidance on how to move forward, maintain perspective, and remain positive. More broadly, it aims to support not only the technical demands of doctoral research, but also your capacity to find satisfaction and growth in the process itself, and perhaps even to love the experience.

The decalogues move from broad subjects to more specialised elements; their titles are designed to make navigation easy. You need not proceed strictly from beginning to end. The list-based structure allows you to dip into particular sections as issues become timely, then return to others as your research develops.

Second, *CAPC* provides a bibliography that includes cited work and suggested reading that align with each decalogue, pointing you towards deeper engagement in each subject area. General resources on thesis research and completing a PhD are plentiful. The suggested reading includes what I consider the most valuable general PhD resources, and those specific to creative arts research and particular topics covered in each decalogue. This approach extends this book's aim beyond the text itself to serve as a launching pad to more detailed and specific texts.

The book also includes a glossary with focused definitions of terminology used throughout *CAPC*, including foundational concepts that are often misunderstood or used ambiguously within creative arts research environments. I have not included vocabulary already familiar from most bachelor's or master's degrees, but rather terms that, in my experience, often become important only at the doctoral level.

Although I haven't outlined each decalogue in this introduction, I note that the conclusion reflects on my own academic journey, supported by a bibliography highlighting works that unexpectedly and dramatically influenced my research, illustrating how tangential works can become central to your research. My hope is that these eleven decalogues will inspire your own exploration of the sometimes serendipitous, unpredictable, and emergent process of embarking on a creative arts PhD and prepare you for what is to come.

## Notes

1 Throughout *CAPC*, I use the term university to refer to the academic institution in which you are enrolled. While some creative arts PhD programmes are offered through independent art colleges, conservatories, or research institutes, the vast majority are housed within universities. The guidance provided applies across institutional contexts.
2 I use the term thesis to describe the PhD output where other countries use dissertation.
3 See Sarah Stollman (2023).
4 The Ten Commandments as given to Moses by God in the Hebrew Bible (*Exodus* 34:28). For an etymology of decalogue, see Klein ([1971] 2003, 193, 428).
5 I note that though the term practice-based is used within other disciplines, I refer to practice here solely in reference to the creative arts.
6 Brabazon uses the US spelling: artifact. I use the more commonly used UK spelling: artefact.
7 A note regarding the adoption of the fine arts and design PhDs in the US. The Master of Fine Arts (MFA), as a studio practice degree, is still considered by many to be a terminal degree in the US, along with the less frequent fine arts PhD. The equivalent to a creative artefact PhD has had a much slower take-up in the US than the UK, Australia, and some European countries. For discussions on the adoption of this

degree in the US, see James Elkins (2014); Jessica B. Schwarzenbach and Paul M. W. Hackett (2016); Barbara Bolt et al. (2025).

8 For varied opinions on the differences and potential similarities between creative artefact research and laboratory-based scientific research, see Brabazon (2020a, 32), Jenny Wilson (2018, 77) and Candy and Edmonds (2018, 126).

9 Many books and articles over previous decades have debated and analysed this form of academic research (in its various forms). *CAPC* does not revisit whether a creative artefact PhD is a valid form of academic pursuit; it proceeds on the understanding that it is an accepted and significant mode of thesis. Readers interested in the broader debate will find relevant sources in suggested readings.

## References

### *Cited works*

Bolt, Barbara, Maibritt Borgen, Geoff Cox et al. 2025. *Challenging Institutionalization: A Propositional Toolkit for Doing Supervision of Artistic and Practice-based Research*. Sternberg Press.

Brabazon, Tara. 2020a. "The Specificity of Creative-led Theses." In *The Creative PhD: Challenges, Opportunities, Reflection*, edited by Tara Brabazon, Tiffany Lyndall-Knight, and Natalie Hills. Emerald Publishing.

Brabazon, Tara. 2020b. "Strategies for Students Considering a Creative-led Doctorate." In *The Creative PhD: Challenges, Opportunities, Reflection*, edited by Tara Brabazon, Tiffany Lyndall-Knight, and Natalie Hills. Emerald Publishing.

Candy, Linda. 2006. "Practice Based Research: A Guide." *Creativity and Cognition Studios Report*, November V1.0. https://www.creativityandcognition.com/wp-content/uploads/2011/04/PBR-Guide-1.1-2006.pdf

Candy, Linda, and Ernest Edmonds. 2011. "The Role of the Artefact and Frameworks for Practice-Based Research." In *The Routledge Companion to Research in the Arts*, edited by Michael Biggs and Henrik Karlsson. Routledge.

Candy, Linda, and Ernest Edmonds. 2018. "Practice-Based Research in the Creative Arts: Foundations and Futures from the Front Line." *Leonardo* 51(1): 63–69. https://doi.org/10.1162/LEON_a_01471

Elkins, James. 2014. "Introduction." In *Artists with PhDs: On the New Doctoral Degree in Studio Art*, 2nd ed. New Academia Publishing.

Frayling, Christopher. 1993. "Research in Art and Design". *Royal College of Art Research Papers* 1 (1): 1–5. https://researchonline.rca.ac.uk/384/

Haseman, Brad. 2007. "Rupture and Recognition: Identifying the Performative Research Paradigm." In *Practice as Research: Approaches to Creative Arts Enquiry*, edited by Estelle Barrett and Barbara Bolt. I. B. Tauris.

Kieślowski, Krzysztof, dir. *Dekalog*. Telewizja Polska (TVP). 1988/2016. In Polish with English subtitles. 4K Blu-ray.

Klein, Ernest. (1971) 2003. *A Comprehensive Etymological Dictionary of the English Language: Dealing with the Origin of Words and their Sense Development thus Illustrating the History of Civilization and Culture*, unabridged, one-volume edition. Elsevier Science.

Latour, Bruno. 2004. "Why Has Critique Run out of Steam? From Matters of Fact to Matters of Concern." In *Things*, edited by Bill Brown. The University of Chicago Press.

Nowotny, Helga. 2011. "Foreword." In *The Routledge Companion to Research in the Arts*, edited by Michael Biggs and Henrik Karlsson. Routledge.

Schwarzenbach, Jessica B., and Paul M. W. Hackett. 2016. *Transatlantic Reflections on the Practice-Based PhD in Fine Art*. Routledge.

Stollman, Sarah Ellen. 2023. "Magical Props: The Cinematic Object and Narrative Magic in Poetic Realist, Surrealist and Magical Realist Film." PhD diss., Curtin University School of Media, Creative Arts and Social Inquiry. http://hdl.handle.net/20.500.11937/94397

Švankmajer, Jan. (1999) 2008. "Decalogue." In *The Cinema of Jan Švankmajer: Dark Alchemy*, 2nd ed., edited by Peter Hames. Translated by Tereza Stehlíková. Wallflower Press.

Wilson, Jenny. 2018. *Artists in the University: Positioning Artistic Research in Higher Education*. Springer Nature.

## *Suggested reading*

Archer, Bruce, Ken Baynes, and P.H. Roberts. 1992. *The Nature of Research into Design and Technology Education: Design Curriculum Matters Series*, edited by Bruce Archer, Ken Baynes and P.H. Roberts. Loughborough University. https://hdl.handle.net/2134/1687 (See "The Nature of Research in Design and Design Education.")

Batty, Craig, and Arezou Zalipour. 2025. "Research, Practice, Knowledge: Introducing the Creative Knowledges Enabling Framework." *Media Practice and Education* 26(4): 461–477. https://doi.org/10.1080/25741136.2024.2384686

Conomos, John, and Brad Buckley. 2009. "Introduction." In *Rethinking Contemporary Art: The Artist, the PhD and the Academy*, edited by John Conomos and Brad Buckley. The Press of the Nova Scotia College of Art and Design. http://doi.org/10.7202/1066794AR

Elkins, James. 2009. "The Three Configurations of Studio-Art PhDs." In *Mapping Landscapes for Performance as Research: Scholarly Acts and Creative Cartographies*, edited by Shannon Rose Riley and Lynette Hunter. Palgrave Macmillan.

Friedman, Ken, and Jack Ox. 2017. "PhD in Art and Design." *Leonardo* 50(5): 515–519. MIT. http://doi.org/10.1162/LEON_e_01472

Galdon, Fernando, and Ashley Hall. 2022. "(Un)Frayling Design Research in Design Education for the 21Cth". *The Design Journal* 25(6): 915–933. http://doi.org/10.1080/14606925.2022.2112861

Greenspan, Andy. 2021. "9 Things you Should Consider Before Embarking on a PhD." *Elsevier Connect* (blog). June 23. https://www.elsevier.com/en-au/connect/9-things-you-should-consider-before-embarking-on-a-phd

Kosinen, Ilpo. 2009. "Throwing the Baby Out or Taking Practice Seriously." In *Reflections and Connection: On the Relationship Between Creative Production and Academic Research*, edited by Nithikul Nimkulrat and Tim O'Riley. University of Art and Design Helsinki.

Scrivener, Stephen. 2011. "Transformational Practice: on the Place of Material Novelty in Artistic Change." In *The Routledge Companion to Research in the Arts*, edited by Michael Biggs and Henrik Karlsson. Routledge.

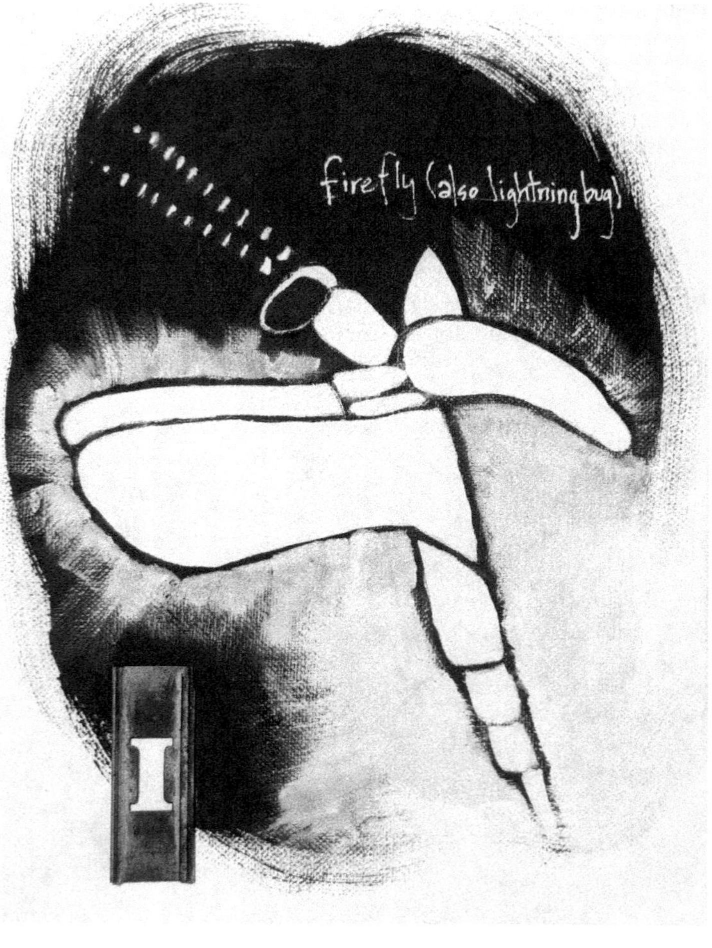
firefly (also lightning bug)
I

# Decalogue I

## TEN PHD THINGS (I WISH I'D KNOWN)

Before committing to a PhD programme, prospective students often face crucial questions that remain unclear even after enrolment. These queries concern the PhD as a structured, finite academic task and the student's place within that space. This opening decalogue addresses initial uncertainties: What motivates you to pursue a PhD? How should you select and refine your research topic? What is a thesis? What research model best suits your work? How does creative work function as research? Who will answer these and other critical questions? Exploring these queries lays the groundwork for everything that follows: from methodology selection to supervisor relationships and issues of wellbeing.

These questions may seem straightforward, but they represent genuine challenges when entering doctoral study. Choosing a topic feels overwhelming when it must be both focused enough to complete and broad enough to sustain years of inquiry. Understanding what distinguishes a thesis from other academic work isn't immediately obvious, particularly in creative fields where research models often continue to evolve.

Beyond initial questions, this decalogue introduces several orienting frameworks for doctoral study in the creative arts, including focus, personal anchors, and the non-linear character of the research process. These ideas are offered as conceptual aids rather than fixed rules. Throughout, I relate them to the standards and expectations that shape original research in creative disciplines.

### 1 Why pursue a PhD?

Scholars pursue a PhD at different life stages and for varied reasons. Some move directly into doctoral study after earlier degrees, while others return after years of professional work. Their motivations may include innovation, deeper knowledge, formal qualification, or some combination of the three.

DOI: 10.4324/9781003584209-2

These different motivations have important implications for topic selection and overall research design. As a rough guide, if you are pursuing doctoral study principally for career advancement, you may find it most efficient to select a topic that you already understand well (approximately 90–95 per cent familiar), leaving a manageable portion for exploration. The remaining 5–10 per cent should be sufficiently challenging to sustain your intellectual engagement throughout the project.

If, instead, your goal is to expand knowledge or explore new terrain, you might choose a topic that is somewhat less familiar, perhaps 70–80 per cent known to you, leaving more room open for discovery. This balance allows for both confidence in your grounding and meaningful growth opportunities. For those aiming for a more streamlined process, building upon prior research, writing, or creative practice can provide a stable foundation for the central argument of the thesis.

Your thesis question emerges from multiple considerations, but the most important is this principle: identify what you want to discover, not what you want to prove. A PhD is an investigation, not a confirmation. At the outset, clarify your thesis's purpose. Is it primarily to demonstrate your research capacity to conduct rigorous research, to make a substantial contribution to the field, or both? This fundamental distinction will shape your research design, methodology, and scope. Available supervisors, potential funding, career goals, and personal circumstances also influence topic selection. Balancing intellectual ambition with realistic constraints ensures your project is both achievable and meaningful.

## 2 Choose a focused topic

Having established why you're pursuing a PhD and what contribution you intend to make, you now face the practical challenge of defining your topic's boundaries. Starting with a concentrated focus serves as insurance against the unknown. Your research likely will take unexpected turns; your analyses or creative practice may reveal unanticipated ideas and concepts. These discoveries demand flexibility and often additional time and resources. A broad topic requiring multiple methodologies can quickly become unmanageable within typical PhD timeframes. In general, it is better to research a narrower topic with greater depth than a broader one with limited depth, both for its potential to yield significant discoveries and for efficient use of time.

Once you've identified a focused research topic, narrow it by half, and then narrow it by half again. Even the most focused topic will expand naturally as your research deepens and as your analytical and creative process unfolds. Writing lists can help. Draft summaries of your initial thoughts, then break them down into component parts, such as key ideas, terms, and concepts. This exercise reveals how many research paths your project might contain, what methodologies you'll need to pursue them, and which ideas are central.

Spreadsheets can also be helpful for this refinement process since they allow you to move terms swiftly between columns and visually indicate connections, hierarchies, and relative significance. This kind of comparison may help clarify your intent and identify where your strongest intellectual investment lies. From there, synthesise your lists into a revised summary of your proposed argument, then narrow the scope by half again. Rather than prematurely constraining your research, this iterative process creates room for unexpected discoveries while maintaining manageable focus.

Umberto Eco offers four useful rules for choosing a thesis topic:

- "The topic should reflect your previous studies and experience".
- "The necessary sources should be materially accessible".
- "The necessary sources should be manageable".
- "You should have some experience with the methodological framework that you will use in the thesis" ([1977]/2015, 7–8).

Eco himself suggests that these rules are obvious; yet they provide an excellent checkpoint. Use them to test whether your refined topic is not only focused but also feasible. With your topic now defined, the challenge shifts from selection to sustained attention.

## 3 Investigate existing research

As you determine your topic, explore published works in your area through library databases, catalogues, thesis repositories, and targeted online searches. Your supervisor and other academics at your university may also help you gauge whether your proposed question remains current and relevant; they may also be aware of forthcoming publications. Conducting this exploratory literature review early is critical as it helps you avoid unintentionally duplicating existing research and positions your study within ongoing conversations in your field.

Establish the practice of checking regularly for new publications, including books, journals, and theses, to maintain awareness of current work in your field. New resources may help you refine your focus, validate your research direction, and clarify what is distinctive about your own approach. This is one of the key functions of the literature review.

Don't be disheartened if you discover a resource that seemingly addresses your research question. Rather than seeing this work as competition, treat it as an opportunity to refine and refocus your approach. While reading the abstract or publisher description may initially cause concern, you will likely find that the publication focuses on different questions, addresses tangentially relevant issues, or treats your topic more briefly than you intend in your own work. This process will help you to clarify the distinctive significance of your question.

In your analysis of any source, consider: What, exactly, are they asking? What is their central argument? Who is the intended audience for these findings? Where can the conclusions be applied? When was this research conducted? Comparing your answers to these questions with your own evolving ideas reveals the distinctive contribution your work will make and lays the foundation for a strong, original thesis argument.

## 4 A thesis is an assignment

Remember that your thesis is fundamentally an assignment, albeit one operating on a much larger and more complex scale than essays written in earlier degrees. This simple reframing is more than semantic; it serves as a critical anchor when your research threatens to expand endlessly or become over-complicated. No matter how emergent or original your ideas may be, your thesis ultimately still must satisfy specific academic requirements and remain within defined parameters. While framing your thesis as an assignment may seem reductive, it offers valuable perspective during challenging moments.

To illustrate this concept, consider your primary audience. Not the broader scholarly community, who may later read and cite your work, but your thesis committee and examiners. These individuals will read, review, and assess your work, determining whether you meet the requirements for the degree: they expect clear academic writing, coherent argumentation, and adherence to established conventions. Originality lies in your contribution to knowledge, not in unconventional structure or presentation. What matters most is clearly articulating your original research findings within given conventions.

Viewing your thesis as an assignment with specific parameters enables you to work through feedback more effectively, recognising what belongs in this project and what represents valuable material for your ongoing scholarly career. A strong PhD thesis need not redefine the field; it must make a meaningful and well-supported contribution within its agreed scope. What is critical is remembering the parameters within which you are working.

## 5 Many thesis models exist

Discuss potential thesis formats with your supervisor early in the process. Determine which model best suits your research while also meeting your university's requirements and expectations. Preferred thesis formats vary across academic fields, universities, and countries. In the creative arts, the most common thesis structures are:

- **Fully written document:** a single monograph.
- **Creative artefact:** a creative work accompanied by an exegesis or critical commentary.

Less common in this field are:

- **Thesis by publication:** compilation of peer-reviewed articles completed during candidature.
- **Book-style thesis:** work formatted for commercial publication.

New models emerge regularly, though institutional adoption can be slow. Whatever model you select, familiarise yourself thoroughly with its structure and content requirements and ensure that your proposed work aligns with these expectations.

One practical benefit of understanding thesis models early is that structural conventions are easier to anticipate, helping you make early practical decisions about when to write or create each component. Meanwhile, familiarise yourself with your programme's general expectations for your chosen thesis model. This foundational knowledge provides a framework for early planning without constraining the creativity of your evolving research.

## 6 Academic research or independent practice?

If you are undertaking creative artefact research, it is important to ask yourself why. As an arts practitioner or artist, why pursue a project whose primary goal is not the creation of an artwork itself, but rather the generation of original knowledge through creative research?

I encountered a student at a recent conference who explained that they were completing a PhD as a means to write a novel. They had received a scholarship that provided time to write and space at the university. They had no interest in developing a research question through their creative process and approach to writing, which suggested that they fundamentally misunderstood the purpose of this doctoral mode. As discussed, the exegesis, the written component that frames, interrogates, and contextualises the creative work, is not an add-on or bureaucratic hurdle, but a core part of the research. As Ariella Van Luyn and Robyn Glade-Wright observe, some candidates perceive the exegesis as "a difficult thing I had to do in order to pass" (2018, 5). This misconception weakens the intellectual and methodological integrity of the creative artefact model.

In this doctoral framework, the creative artefact functions as a research tool: a vehicle for testing ideas, formulating questions, and articulating new insights. Theoretically, it is evaluated not for its artistic merit or commercial value alone, but for the originality and clarity of its contribution to knowledge. The artefact and the exegesis exist in interdependent dialogue: each informing and refining the other.

In practice, many creative artefacts from PhD theses are presented as stand-alone pieces, with minimal attention to the accompanying exegesis.[1] This tendency can undermine the purpose of pursuing research alongside the creation of artistic work, or at least dilute it. Assessment practices do vary across universities. Determine how your programme positions the exegesis and its intended relationship to the completed work.

Maintain detailed notes throughout your creative process from the start, allowing your exegesis to develop organically from your practice. This sustained relationship between work and exegesis is what distinguishes a creative artefact PhD from independent creative work.

## 7 Finding your own answers

In contrast to other levels of study, PhD research requires you to assume full responsibility for your intellectual development: for understanding information, interpreting findings, and developing concepts. No one, including your supervisor, will hand you ready-made answers to your research questions. A central aim of your doctoral study is to cultivate your ability to generate knowledge through inquiry, reflection, and experimentation. Moreover, if your research is genuinely original, your supervisor may not have ready answers to your specific questions. Instead, supervisors typically reflect questions to you; their role is to encourage you to develop answers through your own investigation.

Supervisors may guide this process in several ways: suggesting readings and related research areas, reframing questions to stimulate deeper thought, or recommending short exploratory papers on loosely related but relevant topics. This indirect guidance may feel isolating or frustrating, but it is ultimately empowering. It develops the habits of independent research and critical thinking that doctoral research demands.

Tim Ingold captures this process powerfully: "Know for yourself!" (2013, 1; emphasis in original). Describing his experience working as a young man with the Saami people in Finland, Ingold recounts how he, when left to complete a task on his own, learned a significant lesson: "[t]o know things you have to grow into them, and let them grow in you, so that they become a part of who you are" (1). When told what to do, deep learning doesn't happen. True learning arises when you experience the discovery of knowledge; that learning stays with you.

Returning to your research after grappling with questions independently, you emerge with greater confidence to advance your argument. Tangential research directions suggested by your supervisor often prove invaluable, enriching both your research and argument. Learning to find your own answers is not merely a pedagogical exercise; it is fundamental to becoming an independent scholar capable of making original contributions to your field. Those guiding your research will nudge you towards solutions; however, only your diligent research and critical thinking will achieve meaningful outcomes.

## 8 Refocus, refocus, refocus

You've chosen your topic with care and narrowed it deliberately. Now the real challenge emerges: sustaining that focus over the months and years of research. If you find exciting new research or have ground-breaking ideas, remind yourself of your goal, the thesis argument. If the new material lies beyond this frame, leave it for a later publication. Remember, the thesis has defined parameters and outcomes. When you feel overwhelmed with ideas or their scope, pause, breathe deeply, and refocus on your aims.

Throughout your PhD, you'll develop discernment. You will gain the ability to recognise which ideas support your thesis and which, however brilliant, are tangential. Maintain a document (titled "future ideas" or similar) as a designated space for capturing thoughts, findings, and references that may not directly align with your current research. This practice prevents valuable ideas from being lost or forgotten and creates a useful resource for future proposals. Keep the document well-organised and searchable. Maintaining this perspective helps you to regularly distinguish between ideas central to your thesis and those better suited to future projects.

It is also worth noting that your thesis argument may shift. When changes occur, the "future ideas" document may contain ideas relevant to your revised direction. Returning to this document allows you to recover and develop earlier thoughts without relying on memory alone. This practice requires minimal time but pays significant dividends. Recording, returning, and reassessing ideas becomes part of the recurring discipline of maintaining focus within an evolving project. Such notation also allows you to quickly refocus.

You will rarely regret taking a brief moment to record an idea, but you may regret losing one.

## 9 Finding a cue as your anchor

Whether visual or linguistic, a conceptual cue or metaphor can anchor you when you feel overwhelmed or uninspired, reminding you of your goals and reigniting motivation.

When I need inspiration, I close my eyes briefly and imagine a firefly (lightning bug), drawing from its resilience, adaptability, and magic. This insect flies at night, beautifully radiating yellow light intermittently. As a group, the sky looks as if filled with flying stars. However, fireflies don't emit light constantly, and they spend most of their lives in the dark. Their motivation to "light up" evolves across their life cycle: as a warning, to attract mates, and sometimes for unknown reasons.

This metaphor reminds me that motivation evolves throughout scholarly development. As you progress in your studies, what inspires you shifts based on changing circumstances and questions. The firefly's intermittent illumination always returns, mirroring the process of research itself. Clarity doesn't always arrive conveniently at your desk. Even while taking a break, the brain continues processing in the background. You may be preparing dinner, playing football, or walking the dog, and unexpectedly "light up", finding clarity in a previously muddled concept.

Your cue will be different from mine. It could be a phrase, image, or memory that grounds you. The key is finding something meaningful that reconnects you to your purpose when motivation wanes. Helen Sword captures this idea well, describing metaphors as "the stories that we tell ourselves about our relationship to the world. By changing our metaphors, we can change our stories" (2017, 191). Consider what metaphor might be relevant to your approach to academic study. It might emerge from nature, art, or childhood experience. What matters is that it resonates with you personally. This anchor becomes a quiet companion, reminding you why your work matters even when the path feels uncertain.[2]

## 10 Time is like a spiral

At some point, you will devise a timetable for your PhD, scheduling deadlines, presentations, meetings, and other critical dates. This timetable implies that the PhD process is linear. In the broadest sense, its progression does appear linear: proposal, research, writing and making, submission, examination, acceptance, completion. However, what transpires between those milestones is neither strictly linear nor truly circular. If the process were circular, you would continually cycle through the same steps, each time perhaps at increasingly higher levels. This doctoral research process more closely mimics the movement of a spiral.

As applied to research, the spiral captures the way ideas are revisited from new positions of understanding by winding through thoughts, oscillating back and forth, sometimes returning to earlier concepts before advancing.[3] You go back to ideas, integrate them with new findings, and gather insights from different points along the spiral: all in pursuit of answering your thesis question. This process can feel frustrating. When you revisit material you thought you had finished, it may seem as though you are simply moving in circles, or worse, regressing.

However, when you understand the process as a spiral rather than a circle, you can recognise its forward momentum, revealing the iterative nature of the research process. Each return to earlier material happens at a new level of understanding. My supervisor once suggested that I write a brief essay on an aspect of my topic, not for inclusion in my thesis, but to deepen my knowledge. At first, it seemed like a diversion. In fact, it strengthened my confidence and understanding of my main topic. What feels like regression is actually progression along a three-dimensional path towards your goal, and each return occurs at a higher level of insight. You are not standing still; you are advancing by revisiting.

This motion is evident in the Australian Indigenous way of thinking, Songlines. Lynne Kelly describes Songlines as a dynamic state rather than one of stasis, referring to the motion of time through cycles and spirals: "when you look behind you, you see the future in your footprints" (2020, 80). This image of spiralling movement—around, forward, backward, and through—resonates with the research spiral described here.

## Notes

1 See Tara Brabazon et al. (2020) for a discussion on the misunderstood nature of the exegesis.
2 For other applications of metaphor in research, see Nerida Blair (2019, 203–223) on her research approach, "Lilyology", and Barbara Kamler and Pat Thomson (2014, 34–36).
3 After developing this metaphor, I discovered that Baz Kershaw and Helen Nicholson use a similar framework, describing the learning process as "not linear but spiral" (2011, 1).

## References

### *Cited Works*

Blair, Nerida. 2019. "Lilyology as a Transformative Framework for Decolonizing Ethical Spaces within the Academy." In *Decolonizing Research: Indigenous Storywork as Methodology*, edited by Jo-ann Archibald Q'um Q'um Xiiem, Jenny Bol Jun Lee-Morgan, and Jason De Santolo. Zed Books.

Brabazon, Tara Tiffany Lyndall-Knight, and Natalie Hills, eds. 2020. *The Creative PhD: Challenges, Opportunities, Reflection*. Emerald Publishing.

Eco, Umberto. 1977/2015. *How to Write a Thesis*. Translated by Caterina Mongiat Farina and Geoff Farina. MIT Press.

Ingold, Tim. 2013. *Making: Anthropology, Archaeology, Art and Architecture*. Routledge.

Kamler, Barbara, and Pat Thomson. 2014. *Helping Doctoral Students Write*, 2nd ed. Routledge.

Kelly, Lynne. 2020. "Songlines Spiral Forever." In *Songlines: Power and Promise*, by Margot Neale and Lynne Kelly. Thames and Hudson Australia.

Kershaw, Baz, and Helen Nicholson. 2011. "Introduction: Doing Methods Creatively." In *Research Methods in Theatre and Performance*, edited by Baz Kershaw and Helen Nicholson. Edinburgh University Press.

Sword, Helen. 2017. *Air & Light & Time & Space: How Successful Academics Write*. Harvard University Press.

Van Luyn, Ariella, and Robyn Glade-Wright. 2018. "Changing Tertiary Landscapes for the Artist-Academic: Towards a Framework for Nurturing Creative Arts research beyond the PhD." In *Climates of Change*, edited by Patrick Allington, Piri Eddy, and Melanie Pryor. Special issue, Text 22 (51): 1–14. https://doi.org/10.52086/001c.25586

### *Suggested Reading*

Barrett, Estelle, and Barbara Bolt. 2007. *Practice as Research: Approaches to Creative Arts Enquiry*. I. B. Tauris.

Bell, Desmond. 2018. "The Primacy of Practice: Establishing the Terms of Reference of Creative Arts and Media Research." In *Screen Production Research: Creative Practice as a Mode of Enquiry*, edited by Craig Batty and Susan Kerrigan. Palgrave Macmillan.

Burarrwaŋa, Laklak, Ritjilili Ganambarr, Merrkiyawuy Ganambarr-Stubbs et al. (Gay'wu Group of Women). 2019. *Songspirals: Sharing Women's Wisdom of Country Through Songlines*. Allen and Unwin.

Dijkgraaf, Robbert. 2007. "Interview: Robbert Dijkgraaf." Interview by Annette W. Balkema and Henk Slager. Mahkuzine, Winter 2: 31–37.

Glade-Wright, Robyn, and Elizabeth A. Smyth. 2023. "Metaphors for Doctoral Research: Fundamental Tenets and Creative Courage." *Text* 27 (1): 1–14. https://doi.org/10.52086/001c.75235

Guccione, Kay, and Jerry Wellington. 2017. *Taking Control of Writing Your Thesis: A Guide to Get You to the End*. Bloomsbury Academic.

Jones, Timothy Emlyn. 2006. "A Method of Search for Reality: Research and Research Degrees in Art and Design." In *Thinking Through Art: Reflections on Art as Research*, edited by Katy Mcleod and Lin Holdridge. Routledge.

Jones, Timothy Emlyn. 2013. "Interview with Dr. Timothy Emlyn Jones (Dean, Burren College of Art; Ireland)." Interview by Emma Lough. *Arts as Cultural Diplomacy*, April 29, 2013. https://artsasculturaldiplomacy.wordpress.com/2013/04/29/dr-timothy-emlyn-jones/

Kara, Helen. 2020. *Creative Research Methods: A Practical Guide*, 2nd ed. Bristol University Press. (See Chap. 1, "Introducing Creative Research")

Sullivan, Graeme. 2010. *Art Practice as Research: Inquiry in Visual Arts*, 2nd ed. SAGE Publications.

Vincent, Alison. 2019. "Who Am I, Where Am I Going on This Journey, and Why?" In *The Doctoral Experience: Student Stories from the Creative Arts and Humanities*, edited by Donna Lee Brien, Craig Batty, Elizabeth Ellison, and Alison Owens. Palgrave Macmillan.

Wilson, Mick. 2014. "Between Apparatus and Ethos: On Building a Research Pedagogy in the Arts." In *Artists with PhDs: On the New Doctoral Degree in Studio Art*, 2nd ed., edited by James Elkins. New Academia Publishing.

a process, not a known point
II

# Decalogue II

## TEN RESEARCH THINGS

This decalogue addresses the core aspect of doctoral work: research. It establishes what research means in a creative arts context, how creative practice functions as research, and what distinguishes academic research from independent artistic practice. Understanding these foundational concepts will help you to articulate your approach clearly and position your creative practice within scholarly frameworks.

What, actually, is research? What does it mean to conduct academic research in the creative arts? Answers to these questions may seem obvious, but creative arts research operates at a unique intersection: it demands the rigour and systematic inquiry of traditional scholarship while embracing the exploratory, embodied, and emergent qualities of artistic practice. This dual nature initially can seem contradictory.

Creative artefact research is particularly misunderstood. Some view it simply as "art with an essay attached". Others worry that it diminishes artistic practice by forcing it into academic frameworks. Neither view is helpful. Creative artefact research generates original knowledge through processes that neither independent art practice nor conventional scholarly research can fully replicate on their own. Whether you pursue a written thesis analysing existing work or a creative artefact thesis combining artefact and exegesis, you are engaged in scholarly inquiry that contributes to knowledge in your field.

The creative artefact is not decoration or simply illustrative; it is a site of research, a vehicle for generating insight, and a means of communicating findings that resist reduction to text alone. It contextualises, interrogates, and articulates the knowledge generated through your creative work. Together, artefact and exegesis constitute research.

I begin with fundamental definitions and follow with the distinctive characteristics of creative arts research. One aim of this discussion is to dissolve the false assumption that your identity as a researcher is separate from or opposed to your artistic practice. Research is creative. Creative practice, when conducted systematically to generate shareable knowledge, is academic research.

DOI: 10.4324/9781003584209-3

## 1 What is academic research?

What are the differences between research generally, in academia, in the creative arts, and as a creative artefact? At the level of basic definitions already introduced, the distinctions are not absolute. Instead, they lie in the subject or object studied, the questions asked, the research paradigms used, the methodology, and the role that practice may play in generating knowledge.

Most definitions of academic research include some combination of the following language: generating new knowledge, systematic inquiry, methodological rigour, a specific research question, contribution to a discipline, investigation, exacting academic standards, originality, scholarship, public, or shareable outcomes.

Let's consider how various scholarly works articulate this shared foundation:

- **In general:** "Systematic investigation or inquiry aimed at contributing to knowledge of a theory, topic, etc., by careful consideration, observation, or study of a subject" (*Oxford English Dictionary* 2025).
- **In academic research:** "the art of research" is an opportunity to learn "to reflect on the origins of theories and concepts, how to theorise, how to mesh theory with practice, and how to prioritise and organise a vast quantity of material into a readable text within a restricted period of time" (Grix 2022, 5).
- **In creative artefact research:** "the imaginative and intellectual work undertaken by artists is a form of research that has the potential to make important contributions to contemporary art, culture, and education in the broadest possible sense". (Sullivan 2010, 88).[1]

Although these definitions are from different disciplinary perspectives, they share key elements. Research is a systematic inquiry that generates new knowledge, follows rigorous methodology, and makes its findings public. Where a creative artefact is involved, this work itself can be a site of inquiry and a vehicle for communicating research findings that, alongside the exegesis, articulate research questions, methodologies, and contributions to knowledge.

I therefore offer an inclusive academic definition: Creative arts research is a structured investigation of a formulated question that generates new knowledge and contributes to scholarly discussion in the field, whether through a written thesis or through the creation of an artefact and exegesis. This expansion recognises that knowledge generation can emerge through multiple modes of inquiry while maintaining the fundamental scholarly standards that characterise academic research.

This definition also clarifies what research in an academic context is not: unstructured inquiry where insights remain private, tacit, or intelligible only to the individual practitioner. Research embedded in artistic practice happens both intentionally and organically through making and generates valuable understanding of technique, context, and process. This research directly benefits the creator and their evolving practice, but remains implicit unless it is systematically framed, documented, and communicated. For instance, an artist who conducts research by testing different techniques of paint application may gain insight into their practice; however, unless that inquiry is systematically framed and communicated to others, it is not academic research.

Research conducted through creative practice as part of doctoral study ensures that outcomes are publicly accessible. Documentation, including the exegesis and creative artefact, articulates the research process, methodologies, and findings in forms that others can engage with and build upon. This sharing allows creative practice to operate as scholarly research rather than private inquiry alone.

## 2 What is creative arts research?

In the previous section, I discussed how academic research shares characteristics across fields and proposed a definition of creative arts research that corresponds to general definitions. Now you may ask, how does creative arts research differ from other fields of research? The distinction lies in how it engages with its objects of study. Bruno Latour observes that "the same word *thing* designates matters of fact and matters of concern" (2004, 158; emphasis in original). While some fields focus primarily on matters of fact (such as outcomes from empirical data and measurable properties), creative arts research addresses matters of fact and matters of concern simultaneously: the material reality of artworks and their cultural, emotional, and existential significance.

Henk Borgdorff articulates this idea when he suggests that arts research "focuses not just on what is enacted in creative processes and embodied in art products, but it also engages with who we are and where we stand" (2011, 51). Creative arts research, whether examining existing works or creating new ones, investigates form, technique, and material properties while also exploring questions of meaning, representation, identity, and cultural value.

Academic analysis of artwork typically draws on broader theoretical frameworks such as philosophy, culture, sociology, and psychology, disciplines that explore what it is to be human. The intention, meaning, and affect of a work of art, when questioned and analysed, often serve as a basis for research inquiry in the creative arts. This dual focus on artistic practice (whether existing or created as part of research) and theoretical analysis is what differentiates creative arts research from many other areas of scholarly inquiry.

The sense of the research process as a spiral is especially visible in creative artefact research as the processes of creation, reflection, analysis, and writing are both concurrent and reflexive. Similarly, in a written creative arts thesis, the researcher moves back and forth between experiencing a work (through viewing, reading, and hearing) and analysing its relation to their research question. Desmond Bell calls this process "'discovery-led' rather than hypothesis-driven" (2019, 16), suggesting that discovery, through making or experiencing, drives the formulation of research questions in creative arts rather than hypotheses based on existing knowledge.

Borgdorff similarly summarises that artistic research "creates room for that which is unthought, that which is unexpected: the idea that all things could be different" (2012, 71). Creative research encourages openness to emergence and surprise, characterised by making, intuition, and experiential engagement. It may appear less linear than hypothesis-driven models, but its rigour lies in how carefully the researcher documents, reflects on, and interprets those emergent processes. Borgdorff suggests this research may be more in line with participatory action than humanities research, as "the experimental practice of creating and performing pervades the research at every turn" (2012, 48). This engagement with exploratory investigation is at the heart of creative arts research.

Significantly, the research process itself mirrors its subject matter: creative work. Just as creative practice involves iterative exploration, unexpected discovery, and knowledge that emerges through doing, so too can creative research. The researcher, like the artist, works with materials, ideas, and contexts that reveal insight through engagement rather than observation alone. This mirroring raises the question of creativity's role in research. For creative arts researchers, the concept that artefact research is itself creative is a more natural step than for researchers in other fields, as they are already accustomed to working through exploration, innovation, and new processes. It is precisely this shared creativity between artistic practice and academic inquiry that explains why this form of research is seen as a mismatch to some. However, as Louise Ravelli et al. explain: "It is not that the visual and performing arts are 'unsettled'. Rather, it is that they 'do' research in a different and unfamiliar way" (2021, 222). This difference should not be mistaken for a lack of rigour.

## 3 Research is creative

Research is creative, and as Ken Friedman writes: "Research is also an art" (2014, 257). What does it mean to be creative as a researcher? The adjective "creative" suggests originality, innovation, and a capacity to see new possibilities or connections that lead to a unique and useful idea, theory, or artefact. In this sense, research in all fields can be deemed creative.

This point is particularly significant in creative artefact research, where art practitioners entering academic research can sometimes become disengaged from the academic writing process. They may focus substantially on the "creative" making part and complete the exegesis because "they have to". Recognising research itself as creative dissolves this false separation. As discussed earlier, academic analysis, theoretical investigation, and reflective writing become part of the creative process rather than bureaucratic requirements.

Creativity drives both artefact production and knowledge generation through investigation. Recognising and articulating links between the making, meaning, theory, and practice elements of creative art is itself a creative act. Keeping this idea in mind, the seeming chasm between an examined artefact and thesis, or the making of an artefact and exegesis, vanishes. This framework allows healthy interdependence between research and output, each strengthening the other.

So, how to start? The next four sections address the core elements present in the definition of research offered earlier in this decalogue: investigation, formulated question, new knowledge, and scholarly discussion. These features recur across most research definitions and help clarify what doctoral inquiry requires.

## 4 Research is an investigation

Research is an investigation that rambles through structured exploration. Along the way, ideas are devoured, savoured, rejected, and set aside. This exploratory process sits inside a rigid framework that follows articulated aims and outcomes. While the timetable of this process appears highly linear (start-research/write-make/complete-submit), the actual experience is the spiral described earlier, pulling you in and out, up and down. Eelko K.R.E. Huizingh describes research projects as "adventure trips" (2023, 2), suggesting the presence of a plan that is continually, and happily, interrupted by surprises, unknowns, and revelations. For instance, from the outset, you may have a preliminary notion of resources relevant to your research. When you start to explore these resources, you may suddenly find yourself reading something unexpected, unknown, and initially irrelevant. You can instigate this journey intentionally or allow it to unfold randomly. "Snowballing", a technique of discovering new resources through the bibliographies of publications foundational to your work, will lead you to other relevant sources.[2]

Follow your instinct when something captures your attention, even when it may not seem relevant on the surface. Pick up that random book in the library that catches your eye, read that article that comes up in a search because you changed your terms, or visit an art exhibit that triggers a new perspective. Research is a process, not a known point.

For example, a filmmaker researching visual language in documentary might begin by examining existing theoretical frameworks, then discover through their own practice how design choices contribute to a documentary's visual approach. Design happens whether planned in advance or emerging during filming, whether by a dedicated production designer or by the director and cinematographer. Following this new understanding leads them to interview other documentary makers, discovering a gap in the literature about the operation of design. This approach wasn't exactly their original plan, but investigation means following where the evidence leads.

Your exploration may also guide you to unique research approaches that become critical in your process. For example, research using non-representational theory (NRT) focuses on embodied experience rather than representation or meaning. It explores sensory, affective, or temporal dimensions that shift over time. In the creative arts, this research perspective may naturally allow an exploration of affect as concerns the artist, performer, and audience. Coming across this approach may occur through open exploration that may ultimately shape the direction of your research.

## 5 Formulating your research question

Your research question will guide your investigation, but it will be adjusted, focused, and refined along the way. It demands enough initial flexibility to allow its shape to form. Too much rigidity will not allow your question the space required to develop beyond initial parameters, while too little structure can leave the project shapeless. The challenge is to hold the question firmly enough to guide inquiry while allowing it room to mature. Surprising explorations, findings, and resources will push and stretch you and your question continuously until it settles and solidifies around your true aim.

Huizingh offers a straightforward method in evaluating potential questions by asking the what, the why, the conceptual how, and the practical how (2023, 38).[3] Within this framework, the specific questions you ask will help determine your thesis inquiry, which might include: What am I fascinated by? Why is this research valuable? How will a theoretical perspective guide the research? How will I use methods and tools to analyse and produce elements of research? This method helps you not simply find a question, but one that is researchable, and most critically, one you understand yourself.

For example, you may come up with a question that is too broad: "How does colour affect viewers?" A narrower question leads to an opportunity for deeper investigation, such as: "What associative factors contribute to a viewer's emotional responses to colour in paintings?" The second query specifies the context, the artefact mode, the variables being investigated, and the method of inquiry.

Huizingh's tool is particularly useful when you feel overwhelmed and unsure of the next step in your exploration. Returning to these guiding questions helps clarify your direction and the structure of your argument.

## 6 Generating new knowledge

The contribution of new knowledge is a critical factor in completing any thesis. This expectation distinguishes doctoral research from earlier academic study. Although you cannot guarantee from the outset that your project will lead to new knowledge, you can design a question that creates the conditions for originality. In the creative arts, a compelling question might connect disciplines in atypical ways, consider untested techniques of producing art using experimental methods, or analyse artefacts, existing or new. Your research process uncovers knowledge as you proceed, and your question solidifies as the direction of new knowledge becomes clear. Helga Nowotny describes research as "the curiosity-driven production of new knowledge" (2011, xix). This drive of inquiry is inextricable from the doctoral process.

That curiosity extends beyond academic convention. As Ralph Waldo Emerson observes: "Skill to do comes of doing; knowledge comes by eyes always open, and working hands; and there is no knowledge that is not power" (1870, 303). Knowledge allows a level of expertise, and these key elements—curiosity, perseverance, and discovery through experience—are also those of successful research.

New knowledge is not intended to be solely new to you, as a researcher, but new to the larger discussion in your field, topic, and question. Linda Candy and Ernest Edmonds point out that new knowledge "is expected to have two characteristics: first that it is shared and second that it can be verified or challenged" (2011, 121). I would add a third quality, perhaps assumed, that it is indeed unique within the discourse in your area of research.

New knowledge might emerge, for example, from discovering that the type, amount, or colour of patina on a bronze sculpture affects how a viewer relates to the authenticity and import of the work. This finding may lead to the development of a study of emotional human reaction to a range of patina outside of an artistic context. The knowledge is new not because bronze has never been studied, but because the relationship between patina and viewer affect hasn't been systematically investigated and documented.

Whether ideas and theories constitute new knowledge can be confirmed through your literature review. This critical process requires broad-based research to catch cross-disciplinary discourse, as well as deep research to be fully informed of discussions in your area on your topic. In creative artefact research, it is crucial to be aware of similar work being produced both within and outside academia. Originality depends on being as well-informed as possible about what already exists. As Sullivan observes: "fresh perspectives as much as prior knowledge are determinants in creating and constructing new knowledge" (2011, 100). Essentially, you are responsible for knowing what exists and what could be considered new knowledge.

## 7 Contributing to scholarly discussion

Your research findings will not remain in the little intimate bubble of your computer files, hard drives, and the cloud; they will enter the scholarly domain. Your research thesis will eventually be published, and, prior to that, findings may be disseminated through presentations, papers, discussions, and informal exchanges. Sharing knowledge with colleagues, peers, and your supervisor may seem daunting as a researcher, writer, or practitioner accustomed to working alone at the computer or in the studio.

Your research might contribute to scholarly discussion by challenging existing assumptions, filling a gap, or connecting previously separate conversations. You're not working in isolation; you are entering and extending what others in the field have explored.

Milestone presentations, typically required by your university, help you to articulate your research question and ideas. To prepare for mine, I focused on developing clarity in my expression. I found it useful to explain my question, topic, and inquiry to colleagues, friends, and family with no background in the field. If they understood my explanations, I was confident that my communication was clear. I also read my draft abstract and thesis question aloud. Hearing my words rather than reading them on screen restored critical distance.

Acknowledge the significance of your research contribution. As part of your study, learn to take ownership of your topic and be confident in introducing, discussing, and debating your ideas. Your contribution to scholarly discussion may come primarily through published, exhibited, or performed work. As Carole Gray and Julian Malins explain: "All formal research contributions constitute 'a brick in the wall' of the knowledge base of the discipline" (2016, 177). Given that your contribution takes these public forms, there is a high probability that you will exchange aspects of your findings online, at conferences, at public venues, or through inquiries. The process of academic research does not end at submission. Be prepared.

## 8 Interdisciplinary opportunities

Whether you intend it or not, your research may become interdisciplinary. In the creative arts, it almost certainly will. This approach to research can also be referred to as multidisciplinary, transdisciplinary, or cross-disciplinary; the meanings of these terms, though related, are not synonymous.[4] As described earlier, my thesis branched out into other disciplines in ways I hadn't anticipated. By staying open to unfamiliar theory early in the process, my ideas formed unexpected connections across fields.

Trust yourself to delve into ideas that may not be in your area of expertise. This exploration may make you feel unconfident, or even out of your depth. However, this discomfort is normal, pushes you along in your research, and may reveal interdisciplinary links from your new knowledge. According to Candy et al., "interdisciplinary approaches [...] can enhance understanding and become a rich source of new insights" in creative artefact research (2022, 6).

Breaking down disciplinary boundaries is embraced by explorations of artistic expression, and is why Jonathan Michaels describes the nature of interdisciplinary research as inherently suiting the creative arts (2022, 52). I experienced this process of leaning into other disciplines and feeling unsure of this direction.

Early on in my research, I engaged with complex philosophical ideas that were new to me, and I described them to a colleague. They paused and replied, "just don't go there", perhaps implying that the theoretical frameworks were overused, too far outside my area of expertise, or simply too advanced for me. This person was a respected academic, but their comment initially undermined my confidence; it made me feel I was heading in an irrelevant or unreachable direction. Fortunately, I didn't listen to their warning, and those theories branching across several fields enabled me to establish a rich and innovative research question. The ideas could have turned out to be irrelevant or unnecessarily abstract; however, such a conclusion is one that I needed to discover myself.

This experience only highlights the highs and lows of the exploratory nature of PhD research. Sometimes you need to step outside your area of expertise, listen to your intuition, and push through the unknown to discover your research quest and your thesis question.

## 9 Ethics in creative arts research

Ethics is a core factor in all PhD research, although implications vary across fields, modes, and subject matter. In the sciences, for example, ethical considerations often concern the physical or psychological treatment of humans or animals. Issues of ethical significance may be evident in creative arts research through issues of prejudice, racism, bullying, informed consent and intimacy, or cultural, ability, and gender differences, among others. However, as creative arts research is often interdisciplinary, possible concerns are limitless.

Possible ethical factors also include behavioural considerations, such as respect, confidentiality, fairness, truth, and accuracy (Hübner 2022, 581–82; Flick 2025, 39–58). In creative arts research, these concerns may arise in the act of research, in the content of what is being researched or created, or in the method of dissemination. For example, consider the following: Are there ethical considerations in any of the materials that you use in your artefact? This might include animal fur, human hair, personal ephemera, or photographs of people. Does the content or subject matter raise issues of cultural sensitivity? These may include Indigeneity, land, natural or cultural articles, ethnicity, or gender. Does your research necessitate referencing potentially triggering events? These might include violence, abuse, trauma, suicide, or other psychologically disturbing acts.

Falk Hübner proposes an ethics-based research approach grounded in a realignment of attitude. He suggests a changed awareness where "the researcher perceives ethical behaviour not as an obligation or hindrance but as an invitation to develop and practice empathy, thinking about and being aware of others" (2024, 63). Be aware that ethical issues in creative arts study may arise not only during the research process, but also in the dissemination of the findings through exhibition, performance, or interaction.

Your university will have a formal ethical research practice and procedure for review and approval where required. As some potential ethical considerations may be challenging to identify at the outset, discuss them early with your supervisor and become familiar with your university's ethics process. Submitting your research proposal for ethics evaluation should be mandatory for all candidates, though often it is not required.

## 10 "Work of art (process) and works of art (product)"[5]

Creative arts research encompasses both the process of making art and the effect of that final work. These areas of investigation are present whether the thesis topic analyses existing works or develops artefacts as part of the research itself. Your research, therefore, can sit within a process, a final work, or the intersection of both. Understanding how creative work comes into being and what it means or does once completed is essential to creative arts research.

This dual focus distinguishes creative arts from fields that study only process, output, or cultural context, for instance. You may not know at the start where your research question sits. When you do determine the direction your question takes, further decisions follow. If your thesis includes a creative artefact and you are experimenting with different processes, are multiple finished works required to answer your research question? If your thesis is written and you are analysing audience reaction to completed work, how will you gather evidence? If your artefact thesis assesses a single final work, mapping backward to determine cause and effect, does it require experimenting with an atypical creative process? Whatever form your project takes, ensure your choices support your focus.

The nature of scholarly creative work (originating, making, completing, and presenting) demands reflection and problem-solving alongside analysis and learning. It also requires attention to the experiential aspect of the work for both artist and audience, meaning that the artefact, the human, and the context are considered simultaneously. This integrated approach makes creative arts research naturally interdisciplinary, drawing on philosophy, material studies, cultural theory, embodied practice, and any other area of conceptual thought. The field is rich, diverse, and uniquely positioned to explore questions that emerge at the intersection of theory and artistic practice, questions that cannot be adequately addressed through either making alone or scholarly analysis alone.

### Notes

1 Sullivan contextualises historical discussions of artistic research. This detailed account includes many definitional approaches (2010, 73–92).
2 This usage evolved from a term for a research sampling technique indicating a sample that starts small and systematically expands through connections. See David L. Morgan (2012) for more background on the sampling use of this metaphor and Claes Wohlin et al. (2022) for its use as a technique in literature review.
3 Huizingh adapts this method from a technique developed by Tony J. Watson, originally referred to as a "Watson box" (Watson 1994).

4 For definitional differences see Halina Dunin-Woyseth (2011, 65) and the *CAPC Glossary*.
5 This phrase is borrowed from Stephen Scrivener (2011, 321).

## References

### *Cited works*

Bell, Desmond. 2019. *Research in the Creative and Media Arts: Challenging Practice*. Routledge.

Borgdorff, Henk. 2011. "The Production of Knowledge in Artistic Research." In *The Routledge Companion to Research in the Arts*, edited by Michael Biggs and Henrik Karlsson. Routledge.

Borgdorff, Henk. 2012. *The Conflict of the Faculties: Perspectives on Artistic Research and Academia*. Leiden University Press.

Candy, Linda, and Ernest Edmonds. 2011. "The Role of the Artefact and Frameworks for Practice-Based Research." In *The Routledge Companion to Research in the Arts*, edited by Michael Biggs and Henrik Karlsson. Routledge.

Candy, Linda, Ernest Edmonds, and Craig Vear. 2022. "Introduction to the Handbook." In *The Routledge International Handbook of Practice-Based Research*, edited by Craig Vear. Routledge.

Dunin-Woyseth, Halina. 2011. "Some Notes On Mode 1 And Mode 2: Adversaries Or Dialogue Partners?" In *The Routledge Companion to Research in the Arts*, edited by Michael Biggs and Henrik Karlsson. Routledge.

Emerson, Ralph Waldo. 1870. *Society and Solitude: Twelve Chapters*. The Riverside Press.

Flick, Uwe. 2025. *Introducing Research Methodology: Thinking Your Way Through Your Research Project*, 4th ed. Sage Publications.

Friedman, Ken. 2014. "Now that We're Different, What's Still the Same?" In *Doctoral Writing in the Creative and Performing Arts*, edited by Louise Ravelli, Brian Paltridge, and Sue Starfield. Libri Publishing.

Gray, Carole, and Julian Malins. 2016. *Visualizing Research: A Guide to the Research Process in Art and Design*. Routledge.

Grix, Jonathan. 2022. *The Foundations of Research*, 3rd ed. Bloomsbury Academic.

Hübner, Falk. 2022. "Ethics Through an Empathetic Lens: A Human-Centred Approach to Ethics in Practice-Based Research." In *The Routledge International Handbook of Practice-Based Research*, edited by Craig Vear. Routledge.

Hübner, Falk. 2024. *Method, Methodology and Research Design in Artistic Research: Between Solid Routes and Emergent Pathways*. Routledge. https://doi.org/10.4324/9781003188841

Huizingh, Eelko K.R.E. 2023. *Unlocking PhD Success: How to Acquire Crucial PhD Skills*. Springer Nature.

Latour, Bruno. 2004. "Why Has Critique Run out of Steam? From Matters of Fact to Matters of Concern." In *Things*, edited by Bill Brown. The University of Chicago Press.

Michaels, Jonathan. 2022. "Interdisciplinary Perspectives on Practice-Based Research." In *The Routledge International Handbook of Practice-Based Research*, edited by Craig Vear. Routledge.

Morgan, David L. 2012. "Snowball Sampling." In *The SAGE Encyclopedia of Qualitative Research Methods*, vol. 2, edited by Lisa Given. SAGE Publications. https://doi.org/10.4135/9781412963909.n425

Nowotny, Helga. 2011. "Foreword." In *The Routledge Companion to Research in the Arts*, edited by Michael Biggs and Henrik Karlsson. Routledge.

*Oxford English Dictionary*, "research (*n.1*)," December 2025, https://doi.org/10.1093/OED/1888781292

Ravelli, Louise, Sue Starfield, and Brian Paltridge. 2021. "Re-imaging Doctoral Writing Through the Visual and Performing Arts." In *Re-imaging Doctoral Writing*, edited by Cecile Badenhorst, Brittany Amell, and James Burford. University Press of Colorado. https://doi.org/10.37514/INT-B.2021.1343

Scrivener, Stephen. 2011. "Reflections on Interactive Art and Practitioner Research: 2 Interpretation." In *Interacting: Art, Research and the Creative Practitioner*, edited by Linda Candy and Ernest Edmonds. Libri Publishing Ltd.

Sullivan, Graeme. 2010. *Art Practice as Research: Inquiry in the Visual Arts*, 2nd ed. Sage Publications.

Sullivan, Graeme. 2011. "Artistic Cognition and Creativity." In *The Routledge Companion to Research in the Arts*, edited by Michael Biggs and Henrik Karlsson. Routledge.

Watson, Tony J. 1994. "Managing, Crafting and Researching: Words, Skill and Imaginations in Shaping Management Research." *Special issue, British Journal of Management*, 5(s1): S77–S87. https://doi.org/10.1111/j.1467-8551.1994.tb00132.x

Wohlin, Claes, Marcos Kalinowski, Katia Romero Felizardo, and Emilia Mendes. 2022. "Successful Combination of Database Search and Snowballing for Identification of Primary Studies in Systematic Literature Studies." *Information and Software Technology*, 147. https://doi.org/10.1016/j.infsof.2022.106908

## *Suggested reading*

Adolf, Marian, and Nico Stehr. 2016. *Knowledge: Is Knowledge Power?* 2nd ed. Routledge. http://dx.doi.org/10.4324/9781315543093

Barrett, Estelle. 2007. "Appendix: Developing and Writing Creative Arts Practice Research: A Guide." In *Practice as Research: Approaches to Creative Arts Enquiry*, edited by Estelle Barrett and Barbara Bolt. I. B. Tauris.

Biggs, Michael, and Daniela Buchler. 2008. "Eight Criteria for Practice-Based Research in the Creative and Cultural Industries." *Art, Design & Communications in Higher Education* 7(1): 5–18. https://doi.org/10.1386/adch.7.1.5_1

Booth, Wayne C., Gregory G. Colomb, Joseph M. Williams, Joseph M. Williams, Joseph Bizup, and William T. FitzGerald. 2024. *The Craft of Research*, 5th ed. The University of Chicago Press. (See chap. 1, "From Topics to Questions.").

Candy, Linda. 2006. *Practice Based Research: A Guide*. Creative and Cognition Studios. https://www.creativityandcognition.com/wp-content/uploads/2011/04/PBR-Guide-1.1-2006.pdf

Chapman, Owen, and Kim Sawchuk. 2012. "Research-Creation: Intervention, Analysis and 'Family Resemblances'." *Canadian Journal of Communication Corporation* 37 (1): 5–26. https://doi.org/10.22230/cjc.2012v37n1a2489

Edmonds, Ernest. 2022. "Research, Shared Knowledge and The Artefact." In *The Routledge International Handbook of Practice-Based Research*, edited by Craig Vear. Routledge.

Forrest, David, ed. 2017. *Doctoral Research in Art*. Australian Scholarly Publishing.

Kara, Helen. 2018. *Research Ethics in the Real World: Euro-Western and Indigenous Perspectives*. Policy Press.

Loveless, Natalie. 2019. *How to Make Art at the End of the World: A Manifesto for Research-Creation*. The University of Alberta Press.

Loveless, Natalie, ed. 2020. *Knowings and Knots: Methodologies and Ecologies in Research-Creation*. Duke University Press.

Sullivan, Graeme. 2009. "Making Space: The Purpose and Place of Practice-led Research. In *Practice-led Research, Research-led Practice in the Creative Arts*, edited by Hazel Smith and Roger T. Dean. Edinburgh Press.

III
balance, adapt, plan

# Decalogue III

## TEN MANAGEMENT THINGS

This decalogue addresses the administrative and organisational dimensions of your PhD study, demonstrating that management practices are not peripheral but foundational to intellectual and emotional sustainability.

As you progress through the PhD journey, a range of practical and logistical issues and tasks inevitably arise. Many of these matters are navigated more efficiently with prior awareness. Areas of doctoral management considered include identifying appropriate contacts for inquiries, relevant policies and procedures, identifying options for financial support, adopting effective project and time management approaches, and compiling necessary documentation. Furthermore, this list provides an overview of requirements concerning thesis parameters, permissions for third-party materials, and intellectual property (IP) policies. It also offers guidance on organising and safeguarding digital files and navigating submission processes.

Significantly, this decalogue highlights the value of information available from your research department or faculty, including specific details that can only be provided by your university. Knowing which procedures to follow and preventing administrative tasks from overwhelming your research is critical to successful thesis completion.

As Natalie Hills, Higher Degree by Research Examinations Coordinator, expresses: "Efficiency, accuracy, support and integrity matter" (2020, 162). Effective management is integral to your PhD thesis.

### 1 Know who to ask

Before you arrive at a question, challenge, or crisis in regard to the management of your PhD, determine which department or person you should contact at the university. Introduce yourself to your point of contact in the research office and in your faculty, school, or department. By making

DOI: 10.4324/9781003584209-4

these connections early, the office will be familiar with you and your work, streamlining the process when you need to ask questions. If you have an urgent question, you will know exactly where to go and the process to follow. In addition, you won't need to use up your supervisor's time inquiring about administrative issues.

Although this point sounds basic, I uncovered this information only as I went along and, at a couple of points, found that figuring out the relevant person to speak with was quite stressful. If I had made a list of key contacts for the programme at the outset, I would not have added unnecessary pressure. Significant logistical questions don't need to be stressful ones.

## 2 Know the rules

Each university has similar, but different, processes and procedures governing matters such as extensions, leaves of absence, and deferrals. These policies are generally institution-wide, and your supervisor may not know the answer to every intricate detail. Familiarise yourself early with policies and procedures.

For instance, be clear on the maximum time that the university allows for the completion of your thesis (including any extensions). This clarity is particularly critical if you are studying part-time and have greater possibility of delay due to family or work commitments, known or unexpected.

Be aware of the requirements for the use of digital services to detect plagiarism in your written work. Learn how this system operates and how the feedback is interpreted. This process is not to be feared; it is simply a safeguard to support and protect the originality and integrity of your writing. It also ensures the successful completion of your thesis.

Identify your university's current policies and advice on the use of artificial intelligence (AI) as part of your thesis process. The use of AI, as permitted, is explored in greater detail in the academic tool decalogue.

As discussed, following ethics approval procedures may be a particularly critical aspect of your PhD. While the ethical significance of your research should be examined early, the management task here is to understand your university's required steps, guidelines, and forms, if applicable.

## 3 Finding financial support

If possible, before you enrol, find opportunities for funding that will provide a stipend while you study. Determine what your programme funds are and access the university's list of available financial support opportunities. Subsidy may be available through scholarships, or you may be eligible for grants. If you are currently teaching, enquire whether the university contributes additional salary towards study or will allow research time as part of your workload. Online databases exist that compile lists of opportunities across multiple institutions.

Many universities set aside an expense allowance for each student to cover conferences and research expenses. Some programmes may also contribute towards third-party permissions or professional services such as copy-editing. If you are pursuing a creative artefact PhD, enquire what funding your programme covers towards the realisation of the artefact. This knowledge allows you to plan and determine what you may need to fund yourself.

## 4 Managing your time

Efficient time management is critical to ensuring a smooth process throughout your thesis journey. Begin by determining the stages and tasks that need to be factored into a schedule, and clarify what is required for your submission. Identify the expected timeline for each stage of your candidature in line with your university's requirements. Although some of these significant dates may seem far away, soon they will be upon you. Be aware of milestones, required presentations, submission requirements, annual report requirements, and your agreed-upon completion date.

Early in your candidature, ask either your supervisor or the research office whether you can see a former PhD candidate's schedule document. This example will highlight significant dates and also the process involved in draft submission, revision, and pre-submission planning. For instance, I hadn't realised until late in my candidature how many times drafts typically go back and forth between supervisor and candidate. Had I realised earlier, I would have had fewer surprises in my submission process. Once you understand the main stages of your candidature, you can develop a realistic timetable including deadlines, meetings, milestones, and progress dates.

My initial schedule was a skeleton compared to my final draft. My first version indicated meeting times, a completion date for a progression of drafts, and a submission date. My final schedule listed each stage of a chapter draft submission and revision, indicating overlaps of different chapter stages and showing which chapters were with my supervisor. It also included the final process of submitting the final draft to supervisor(s), copyeditor, back to supervisor, and full submission, while indicating time for revisions in between.

The schedule is not a static document. More detail emerges as your research progresses, and timetables shift accordingly. Hills describes an effective technique of "backward mapping" that starts from the final submission date and works backward, plotting each milestone, ensuring that time allocated for each task is realistic (2020, 144, 154–158). By entering your anticipated time for each stage into the timetable and working backward, you discover whether your expectations are achievable or unrealistic. This kind of planning, while still allowing for change, alleviates unnecessary stress.

To be realistic in your timetable, build in contingency. Map out the time you need for each stage and add at least half the time again. There will always be something to cause a delay. My own candidature included unexpected events ranging from increased hours of paid employment to a ruptured appendix. Because I built contingency into my schedule, and my university granted a medical extension, I was able to submit as agreed.

If your creative artefact is non-distributable (for example, a dance performance), specialised timetabling will be required. Build this requirement into your timeline as early as possible. Other reasons for contingency: Your initial arguments may evolve greatly, you might experience a prolonged block, or your supervisor might take research leave. If the contingency is not needed, you will have more time to finalise your research, or possibly complete earlier than planned: a pleasant surprise rather than a critical one.

Review and adjust your timetable as deadlines and your completion date approach. Your schedule, as a flexible document, provides goals to strive for while remaining adaptable enough to support your evolving research.

## 5 Know the parameters (and when to challenge them)

Before you begin your research, determine the expected word count for your thesis or exegesis and any parameters that exist for your creative artefact. You may have a valid reason to work outside these parameters, and this rationale may be approved. However, it is essential to be aware of expectations and requirements before you deviate from them.

This information may not be as straightforward or forthcoming as expected. For my thesis, I wanted to know absolute expectations and limits as to the thesis word count. Both the graduate research office and my supervisor were vague and responded with generalisations. Perhaps my supervisor wanted to grant me freedom to write initially without limit. As a result, I wrote way too much; however, in the process, I also learned a great deal. In the end, I struggled to reduce my thesis length to 115,000 words, exceeding the official limit by 15,000 words. I was approved for the overage, but the research office warned that some examiners may be annoyed at the length. I passed, but it was not without risk.

The key takeaway here is to keep in mind the allowable word count range, but don't let it dominate early inquiry. Some topics require shorter written work, and others require longer analyses. Rules matter, but at the exploratory stage, they should not overwhelm the development of ideas. At some point, however, it becomes critical to shape the work within the approved parameters or to seek formal approval to depart from them.

The same principle applies to the creative artefact. Clarify any parameters early, but keep them in the background during initial stages, enabling development of ideas, practice, and artefact without restriction. Focusing narrowly on form or output too soon closes off experimentation, possibilities of lateral thinking, and the pushing of boundaries. Once the form and direction of your research become clearer, revisit those parameters and shape the work accordingly.

## 6 Who owns your work?

Understanding IP rights for your thesis is essential. IP refers to created works requiring legal protection through copyright, patents, or trademarks. For creative arts theses, this includes both your written work (written thesis or exegesis) and your creative work (artefact), which may require separate copyright or patent protection.

Institutional policies vary significantly, even in the same country. Before you enrol, investigate whether copyright of your written thesis remains with you or transfers to the university, whether IP for creative work or inventions is treated separately from written work, and what rights you retain for exhibiting, publishing, screening, or commercialising your artefact.

Request written guidance about your rights before enrolment to ensure policies are acceptable for your situation. Discovering unfavourable IP terms after beginning your PhD can limit your professional options.[1]

## 7 Getting third-party permissions

Any copyrighted material included in your thesis requires permission from the owner of the copyright. This third-party material may be photographs, artwork, charts and diagrams, tables, or extended extracts from creative written works. Apply for permissions as soon as you know what you wish to include. This process can be lengthy, particularly if it's unclear who holds the copyright.

Don't integrate work before securing permissions. If your thesis analyses a particular artist's work, approach the artist or copyright owner immediately to obtain rights for a group of works. You can confirm the exact images later. Completing a thesis about an artist's body of work without including any images of that work would be an enormous challenge, so address permissions early.

If you don't have permissions at the time of submission, the images or full thesis will be embargoed until permissions are acquired. Be aware that some permissions incur fees, even though the thesis is non-commercial and intended for educational use. Many countries follow "fair use" policies, though these can be vague and may not be acceptable to your university's requirements.

Carefully consider your material selections before becoming attached to specific works. If fees are involved, estimate costs and enquire whether your university can cover them. This issue has grown more significant as theses that were once bound and shelved in a library are now widely accessible as digital downloads.

My thesis required permission for film stills. I mistakenly assumed that film images would fall under educational use. They didn't. While two filmmakers readily agreed, the third required extensive tracking down to determine the current rights holder. I eventually located the distribution company and secured permission, though an administrative fee was required, negotiated down from an even higher initial price. During this lengthy process, I began considering how to reframe my thesis without these images. Fortunately, it didn't come to that, though my thesis was embargoed briefly while I waited to receive the final signed document. This experience reinforces how beneficial it is to begin this process early.

## 8 Data management

As with most topics I have discussed in this decalogue, adopting effective data management systems early reduces stress. Three of the more critical issues are efficient resource organisation, data security and protection, and foolproof backup and storage.

Organise materials clearly and consistently. Your thesis may include resources in multiple formats: created files, physical artefact elements, hard copies in your collection, library, or museum materials, digital files stored remotely or accessible online, thesis drafts, notes, lists, analytical data, interview material, working bibliographies, forms, institutional documentation, sketches, and handwritten elements. Consider what organisation and file structure will allow you to find these things easily.

Design your system early, then develop it as needs evolve. My initial mistake was creating vague files that lumped together resources, notes, and administrative information without clear delineation. I didn't grasp the exponential growth of resources. I saved articles with meaningless auto-generated filenames, assuming I'd remember why I saved each one.

Returning to my thesis after several leaves of absence, I couldn't find anything: computer file chaos.

I eventually reorganised everything with descriptive, uniform filenames: "author surname_first name_article name" for resources; "Chp#_Draft#_date" for chapter drafts. Files became more easily searchable. I created empty folders for content that I knew was coming, which also served as direction reminders. Recognise that you can't always pause to file as you research and set up a regular time in your week to update files and organise your computer and drives. Rigorous organisation saves time.

Data protection is critical, even when your research does not seem to involve sensitive information. You might conduct interviews, collect personal information, or gather IP data. All work should be protected from misuse or unauthorised access. Review your university's policy on data protection and research the safety of storage options, including external drives, remote servers, cloud services, and databases. Storage innovation is constant; keep up to date.

Implement a foolproof backup system from day one and keep your data in at least two locations beyond your computer. Use two mirrored external drives dedicated to your PhD, an external drive plus cloud storage, or a remote server or database (or current best option). This duplication is critical: working files plus two complete backup copies. Archive your work regularly, ideally at the end of each session. Small lapses in discipline can lead to catastrophic loss. I once deleted a partially saved desktop file while tired and emptied the trash before noticing. I now fastidiously check my computer bin before emptying it and always maintain two copies of critical data.

## 9 Preparing for examination

In this section, I address the procedural side of the submission preparation: what to consider in planning your time, formats, and expected outcomes. The practice decalogue discusses the more detailed practical aspects of written submission, artefact submission, and oral examination.

### *Planning*

You should know your expected deadline for submission from the day you begin your PhD. It is typically noted in your record of enrolment. This date will not change unless you successfully apply for an extension or leave of absence.

Your university's examination preparation includes the thesis committee's selection, selection and confirmation of examiners, scheduling of any required performance or exhibition (if creative artefact research), and verification that all policies and procedures have been followed.

In some countries, including the UK and Australia, your supervisor will typically confer with you to nominate a number of possible academics as external examiners for your thesis. The thesis committee typically determines the final selection based on your proposed list. These external experts will examine your work independently. Suggest academics who are experienced, knowledgeable in your area, highly regarded in the discipline, and who have been influential to your research and cited in your work.

To assist in your planning, be clear on what aspects they're assessing, such as contribution to knowledge, methodology, writing quality, and artefact quality. Also, ensure you are aware of the time between submission and examination outcome and the expected revision period if corrections are required.

### *Examination format requirements*

- **Written work:** All candidates submit a written thesis or exegesis in the format prescribed by the university. Confirm requirements for document format, accepted length, method of presentation (digital, bound, or both), and required inclusions such as declarations, abstracts, and acknowledgements. These elements are detailed in the writing decalogue.
- **Creative artefact:** If your thesis is creative artefact research, determine how it will be examined. Distributable works (novels, recordings, and portfolios) are typically submitted alongside the exegesis. Non-distributable works (performances, exhibitions, and installations) require specific scheduling allowing examiners to attend. Begin these logistical arrangements as soon as your artefact form becomes clear. See the artefact decalogue for further notes on artefact examination.
- **Oral examination:** Some institutions require an oral defence or *viva voce*. If required, you will present your research and respond to the examiners' questions. The format, duration, and expectations vary by university and country. Preparation strategies are discussed in the practice decalogue.

### *Possible outcomes of examination*

Following your examination, you will receive a result. The timeline from submission to outcome typically ranges from three to six months. Being aware of likely results will ready you for your assessment. Possible outcomes include:

- Pass without corrections
- Pass subject to minor corrections
- Pass subject to major corrections and revisions (also called a referral)
- Deferred decision, neither a pass nor a fail, requiring substantial revisions
- Not awarded a degree, but may resubmit
- Not awarded a degree and not permitted to resubmit

The first outcome is rare; some corrections are normally required. The last three possible outcomes are extremely rare. In some cases, you may be able to appeal your examiners' outcome.

## 10 When you reach the end, press submit

The submission of your thesis may seem like a distant fiction at this moment, but it is so critical to understand the process early. Familiarise yourself with submission procedures from the start of your research so that the final stage does not bring avoidable surprises. This task involves a continual juggling of time, adaptation, and plans.

You will be exhausted once you have completed your work, so read the submission procedures at the start of your research. Your university will provide a template detailing title page requirements, inclusions in front matter, document order, submission method, and required forms. Your documents and creative artefact must be submitted precisely as requested and made available for examination exactly as agreed. These procedures ensure that you, your supervisor, your thesis committee, the examiners, and the research office all receive a submission that complies with current policy.

The principle is simple: The more you know at the start, the fewer surprises you will encounter and the more confident you will feel in your work. Early familiarity with submission requirements allows you to focus on your research rather than administrative uncertainties.

## Note

1 See Estelle M. Phillips and Colin G. Johnson (2022, 246–249) for further detail.

## References

### *Cited works*

Hills, Natalie. 2020. "Creative Examinations and the Administrator's Perspective." In *The Creative PhD: Challenges, Opportunities, Reflection*, edited by Tara Brabazon, Tiffany Lyndall-Knight, and Natalie Hills. Emerald Publishing.

Phillips, Estelle M. and Colin G. Johnson. (1987) 2022. *Phillips and Pugh's How to Get a PhD: A Handbook for Students and Their Supervisors*, 7th ed. McGraw-Hill Open University Press.

### *Suggested reading*

Cook, Margaret. 2019. "Building Confidence about the Academic Journey." In *The Doctoral Experience: Student Stories from the Creative Arts and Humanities*, edited by Donna Lee Brien, Craig Batty, Elizabeth Ellison, and Alison Owens, 75–87. Palgrave Macmillan. https://doi.org/10.1007/978-3-030-18199-4_5

Cooksey, Ray and Gael McDonald. 2019. *Surviving and Thriving in Postgraduate Research*, 2nd ed. Springer Nature.

Costello, Brigid Mary. "Finding the Groove: The Rhythms of Practice-Based Research." In *The Routledge International Handbook of Practice-Based Research*, edited by Craig Vear. Routledge.

Doyle, Rosie and Fraser Robertson. 2024. *The PhD Handbook: How to Take Care of Yourself, Your Research Project and your Future*. McGraw-Hill Open University Press.

McChesney, Katrina, James Burford, Liezel Frick, and Tseen Khoo. 2024. *Doing Doctoral Research at a Distance: Flourishing in Off-Campus, Hybrid, and Remote Pathways*. Routledge. (See chap. 2, "Beginning Work: Deciding to Study at a Distance and Getting Off to a Flying Start.")

Mewburn, Inger. 2019. *How to Tame your PhD*, 2nd ed. Acton ACT: Thesis Whisperer Books. https://thesiswhisperer.com/

Mewburn, Inger, Pat Thomson, Helen Kara, and Aimee Grant. 2026. *Managing your Research Project: A Guide for Researchers*. Routledge. (See chap. 5, "Time Management for Projects.")

Nelson, Robin. 2022. *Practice as Research in the Arts and Beyond: Principles, Processes, Context, Achievements*, 2nd ed. Palgrave Macmillan. (See chap. 6, "PaR Doctorates: A Guideline/*Clew* to a Successful Outcome for All (Candidates, Examiners, Supervisors, Administrators, Regulators).")

Rugg, Gordon and Marian Petre. 2020. *The Unwritten Rules of PhD Research*, 3rd ed. McGraw-Hill Open University Press. (See chap. 2, "The Many Shapes of the PhD.")

Wilson, Jenny. 2018. "Artistic Research and University Research Management Practices." In *Artists in the University: Positioning Artistic Research in Higher Education*. Springer Nature. https://doi.org/10.1007/978-981-10-5774-8 (See chap. 6, "Artistic Research and University Research Management Practices.")

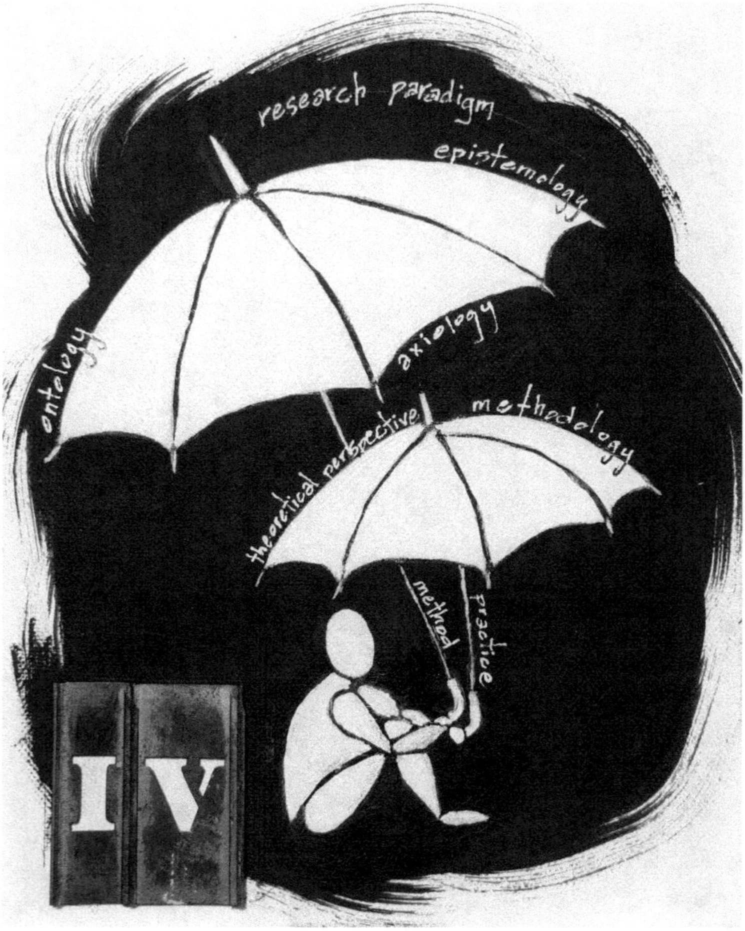
research paradigm
epistemology
ontology
axiology
theoretical perspective
methodology
method
practice
IV

# Decalogue IV

## TEN METHODOLOGY THINGS

This decalogue aims to clarify common confusions and misconceptions about methodology in creative arts research, presenting it as an evolving framework rather than a fixed template. Methodology is a research strategy and system of logic. This framework holds together methods and techniques, providing a theoretical rationale for how you find out what you need to know. For many scholars, particularly those with a practitioner background, identifying and defining a methodology can seem opaque. The terminology is often left unexplained, with an assumption that it is inherently clear to incoming PhD students. It is not, and acknowledging that is the first step.

When I began my PhD, I went straight to methodology without consciously thinking through the foundational tiers of research that sit above it. My misconception wasn't a failing of my university or supervisor; at this level of study, independent navigation is expected. However, I didn't fully appreciate the complexity of research as a discipline in its own right, and I paid for that assumption in lost time and unnecessary confusion. This decalogue exists to give you what I, as a practitioner, didn't have: a clear map before the journey begins.

To provide context for methodology, this decalogue describes a research framework hierarchy: a progression of research elements from the broadest worldview down to specific practice. These elements, and the relationships between them, are introduced briefly here and explored throughout the decalogue. I refer to Jonathan Grix to introduce this framework: "If ontology is about what we may know, then epistemology is about how we come to know what we know" (2022, 57).

### Research Framework Hierarchy

- **Research Paradigm**: Belief system (worldview)
- **Ontology**: What exists (reality)
- **Epistemology**: How we know (knowledge)

DOI: 10.4324/9781003584209-5

- **Axiology**: What we value (ethics, aesthetics, spirituality)
- **Theoretical Perspective**: How we think (lens)
- **Methodology**: How we find out (plan)
- **Methods**: How we implement (tools, techniques, procedures)
- **Practice**: What we do (analysis, writing, making—and how we sustain the doing)[1]

Think of the research hierarchy as two nested umbrellas being held beneath the sky, representing the research paradigm, the whole worldview of research. Ontology, epistemology, and axiology form the first umbrella, theoretical perspective and methodology the second, with methods and practice suspended beneath on the stems.[2] In principle, you work from the outermost inward, considering worldview first and specific practice last. Falk Hübner defines "methodology as the 'discipline of methods', including the underlying ideas of and world views of a research strategy and their philosophical and ethical bases" (2024, 25). Therefore, in practice, many researchers, particularly practitioners, move instinctively towards methodology without consciously examining the foundational tiers. Understanding those tiers, even retrospectively, clarifies and strengthens your research design.

This decalogue outlines conventional understandings of methodology while also introducing emergent approaches, including those that consider the elements of a research framework as intertwined rather than separate. These alternative paradigms, significant for creative arts research, are explored in Section Eight.

## 1 Research paradigm, ontology, epistemology

The research paradigm is, as Egon G. Guba and Yvonna S. Lincoln describe, that which "represents a worldview that defines, for its holder, the nature of the 'world', the individual's place in it, and the range of possible relationships to that world and its parts" (1994, 107). Two broad branches of the paradigm are qualitative and quantitative. Qualitative approaches are typically further defined as constructivist, critical theory, interpretivist, or transformative worldviews; quantitative approaches as critical realist, positivist, or post-positivist worldviews.[3] These terms can be confusing as they are also used to describe techniques and methods within a particular methodology. Creative arts research is typically qualitative, foregrounding analytical and experiential learning, rather than empirical measurement, though a mixed methods approach incorporating both is not uncommon.

Discipline typically determines research paradigm, ontology, and epistemology, which is why researchers often move directly to theoretical perspective and methodology. In interdisciplinary research, however, the paradigm may need to shift to accommodate two or more methodologies founded outside your primary discipline. This multimethodological approach is particularly common in the creative arts.

Ontology, epistemology, and axiology (addressed in the next section) are all defined as branches of philosophy. Ontology examines the nature of reality and what is said to exist, while epistemology considers theories of knowledge and how humans know what they know.

As you develop your proposal, consider your research paradigm explicitly. Can it be described as interpretivist, constructivist, critical realist, transformative, or otherwise? What are your ontological and epistemological frameworks? As pointed out, creative arts research lends itself to multiple interpretations of these terms; the goal is not to find a single correct answer but to develop a conscious and defendable position that supports your research question.

## 2 Axiology

Axiology examines what each person values in research: ethically, aesthetically, and spiritually. More precisely, as a theory and study, it concerns how a person's values influence the research process, from initial design through to the interpretation of findings. Not all research frameworks treat axiology as a distinct element; its concerns are often embedded within the research paradigm or theoretical perspective.

In creative arts research, however, axiology is rarely peripheral. Creative practice and analysis inherently involve value judgements: ethical considerations in representation, aesthetic choices, and questions of meaning and significance are central to the work itself.

Lincoln et al. position axiology as a foundational research element using the term "religion" to broadly include spirituality and questions of meaning in human inquiry. They argue that "axiology has been 'defined out' of scientific inquiry for no larger a reason than that it also concerns religion" (2018, 230). Spiritual dimensions, understood not as traditional religious belief but as fundamental questions of meaning, purpose, and what constitutes a life worth living, remain central to creative practice regardless of a researcher's personal worldview. Whether you are part of a religious institution, agnostic, secular, or atheist, these existential concerns are most probably present in your work.

Developing awareness of how your values shape your research, and how different frameworks address axiology, will strengthen both your research design and your navigation of diverse methodological literature.

## 3 Theoretical perspective, methodology

The relationship between theoretical perspective and methodology is full of assumptions that experienced academics often leave unclarified. These terms are also used differently across universities and disciplines, compounding the confusion. Many academics conflate theoretical perspective with methodology, which overburdens methodology by forcing it to function both as an interpretive lens and as a general research approach. Returning to the research framework hierarchy: theoretical perspective (how we think) and methodology (how we find out) are distinct tiers. Treating them independently clarifies your research design from the outset.

Similarly, the distinction between methodology and method is often overlooked. Gillian Rose clarifies:

> A research *method* is a series of practical steps that produce particular kinds of data, evidence and results. A methodology is more comprehensive. *Methodology* refers to the rationale for those practical steps; it is the justification for the research method you use.
>
> *(2023, 1; emphasis in original)*

Methods are the tools, techniques, and procedures that put your methodology into practice. Practice refers to the actual doing of the research.

Distinguishing each step early may seem overly meticulous, but this thoughtfulness benefits your entire project, from chapter structure to individual lines of writing and every detail of the artefact. The more knowns you establish, the more streamlined the process becomes, and any necessary directional shifts become more apparent.

Methodology is not assigned by you, your university, or your supervisor, but becomes clear through early reading and develops as your research question is refined. Allow time to test your chosen methodology against your evolving question before committing. Consider reviewing similar research, writing a sample paragraph with this methodology in mind, or stepping away for perspective. Be clear on your methodology before your first draft, while remaining open to the possibility that it may evolve.

## 4 Depth over breadth

A thesis typically employs one or two methodologies, with one most often primary. In interdisciplinary research, two methodologies may also carry equal weight, and as discussed, this approach is common in the creative arts. One framework might address the specific area of the arts practice or analysis, paired with a cultural, philosophical, historical, or science-based methodology. When two methodologies are used, be clear on how they function in relation to each other: whether they address different aspects of your research question, operate at different scales of analysis, or complement each other through different disciplinary perspectives. Using more than two methodologies is generally not advised: research becomes too broad and risks superficiality. The fundamental principle here is one that applies across the entire PhD: go deep, not wide.

Methodologies are typically articulated early in your written thesis or exegesis. Institutional expectations vary, with some requiring the framework to be located in your introduction and others preferring a dedicated methodology chapter or chapters.

## 5 Methodology guides research

A "Catch-22" of the research process is evident in the choice of methodology. This productive paradox is at its heart: research guides your methodology, and methodology guides your research. How do you begin? Your topic formation prompts initial research, but the topic itself doesn't determine methodology. Rather, methodology becomes clear through engagement with the broader research process. Your paradigm, ontology, epistemology, axiology, and theoretical perspective may be determined intuitively, organically, or more deliberately; either way, your approach at each level informs your methodological choice. Systematic research coupled with organic exploration enables a theoretical context to develop through doing.

In practice, these steps often mean following unexpected connections through the literature: one text leads to another, ideas branch out in seemingly random directions, and you might find yourself reading about materiality, then phenomenology, then affect theory. This process isn't a distraction. Lincoln and Guba call this "emergent design" (1985, 41), where understanding unfolds through the research process itself. Their notion of "naturalistic paradigm" values "indeterminacy" in research design, suggesting the process is "'played by ear'; it must unfold, cascade, roll, emerge" (208–209). Your reading leads to new questions; new questions lead to new reading. This movement is responsive rather than random, following the logic of your developing inquiry. Following these threads is productive. Your mind forms relationships, building connective theories and ideas.

### *The emergence of methodology*

- **Norman K. Denzin and Lincoln** describe this interdisciplinary reaching as bricolage: "a pieced-together set of representations that are fitted to the specifics of a complex situation" (2018, 45).

- **Patti Lather** embraces the productive disorientation of this phase that suggests "practices of getting lost as fertile space for shifting imaginaries" (2007, xii): purposeful confusion that tends to reveal stimulating associations and hybrid ideas.
- **Tim Ingold** describes a complementary process of finding as "wayfaring" as a practice of "combining movement and attention" ([2007] 2016, xvi). This approach enables you to discover your path rather than following a predetermined route. You may begin in one area of the literature and find yourself drawn into entirely unexpected territory as your mind makes new associations.

This exploratory phase, whether you experience it as emergent design, bricolage, getting lost, or wayfaring, is not a diversion from determining your methodology. It is the process through which your methodology becomes clear. Ingold's description of wayfaring as "neither placeless nor place-bound but placemaking" ([2007] 2016, 104) captures something essential: openness to the unknown journey is more critical than advance knowledge of an endpoint. The methodology you arrive at through this process will be more authentically yours than one selected from a list at the outset.

## 6 Creative arts methodologies

As pointed out, methodology in the creative arts rarely relies on a singular approach. It typically draws on a repertoire of frameworks shaped by research question and artistic practice, and may incorporate subject, content, and methodology from virtually any field through interdisciplinary, multidisciplinary, or multimodal strategies. Broadly speaking, creative arts research is qualitative, foregrounding theoretical and interpretive frameworks, rather than the systematic and replicable procedures more common in the sciences.

A concrete example illustrates how this approach works in practice. Consider a research topic examining the work of a nineteenth-century Australian painter whose work typically depicts rural scenes. A research question might analyse cultural issues evident in rural scene paintings: colonisation, Indigenous histories, feminist and gender attitudes, agricultural history, or treatment of animals. This topic draws the researcher towards a transformative methodology, an approach developed in the social sciences, where the paradigm aims to create social change through the research process itself. As Donna Mertens explains, a transformative methodology does not simply raise issues of social injustice but identifies strategies for change (2022, 73). Paired with an interpretivist methodology, which seeks to grasp meaning through existing works and realities, the two frameworks address different dimensions of the same research question: one concerned with meaning, the other with action. This example demonstrates both the range of methodological possibilities available to creative arts researchers and the importance of articulating clearly how two methodologies function together and how each contributes to answering your research question.

In creative arts research, as Robin Nelson explains, "practice (*praxis*) is at its heart and it embraces experiential modes of knowing (tacit, embodied cognition, performative)" while reaching out to make use of other knowledge, other methodologies (2022, 47).

## 7 Creative artefact methodologies

Creative artefact methodologies, described variously as practice-based, practice-led, or arts-based, indicate that the research methodology is connected in some way to the creative arts.[4]

Linda Candy, writing within interactive arts, observes that such fields are "fundamentally inter-discipline and practitioners are continually exposed to alternative perspectives" (2011, 41), a statement applicable across all creative arts. In determining methodology, Candy identifies two discrete pathways "first, the practitioner's own reflections upon the creative process and the artefact outcomes; and second, the search for understanding about the nature of audience experience with the artworks" (42). These two pathways offer a practical starting point for identifying which additional methodologies your research might require.

Creative artefact methodology is inherently resistant to conventional theoretical frameworks. Brad Haseman and Daniel Mafe describe this approach as "unruly, ambiguous and marked by extremes of interpretive anxiety for the reflexive researcher", characterised by ambiguity and a "deeply emergent" nature (2009, 220). For this reason, though creative artefact research can be described at the methodological or method level, it is helpful to return to the paradigm level: a worldview of research. Rather than treating these qualities as obstacles, understand them as methodological strengths: this inherent openness enables creative artefact methodology to combine productively with virtually any other framework, depending on your thesis subject matter, topic, and form. The research questions you bring to your artefact will guide which combinations make sense.

## 8 Emergent and emerging methodologies

Creative arts research has a particular affinity with emergent methodological approaches that resist conventional structure and instead prioritise practice, embodiment, relationality, and diverse ways of knowing. These approaches may feel more aligned with your creative instincts than conventional qualitative frameworks, and that alignment is methodologically appropriate and intellectually rigorous.

I arrived at several of these frameworks not by choosing them deliberately but by following my literature review wherever it led. I discovered later that what I had been doing instinctively had theoretical grounding I hadn't yet named. If you find conventional methodological frameworks feel constraining for your creative work, this section may help you articulate what you've been doing all along.

The example approaches discussed in this section—decolonising methodologies, arts-based research (ABR), non-representational theory (NRT), agential realism/new materialism, and cultural analysis—are not equally relevant to every researcher. Rather than reading this section as a checklist, use it as a field guide: identify the approach that resonates with your practice and research question, then follow that thread into deeper reading. If these frameworks don't resonate with your work, they may lead you to others, or your research may be better served by conventional methodologies discussed earlier in this decalogue.

### *Decolonising methodology*

Decolonising methodologies encompass research approaches founded in Indigenous ways of knowing that challenge the dominance of Western epistemologies. They reject Western methodology where unsuitable while incorporating conventional techniques where appropriate. Crucially, as Jo-ann Archibald Q'um Q'um Xiiem et al. emphasise, these approaches cannot be reduced to a singular theory: the diversity of First Nations peoples and struggles around the world means decolonising methodologies are necessarily plural (2022, 6). I am a non-Indigenous scholar offering an overview of these frameworks and, therefore, look to First Nations academics to serve as guides through this sub-section.

These methodologies emerged from First Nations sovereignty movements and anti-colonial struggles. As Larissa Behrendt explains: "We place ourselves in the world as an act of sovereignty and it reinforces our worldview. In our research approaches, we take this on by not pretending that we are neutral" (2022, 185). This refusal of neutrality is foundational to this methodology.

The goal is not to position Indigenous thinking as an alternative to Western thought, but to establish the approach as a complete, holistic, and authentic epistemological system in its own right. Linda Tuhiwai Smith describes this distinction precisely: her book on decolonising research focuses not on method selection, but "the context in which research problems are conceptualized and designed, and with the implications of research for its participants and their communities" (2021, 286). Her work has, as she explains, "'talked back to' and 'talked up to' research as an institution of knowledge that is embedded in a global system of imperialism and power" (286).

A holistic approach to worldview that encompasses ontology, epistemology, axiology, and methodology is naturally exemplified through the Australian Aboriginal knowledge system, Songlines. In this worldview, "things" are regarded as "containers of energy" (Page 2021, 22). Objects are not only living but also gain vitality through story and experience.[5] Songlines encompasses this reality as a "oneness of all things" (Neale 2020, 11). Songlines trace knowledge sites that are inextricable to the land (11). As a methodology, this worldview allows a researcher to map out concepts and ideas in interconnected relationships across time, place, and community.

Relationality and story are central to First Nations methodologies: Relationality and story are central to First Nations methodologies

- **Shawn Wilson** captures this ontological foundation: "Indigenous research is a life changing ceremony" (2008, 90).
- **Margaret Kovach** identifies "the tribal epistemology at the heart of this approach and a decolonizing aim, both of which are born of a unique relationship with Indigenous lands" (2009, 35).
- **Robin Wall Kimmerer** extends this insight: "stories are living beings, they grow, they develop, they remember" (2013, 386).

Some First Nations stories drawn through practice and developed through research emerge through "storywork", a methodology identified and embraced by Archibald Q'um Q'um Xiiem (2008). Her later collaborative text describes story as "the most powerful intergenerational manifestation of hope" and "a knowledge journey that harmonizes heart, mind, body, and spirit. It is the tree of life" (Archibald Q'um Q'um Xiiem et al. 2022, 13).

The significance of decolonising methodologies for creative arts research lies in the central role of storytelling and making in First Nations cultures. This approach holds a natural resonance with creative artefact practice. Nerida Blair describes Indigenous ontologies as "holistic, yet integrated, contextual and experiential. Our Knowings are conveyed through story. Listening to, and feeling Story" (2022, 115), suggesting a mutually generative relationship between these research approaches and creative artefact research. For non-Indigenous researchers, engaging with these frameworks requires careful attention to positionality and genuine respect for the epistemological sovereignty they represent.

A key question for non-First Nations researchers to consider: What are principled, acceptable, and ethical approaches to pursuing any research with First Nations content? The answer depends on many factors, including your thesis question, your own experience, whether you are collaborating with First Nations peoples, and your research aims. If your research engages with First Nations content, consult with First Nations academics in your field, and explicitly state your positionality.

### *Arts-based research methodology*

If your creative practice is central to your research process, but not primarily to its outcome, ABR may be your most natural methodological home.[6] An ABR methodology uses creative form as a means of inquiry: making as a technique is primary, suggesting that the artefact is not an articulation of a research question but a means of arriving at findings. Significantly, the topic and research question may reside in any field. The creative form is the investigative framework, and the researcher is not necessarily a practitioner artist.

The term *arts-based research* was coined by Elliot W. Eisner in 1993 within education, as a means of exploring what "research guided by aesthetic features might look like" (Barone and Eisner 2012, 8). After three decades, ABR is well-established but still not universally acknowledged across disciplines. Eisner identifies four ways the arts generate knowledge: by revealing aspects of life that may go unnoticed; by generating empathy that enables action; by providing a fresh perspective; and by revealing our capacity for affective response (2008, 11). These four qualities, taken together, describe why creative practice constitutes genuine research methodology rather than simply supporting written argument.

ABR is not confined to the creative arts. It has emerged as a valuable approach in science, education, history, politics, and social sciences precisely because practice often intersects with disciplines outside the arts. Each artistic form generates knowledge through its own process. A filmmaker's research journey varies from a poet's because cinematic and poetic forms operate through different modalities, materials, and conventions. Examples include performative inquiry (using performance as both research process and outcome), poetic inquiry (where poetry shapes knowledge creation), and choreographic inquiry (privileging movement as communication). These methodologies correspond to specific methods, as discussed in the next decalogue.

The field remains dynamic, with new frameworks developing as practitioners articulate their research processes. There is a notable overlap between ABR and non-representational inquiry, a connection explored in the following subsection.[7]

### *Non-representational research inquiry*

If your creative practice involves embodied experience, atmosphere, movement, or affect, and you've found that conventional research frameworks struggle to capture what actually happens in the making, NRT may offer the language you are looking for. Its central questions are deceptively simple: What does this do? How does this feel? What happens in the doing?

Nigel Thrift, who coined the term within his field of geography, describes NRT as "based on the leitmotif of movement in its many forms" (2008, 5). Its key principles include a focus on ordinary life and pre-cognitive experience, on material bodies of work in practice and action, on affect and sensation, and on spatial and atmospheric dimensions of experience. (5–14) Crucially, NRT holds that not everything can be captured through language or representation, and its experimental nature gives "equal weight to the vast spillage of things" (9). It privileges direct engagement with action, movement, bodily experience, and atmosphere over the interpretation of meanings and symbols.

Phillip Vannini describes NRT as "a synthesizing effort to amalgamate diverse but interrelated theoretical perspectives" (2015, 3), suited to research concerned with events, relations, doings, affects, and atmospheric backgrounds. These are research areas that seek to "make us feel something powerful, to give us a sense of the ephemeral, the fleeting, and the not-quite-graspable" (6): territory that will feel immediately familiar to many creative arts researchers.

NRT shares commitments with both ABR and the following framework, agential realism, which similarly challenges representation and foregrounds material process and embodiment. These overlaps mean the frameworks can be used in combination or can serve as entry points into each other's literature. For creative arts researchers whose work engages with materials, objects, space, or process, moving between these frameworks often feels less like choosing between them and more like triangulating towards the same territory from different directions.

### *Agential realism and new materialism inquiries*

If your research involves the relationship between maker and material, between objects and meaning, or between practice and knowledge, Karen Barad's agential realism offers a framework that may articulate what you've been experiencing but haven't yet named. Iris van der Tuin captures its practical implication simply: "A piece of clay is agential, because what is in the hands of the worker has as great an impact on the emergence of the artefact as what is in her mind" (2014, 262). This insight is foundational. Materials are not passive; they participate in the making of meaning.

Agential realism emerged from Barad's book, *Meeting the Universe Halfway: Quantum Physics and the Entanglement of Matter and Meaning* (2007), developed from their work in quantum physics and feminist theory. It sits within the broader framework of new materialism, a term coined independently by philosophers Rosi Braidotti and Manuel DeLanda in the late 1990s, in response to what was perceived as an overemphasis on language and discourse in poststructuralism.[8] Barad's contribution, though they don't use the term *new materialism* explicitly, was to ground these ideas in material practice rather than purely theoretical argument.

The framework's central concepts are *intra-action* and *diffraction*. Where conventional research thinks in terms of interaction between pre-existing entities, Barad proposes intra-action: "distinct agencies do not precede, but rather emerge through, their intra-action" (2007, 33). In other words, the maker and the material, the researcher and the research, are not separate entities that subsequently meet. They constitute each other through the process of engagement. As Barad states: "matter and meaning cannot be severed" (as interviewed by Dolphijn and van der Tuin 2012, 69). This notion opens a new, "entangled intra-relating" (2007, ix) way of thinking.

Rather than adopting a practice of reflection or reflexivity, Donna Haraway proposed employing diffraction as a way of tracing "difference patterns" in the world rather than simply reflecting the same thing elsewhere (1997, 268). This notion was further developed by Barad as a research approach concerned with difference rather than binary relationships (Bozalek and Murris 2022, 54). Where reflection looks for sameness and correspondence, diffraction attends carefully to what happens when ideas come together and move apart, making new patterns. For creative artefact researchers, this idea is a particularly generative way of thinking about how practice and theory illuminate each other.

Barad describes this framework as ethico-onto-epistemological, or a "relational ontology" (as interviewed by Dolphijn and van der Tuin 2012, 54), that intertwines ontology, epistemology, and ethics. This framing connects directly to the research framework hierarchy introduced at the beginning of this decalogue, suggesting that for some creative arts researchers, these elements cannot be treated as separate tiers at all.

### *Cultural analysis methodologies*

If your research engages with cultural objects, whether you are analysing existing works or creating new ones, Mieke Bal's cultural analysis offers a flexible and generative framework. Bal, a cultural theorist and video artist, maintains that cultural objects are not passive in their encounters with humans: they participate actively in the production of meaning. This insight resonates strongly with creative artefact research, where the work itself is both subject and object of inquiry.

Bal describes this methodology as "concept-based": "concepts are products of philosophy and tools of analysis; they are also embodiments of the cultural practices we seek to understand through them. This circularity is perhaps best understood through the metaphor of travel – with a rough guide" (2002, 21). Like a traveller who allows the journey to shape the destination, cultural analysis follows concepts wherever they lead, across disciplines, time periods, and forms.

The key characteristics of cultural analysis include interdisciplinarity, social relevance, and a rejection of binary thinking. Bal proposes what she calls "pre-posterous history": an "intertwinement" of current and historical perspectives that resist linear chronology (2025, 35). Her characterisation of temporality as an "octopus, with tentacles going in all directions" (25) captures the methodology's embrace of non-linear, associative thinking, a quality that will feel intuitive to many creative arts researchers. Central to the approach is detailed analysis that treats "the object as (also) a subject" (34), an idea that connects directly to agential realism's insistence on material agency.

Cultural analysis shares qualities with conventional qualitative inquiry while also bridging towards post-qualitative approaches through its emphasis on material engagement and conceptual flexibility.

### *Closing reflections*

These emergent methodologies are included here not only because I consider them to be significant for creative arts research, but also because I experienced an overlap of some of their characteristics with my own PhD, which considers the role of "things", space, and affect. I did not intentionally adopt some of these frameworks; I arrived at them through my literature journey. Intuition and pre-cognitive thinking were perhaps also at play.

These methodologies have been developing for decades, some for millennia, and they differ significantly in their driving forces. Decolonising methodologies carry distinct epistemological and political commitments grounded in Indigenous sovereignty. ABR, NRT, and agential realism/new materialism share commitments to practice, embodiment, and material agency, and have contributed to what some scholars refer to as post-qualitative inquiry (PQI). Lisa A. Mazzei describes PQI "as happening in the middle of things, in the threshold" (2021, 198): not bound to one approach, it is a methodology of becoming. Cultural analysis, while sharing qualities with conventional qualitative inquiry, bridges towards PQI through its emphasis on material engagement and conceptual flexibility.

The most significant takeaway from this section is this: If you find yourself drawn to these frameworks, that instinct is worth following. These methodologies emerged from philosophical challenges to dominant research paradigms, and creative arts researchers have found in them a natural resonance. These, or other emerging frameworks, may give your work its clearest voice.

## 9 Determining your methodology

The practical question underlying this entire decalogue is: How do you actually determine your methodology? The answer lies in the spiral process. Begin with informed awareness: an initial scan of methodological possibilities builds foundational knowledge and opens your thinking. Then, set these thoughts aside while you develop and refine your thesis question. When your subject, topic, and research question are clear, return to the literature to construct or confirm your methodological framework. This movement between exploration and consolidation keeps you informed without becoming prematurely prescriptive.

### *An example: Autoethnography*

Autoethnography illustrates how this spiral process works in practice. Widely used in creative arts research, this approach aligns naturally with art practice analysis, as it concerns the self and culture, two central elements of creative work. Stacey Holman Jones describes autoethnography as merging "the practices of autobiography—writing about the self—and ethnography—the study of and writing about culture" (2018, 4–5). In practice, a researcher might explore aspects of their personal history, within a particular place, culture, and time, which have informed and inspired their creative practice.

Consider a creative artefact researcher exploring how childhood immigrant experiences shape their work, theorising notions of place, culture, identity, and diaspora through the creative artefact itself.[9] The work becomes both a site of inquiry and a means of knowledge generation, shaped by the artist's interior life and external experience. When paired with an interpretive framework, autoethnography encompasses both dimensions. As Marjorie Elaine Faulstich Orellana explains: "Auto-ethnography is not just about looking in the mirror; it is about refracting our views both inward and outward as we use the relationship between the self and the world to understand the world and ourselves" (2020, 146). This dual focus, concurrent introspection, and external awareness reveal how autoethnography naturally enables the development of creative arts questions.

This researcher might not have chosen autoethnography from a list at the outset, but arrived at it through their literature journey as the framework that best articulated what their practice had always been doing. The spiral process in action.

## 10 Methodology, method, practice

Once your research framework and methodology are in place, decisions about methods and practice become significantly clearer. Although the range of possible methods, considered in isolation, is arguably endless, methodology acts as a filter; it narrows and focuses your choices, making selection feel purposeful rather than arbitrary.

Hübner proposes a useful intermediate tier between methodology and methods, which he calls research strategy: "the concrete planning and path, which includes a designed set and structure of methods" (2024, 33). While I prefer to consider research strategy a function of methodology rather than a separate tier, Hübner's distinction is helpful in clarifying why qualitative, quantitative, and mixed methods are alternatively referred to as methodologies and as methods. As he explains, "a research strategy provides an overarching organisation of methods, methodology provides an overarching perspective on research strategy" (34). The key takeaway is practical: when your methodology is determined, your methods flow naturally from it.

Practice, similarly, may be shaped as much by PhD guidelines and your own professional background as by methodology. In a written thesis, practice often follows a more conventional path. In a creative artefact thesis, practice is commonly related to the researcher's established creative work and may, in turn, inform methods rather than simply emerging from them. Hübner suggests leaving "time and space in the *planning* of a research project for the unexpected and emergent" (134; emphasis in original): a reminder of the iterative relationship between methodology, methods, and practice.

This back-and-forth movement is, ultimately, what this decalogue has been describing throughout. You will move between your research question, your framework, your methodology, and your practice many times before your thesis takes its final shape. That is not uncertainty; it is the research process working as it should.

## Notes

1 Practice here refers both to the specific doing of research (analysis, writing, and making) and to the broader conduct of research (habits, relationships, and milestones) that sustain those processes.
2 See Grix (2022) for clear a discussion of research paradigm terminology, both historically and in practice. See Susan Kerrigan (2018) for similar, in relation to screen production research.
3 Some scholars use the terms interpretivist and constructivist synonymously, conflating their meanings, while others distinguish the terms; see *CAPC Glossary*.
4 See Appendix A for a table outlining the nuanced methodologies of these and related terms.
5 See *Blackfoot Physics: A Journey into the Native American Worldview* by F. David Peat (2002) for further discussions on First Nations' ways of being and object animacy (Page 2021). Similarly to Karen Barad, Peat combines his background in physics with, in this case, First Nation's worldviews in acknowledgement of methods from both experiences operating effectively "side by side" (xiv).
6 This term originated in relation to creative artefact research and has expanded to embrace all fields. See Owen Chapman and Kim Sawchuk (2012), and Natalie Loveless (2020, 2019). Related terms include "art-based": see Shaun McNiff (2013), and "research-creation", a similar research approach in Canada.
7 Also see Manning (2015, 52–71).
8 See Braidotti (2002) and DeLanda (1997).
9 See "Decalogue IX: Ten Writing Things", sec. 5, "Multiple voices"; and Mahsa Makki Alamdari (2025).

## References

### *Cited Works*

Archibald Q'um Q'um Xiiem, Jo-ann. 2008. *Indigenous Storywork: Educating the Heart, Body, and Spirit*. UBC Press.

Archibald Q'um Q'um Xiiem, Jo-ann, Jenny Bol Jun Lee-Morgan, and Jason De Santolo. 2022. "Introduction: Decolonizing Research: Indigenous Storywork as Methodology." In *Decolonizing Research: Indigenous Storywork as Methodology*, edited by Jo-ann Archibald

Q'um Q'um Xiiem, Jenny Bol Jun Lee-Morgan, and Jason De Santolo. Bloomsbury Academic.

Bal, Mieke. 2002. "Introduction." In *Travelling Concepts in the Humanities: A Rough Guide*. University of Toronto Press.

Bal, Mieke. 2025. "Cultural Analysis: Critical Encounters in Time, Space, and Thought." In *The Future of Cultural Analysis: A Critical Inquiry*, edited by Murat Ayemir, Noa Roei, and Aylin Kuryel. Routledge. https://doi.org/10.5117/9789048559794

Barad, Karen. 2007. *Meeting the Universe Halfway: Quantum Physics and the Entanglement of Matter and Meaning*. Duke University Press.

Barone, Tom, and Elliot W. Eisner. 2012. *Arts Based Research*. SAGE Academic Books.

Behrendt, Larissa. 2022. "Indigenous Storytelling: Decolonizing Institutions and Assertive Self-determination: Implications for Legal Practice." *In Decolonizing Research: Indigenous Storywork as Methodology*, edited by Jo-ann Archibald Q'um Q'um Xiiem, Jenny Bol Lee-Morgan, and Jason De Santolo. Bloomsbury Academic.

Blair, Nerida. 2022. "Lilyology as a Transformative Framework for Decolonizing Ethical Spaces within the Academy." *In Decolonizing Research: Indigenous Storywork as Methodology*, edited by Jo-ann Archibald Q'um Q'um Xiiem, Jenny Bol Lee-Morgan, and Jason De Santolo. Bloomsbury Academic.

Bozalek, Vivienne, and Karin Murris. 2022. "Diffraction." In *A Glossary for Doing Postqualitative, New Materialist and Critical Posthumanist Research Across Disciplines*, edited by Karin Murris. Routledge.

Braidotti, Rosi. 2002. *Metamorphoses: Towards a Materialist Theory of Becoming*. Polity Press.

Candy, Linda. 2011. "Research and Creative Practice." In *Interacting: Art, Research and the Creative Practitioner*, edited by Linda Candy and Ernest Edmonds. Libri Publishing Ltd.

Chapman, Owen, and Kim Sawchuk. 2012. "Research-Creation: Intervention, Analysis and 'Family Resemblances'." *Canadian Journal of Communication* 37 (1): 5–26. https://doi.org/10.22230/cjc.2012v37n1a2489

Delanda, Manuel. 1997. *A Thousand Years of Nonlinear History*. Zone Books.

Denzin, Norman K., and Yvonna S. Lincoln. 2018. "Introduction: The Discipline and Practice of Qualitative Research." In *The Sage Handbook of Qualitative Research*, 5th ed., edited by Norman K. Denzin and Yvonna S. Lincoln. Sage Publications.

Dolphijn, Rick, and Iris van der Tuin. 2012. *New Materialism: Interviews and Cartographies*. Open Humanities Press.

Eisner, Elliot. 2008. "Art and Knowledge." In *Handbook of the Arts in Qualitative Research: Perspectives, Methodologies, Examples, and Issues*, edited by J. Gary Knowles and Ardra L. Cole. SAGE Publications.

Faulstich Orellana, Marjorie Elaine. 2020. *Mindful Ethnography: Mind, Heart and Activity for Transformative Social Research*. Routledge.

Grix, Jonathan. 2022. *The Foundations of Research*, 3rd ed. Bloomsbury Academic.

Guba, Egon G., and Yvonna S. Lincoln. 1994. "Competing Paradigms in Qualitative Research." In *The SAGE Handbook of Qualitative Research*, 1st ed., edited by Norman K. Denzin and Yvonna S. Lincoln. Sage.

Haraway, Donna J. 1997. *Modest_Witness@Second_Millennium. FemaleMan©_Meets_OncoMouse™: Feminism and Technoscience*. Routledge.

Haseman, Brad, and Daniel Mafe. 2009. "Acquiring Know-How: Research Training for Practice-led Researchers." In *Practice-led Research, Research-led Practice in the Creative Arts*, edited by Hazel Smith and Roger T. Dean. Edinburgh Press.

Holman Jones, Stacy. 2018. "Creative Selves/Creative Cultures: Critical Autoethnography, Performance, and Pedagogy." In *Creative Selves/Creative Cultures: Critical Autoethnography, Performance, and Pedagogy*, edited by Stacy Holman Jones and Marc Pruyn. Springer.

Hübner, Falk. 2024. *Method, Methodology and Research Design in Artistic Research: Between Solid Routes and Emergent Pathways*. Routledge.

Ingold, Tim. (2007) 2016. *Lines: A Brief History*. Routledge.

Kerrigan, Susan. 2018. "A 'Logical' Explanation of Screen Production as Method-Led Research." In *Screen Production Research: Creative Practice as a Mode of Enquiry*, edited by Craig Batty and Susan Kerrigan. Springer Palgrave Macmillan.

Kimmerer, Robin Wall. 2013. *Braiding Sweetgrass: Indigenous Wisdom, Scientific Knowledge, and the Teachings of Plants*. Milkweed Editions.

Kovach, Margaret. 2009. *Indigenous Methodologies: Characteristics, Conversations, and Contexts*. University of Toronto Press.

Lather, Patti. 2007. *Getting Lost: Feminist Efforts Toward a Double(d) Science*. State University of New York Press.

Lincoln, Yvonna, Susan A. Lynham, and Egon G. Guba. 2018. "Paradigmatic Controversies, Contradictions, and Emerging Confluences, Revisited." In *The Sage Handbook of Qualitative Research*, 5th ed., edited by Norman K. Denzin and Yvonna S. Lincoln. Sage Publications.

Lincoln, Yvonna S., and Egon G. Guba. 1985. *Naturalistic Inquiry*. SAGE Publications.

Loveless, Natalie. 2019. *How to Make Art at the End of the World: A Manifesto for Research-Creation*. Duke University Press.

Loveless, Natalie. 2020. "Research-Creation Interdisciplinary Praxis: Natalie Loveless in Conversation with Erin Manning." In *Knowings and Knots: Methodologies and Ecologies in Research-Creation*, edited by Natalie Loveless. University of Alberta Press.

Manning, Erin. 2015. "Against Method." In *Non-Representational Methodologies: Re-Envisioning Research*, edited by Phillip Vannini. Routledge.

Mazzei, Lisa A. 2021. "Postqualitative Inquiry: Or the Necessity of Theory." *Qualitative Inquiry* 27(2): 198–200.

McNiff, Shaun, ed. 2013. *Art as Research: Opportunities and Challenges*. Intellect. https://doi.org/10.1177/1077800420932607

Mertens, Donna M. 2022. "Mixed Methods Integration for Transformative Purposes." In *The Routledge Handbook for Advancing Integration in Mixed Methods Research*, edited by John H. Hitchcock and Anthony J. Onwuegbuzie. Routledge.

Neale, Margot. 2020. "First Knowledges: An Introduction." In *Songlines: Power and Promise*, edited by Margot Neale and Lynne Kelly. Thames and Hudson Australia.

Nelson, Robin. 2022. *Practice as Research in the Arts (and Beyond): Principles, Processes, Contexts, Achievements*, 2nd ed. Palgrave Macmillan.

Page, Alison. 2021. "Objects and Spirituality: Building on Country." In *Design: Building on Country*, edited by Alison Page and Paul Memmott. Thames and Hudson Australia.

Peat, F. David. 2002. *Blackfoot Physics: A Journey into the Native American Worldview*. Phanes Press.

Rose, Gillian. 2023. *Visual Methodologies: An Introduction to Researching with Visual Materials*. Sage Publications.

Thrift, Nigel. 2008. *Non-Representational Theory: Space, Politics, Affect*. Routledge.

Tuhiwai Smith, Linda. 2021. *Decolonizing Methodologies: Research and Indigenous Peoples*, 3rd ed. Zed Books.

van der Tuin, Iris. 2014. "The Mode of Invention of Creative Research: Onto-Epistemology." In *Material Inventions: Applying Creative Arts Research*, edited by Estelle Barrett and Barabara Bolt. I. B. Tauris.

Vannini, Phillip. 2015. "Non-Representational Research Methodologies: An Introduction." In *Non-Representational Methodologies: Re-Envisioning Research*, edited by Phillip Vannini. Routledge.

Wilson, Shawn. 2008. *Research is Ceremony: Indigenous Research Methods*. Fernwood Publishing.

## *Suggested Reading*

Aloi, Giovanni, and Susan McHugh, eds. 2021. *Posthumanism in Art and Science: A Reader*. Columbia University Press.

Barad, Karen. 2012. "On Touching—the Inhuman That Therefore I Am." *Differences* 23(3): 206–223. https://doi.org/10.1215/10407391-1892943

Braidotti, Rosi. 2019. *Posthuman Knowledge*. Polity Press. (See chap. 5, "How to Do Posthuman Thinking.")

Chilisa, Bagele. 2020. *Indigenous Research Methodologies*, 2nd ed. SAGE Publications.

Darder, Antonia. 2019. "Decolonizing Interpretive Research." In *Decolonizing Interpretive Research: A Subaltern Methodology for Social Change*, edited by Antonia Darder. Routledge.

González, Maria Cristina. 2000. "The Four Seasons of Ethnography: A Creation-centered Ontology for Ethnography." *International Journal of Intercultural Relations* 24(5): 623–650. https://doi.org/10.1016/S0147-1767(00)00020-1

Kovach, Margaret. 2015. "Emerging From the Margins: Indigenous Methodologies." In *Research As Resistance: Revisiting Critical, Indigenous, and Anti-oppressive Approaches*, 2nd ed., edited by Susan Strega and Leslie Brown. Canadian Scholars' Press.

Leavy, Patricia, ed. 2014. *The Oxford Handbook of Qualitative Research*. Oxford University Press.

Longo, Mariano, Corrado Punzi, and Matteo Jacopo Zaterini, eds. 2025. *Creativity and Sociology: Doing Social Research with and on Artistic Sources*. Routledge.

Maisuria, Alpesh, and Grant Banfield, eds. *Working with Critical Realism: Stories of Methodological Encounters*. Routledge.

Marshall, Judi. 2018. *First Person Action Research: Living Life as Inquiry*. Sage Publications.

Murris, Karin. 2022. *Karen Barad as Educator: Agential Realism and Education*. Springer Nature.

Methods along the path
V

# Decalogue V

## TEN METHOD THINGS

Building on the previous decalogue's discussion of methodology as a framework, this decalogue addresses methods as the specific tools and techniques that enact your research.

When I began my PhD, I understood, in a general sense, that research involved methods. I had investigated ideas, constructed materials, and kept notes throughout my creative practice. What I didn't fully comprehend was that methods aren't simply activities you perform during research; they are the means through which your methodology becomes practice. I attributed my choice of methods simply to a reaction to immediate requirements. Now I know that methods flow from the methodological framework rather than arising arbitrarily, and that it is entirely appropriate to borrow from other disciplines or develop approaches specific to an inquiry. I came to this understanding, as I discovered much in my PhD, by doing rather than through instruction.

This decalogue addresses that gap. It won't tell you which methods to use; that determination belongs to you, your research question, and your methodology. What it will do is help you understand what methods are, how they emerge from methodology, and how to approach the process of selecting, combining, and sometimes inventing the tools that will make your research possible.

The range of methods available to creative arts researchers is remarkably diverse. Conventional methods that "attempt to capture, codify and categorise knowledge" (Kershaw and Nicholson 2011, 1) don't always provide an appropriate fit for the field, though foundational qualitative and quantitative traditions remain relevant and useful. Beyond these, mixed methods, performative approaches, and emergent inquiry frameworks have significantly expanded what is considered rigorous research practice in creative arts.

A reference guide to methods by category is available in Appendix B, and key terms are defined in the *CAPC Glossary*. The appendix provides

DOI: 10.4324/9781003584209-6

breadth across categories by way of lists, while the glossary offers definitions of methods most relevant to creative arts research. As you explore this range, keep in mind Helen Kara's reminder: "the terminology of creative research methods is very fluid" (2020, 5).

## 1 What is method?

In the previous decalogue, Gillian Rose's distinction between methodology and method was introduced: methodology is the rationale, methods are the practical steps (2023, 1). It is worth returning to that distinction here as the two terms are frequently used interchangeably, even by experienced researchers.

A method is a specific tool, technique, strategy, or procedure used to gather and analyse material in the service of your research question. Again, where methodology answers "how will I approach this inquiry?", method answers "what will I actually do?" Falk Hübner offers this vivid distinction: methods are "the locus of concrete activity, the space in which the researcher encounters her research subjects, objects, and entities, the space from where most unexpected ideas within the research process emerge. In short, this is 'where it happens'" (2024, 32). That phrase, "where it happens" is worth returning to. Methods are not procedural requirements to be filled in on a research proposal. They are the lived experience of research: the interviews conducted, the sources searched, the performances staged, the material handled, the journals kept. They are where your research question meets the world.

Importantly, the determination of methods is itself a creative act. Methods may be borrowed from other disciplines, adapted for your specific context, or developed specifically for your inquiry. As you will see in this decalogue, some of the most generative methods in creative arts research emerged precisely because conventional approaches couldn't accommodate what practitioners were already carrying out.

## 2 Methods emerge from methodology

The relationship between methodology and method, as described above, is one of rationale to action: methodology justifies, method enacts. But in practice, the relationship is more dynamic than that sequential description suggests. Methods don't simply follow from methodology like instructions from a manual. They emerge from it, often gradually, sometimes unexpectedly, through the same spiral process described in previous decalogues.

Think of methodology as a filter. Once your methodological framework is in place, the vast range of possible methods narrows considerably. An interpretivist methodology orientates you towards methods that explore meaning: interviews, textual analysis, and reflective writing. A transformative methodology orientates you towards methods that examine and challenge structures of power: participatory action research, community engagement, and oral history. A grounded theory, as a methodology and method, uses a structured set of techniques to determine a theory from particular data. An agential realist framework orientates you towards methods that attend to material agency and entanglement: diffractive analysis, intra-active interviewing, apparatus analysis. The methodology doesn't choose your methods for you, but it leads the way, making the choice purposeful rather than arbitrary.

In creative arts research, this process is rarely linear. You may begin with a provisional methodology, start working with certain methods, and discover through that work that your methodology needs to shift. Or you may find that a method you've been using intuitively in your practice turns out to have a name and a theoretical framework you weren't aware of. Both of these experiences are normal. The spiral continues: informed awareness, organic exploration, then consolidation.

My own PhD illustrates how methodology shapes method, and how that process is rarely straightforward. As described, my research explores magical cinematic objects: the sets, props, and things of film that carry intent and agency. My methodology was qualitative, combining textual and modal analysis with theoretical application. My methods included close textual analysis of three films, each representing a different filmic mode, alongside theoretical analysis drawing on phenomenology, thing theory, and design concepts. My background in production design guided the theoretical component almost instinctively: my experiential knowledge led me towards research in objects and thing theory before I fully understood why.

What I didn't anticipate was the structural problem that instinct would create. I originally wrote three methodology chapters: cinematic objects and thing theory, phenomenology, and film modes. I had researched and written substantially across all three before my supervisor pointed out, gently but clearly, that my research should embrace only two methodologies. I was frustrated, and if I am honest, briefly shattered. I had invested significant time and thought in three frameworks that I believed were all essential.

I returned to my sources, watched more films, and studied my circumstances carefully. The solution, when it came, was straightforward. For my research, phenomenology was not a separate methodology but a theoretical lens that directly supported my investigation of the object, in and out of film. It belonged within my thing theory methodology, not alongside it. The two frameworks, thing theory and film modes, served my research question together. I restructured my approach into two chapters.

For a time, I viewed the discarded third chapter as a failure and wasted effort. As my thesis continued to develop, I came to understand it differently. Had I not researched and written those three chapters, I would never have gained the depth of knowledge required to argue my research question with confidence. The apparent detour was the foundation. This result is the spiral process at work again: you may need to go further than necessary in order to discover where the boundaries of your inquiry actually lie. Your methodology filters your methods, but sometimes the resulting selection only reveals itself through productive overload, trying too much before you see what fits.

You don't need to know your methods before you begin researching. What you need is a methodology that will guide you towards them. The methods become clearer as your research question sharpens and your methodological framework develops. Trust the process.

## 3 Quantitative and qualitative methods

The two foundational traditions of research methods are quantitative and qualitative, and understanding the distinction between them is essential even if, as is typical in creative arts research, you work primarily within qualitative methods.

Quantitative research is about counting and measuring. If you're gathering data that is expressible in numbers, such as audience sizes, frequency of themes, survey responses, or statistical patterns, you're working quantitatively. Although the relevance of quantitative methods may not be immediately apparent for creative arts research, they have definite applications. A creative artefact researcher examining historical trends in production design might use quantitative analysis of archival records. These methods become relevant when your research question requires evidence that can be counted, compared, or measured.

Qualitative research is about understanding and interpreting. If you're exploring meanings, experiences, processes, or contexts through words, images, performance, or descriptions, you're working qualitatively. Most creative arts research is qualitative for good reason. The questions that animate creative practice, such as what does it mean, how does it work, what does this experience feel like, and what cultural forces are at play, are inherently interpretive rather than measurable. Qualitative methods are typically grouped into three categories: interpretive (analysing and interpreting texts), contextual (examining context as an integral element of research), and participatory inquiry (conducted with people rather than on them).

The distinction between qualitative and quantitative is instructive without being prescriptive. These same terms can describe paradigms, methodologies, and methods, sometimes simultaneously, and their boundaries are more permeable in practice than in theory. What matters is that you understand which tradition your primary methods belong to and can articulate why those methods serve your research question.

## 4 Mixed methods

Mixed methods research (MMR) emerged in the 1980s and established itself as a distinct approach in the 1990s. MMR combines quantitative and qualitative methods not as separate parallel elements but as techniques functioning together to generate richer findings than either approach could produce alone (Johnson et al. 2007). For creative arts research, where questions often span interpretive, contextual, and measurable dimensions, MMR offers a flexible and well-founded framework. In any field, using more than one method to investigate a research question, known as triangulation, can strengthen the credibility and validity of findings.

Abbas Tashakkori and Charles Teddlie identify nine characteristics of MMR that distinguish it from simply using both quantitative and qualitative techniques side by side. Among these, the most significant for creative arts research are methodological eclecticism (drawing freely from multiple traditions), paradigm pluralism (refusing to be constrained by a single worldview), an iterative and cyclical approach, and a reliance on visual representations (2010, 8–11). That last characteristic is particularly relevant in the arts and design. Where other disciplines might rely on tables and diagrams, visual communication in a creative arts MMR context can encompass a much broader range of representational forms.

What unifies these characteristics is an absence of binary thinking. MMR doesn't ask you to choose between counting and interpreting, between objectivity and subjectivity. It asks you to deploy whichever approaches best serve your research question, in whatever combination generates the most illuminating findings. For interdisciplinary creative arts research, where questions often don't fit neatly into a single methodological tradition, this flexibility is genuinely liberating.

MMR has gained significant acceptance across academic disciplines, evidenced by dedicated publications, conferences, and a growing discourse around integrated methods.[1]

## 5 Performative methods

The performative research approach, originally proposed in the social sciences, was swiftly and naturally adopted in the creative arts. Norman K. Denzin is generally credited with introducing the term to social science research (2001). His description of its ambition captures why it translates so readily to creative practice:

> I seek an interpretive social science that is simultaneously autoethnographic, vulnerable, performative and critical. This is a social science that refuses abstractions and high theory. It is a way of being in the world, a way of writing, hearing and listening. Viewing culture as a complex performative process, it seeks to understand how people enact and construct meaning in their daily lives.
>
> *(43)*

Following Denzin, Brad Haseman proposes performative research as a distinct paradigm for creative artefact research, defining methods independent of the conventional quantitative and qualitative binary and outside the scope of mixed methods (2006). Performative research, as Haseman explains, "sees the material outcomes of practice as all-important representations of research findings in their own right" (103). Practice itself becomes the means of research articulation. Elena Vacchelli extends this notion, describing the performative method as reflecting "on the complex nature of the spatial scale of the physical body as the site of perceived experiences and subjectivity" (2018, 185). Embodied exploration as a performative method gives creative arts researchers access to knowledge that lives in the doing before it can be spoken.

Not all scholars accept performative methods as a distinct category; many position them as a subset of qualitative research. This view is reasonable as the overlap is genuine. What Haseman's framework offers, however, is explicit recognition that creative practice outcomes are not merely data or illustrative: they are findings. That distinction matters for creative artefact researchers whose work has sometimes been positioned as supplementary to rather than constitutive of their research contribution.

Kathleen Gallagher's research with youth in the performing arts captures what performative methods make possible.[2] Writing about Gallagher's work, Helen Cahill observes that it

> highlights the ways in which the creative and performative methods permit for investigation of the fluid, emergent, and social nature of identities and offer a unique way to investigate hope, as it emerges at the 'borderland between real and imagined'
>
> *(2020, ix)*

For creative arts researchers, this borderland is familiar territory. Performative methods are what give that territory scholarly legitimacy.

## 6 Emergent and emerging methods

Beyond established methods, distinct clusters of research techniques are expanding the landscape of creative arts research. Methods discussed here link directly to the emergent methodologies explored in the previous decalogue. Each methodology generates its own characteristic methods, and understanding that connection helps you identify which approach might serve your inquiry.

As with their corresponding methodologies, some of these methods have been emerging for decades, others for millennia. They are presented here not as comprehensive guides but as an orientation: enough to recognise whether a particular approach resonates with your practice, and to send you towards deeper reading.

### *Decolonising research methods*

Decolonising research methods adapt long-established cultural and community traditions of communication, storytelling, and thought as applied to the context of academic research. Conventional Western methods are then often selected to augment culturally grounded approaches where appropriate. Margaret Kovach's observation that Indigenous research "shape shifts in the form of theory, methods, and ethics" (2005, 32) is worth holding as a guiding principle: these methods resist fixed definition by their very essence.

Riadh Ghemmour raises the need for methods that foreground care, ethics, and the examination of power by addressing a rebalancing of knowledge production by "[t]hinking through a decolonising lens" (2024, 225). This orientation shapes not only what is researched but also how. The methods themselves carry ethical and relational weight.

Two examples illustrate how decolonising methods transfer to practice. Victor Steffensen describes a navigation technique taught to him as a boy by his Elder: "you have to have *praction*" (2022, 226, emphasis added). This combined word describes a practice of action central to the skill of observation. While researching, Steffensen realised that "[i]t was the word for teaching and applying traditional practical knowledge to everything in the natural and cultural world. It was the doing" (226). Jason De Santolo's research, *Yarnbar Jarngkurr*, meaning "talking and storying" (2022, 174), explores this method "as a resonating story continuum across the generations" (2022, 239), giving rise to the term "story research process" (242). De Santolo describes this scholarly inclusion of story: "meaning-making as a spiralling process, as reflected in Elders' ways of teaching through story and action" (2022, 250). Both approaches bring together story and practice in investigation. This convergence will resonate with a range of creative artefact researchers as the approach of learning by doing has deep roots in many cultures.

As a method, Songlines offers a means of self-discovery and relational understanding. It supports research naturally, as Margot Neale describes: "Songlines divulge powerful lessons about what it means to be human and to live on this earth. They offer us the promise of connectivity to each other and our planet in a fragmenting world" (2020, 139). As such, it provides an integrated mapping of questions, observations, and findings.

Underlying these methods is political as well as methodological intent. Leola Roberta Rainbow Tsinnajinnie describes this research as acknowledging "what our peoples have gone through, the impact of colonization", and as actively reclaiming research space, "it's pushing back. It's claiming our space as our own" (Tsinnajinnie et al., 2019, 39). The research methods that emerge through this reclaiming, including learning circles, oral traditions, relational accountability, Songlines, storywork, and storytelling, are as varied as the cultures and communities from which they arise.

### *Arts-based methods (including art-based and research-creation)*

Arts-based methods are driven by artistic form and function alongside many conventional qualitative methods. Through the lens of the art form, a method may draw from the relationship between form and maker, audience, or teacher. An art form may serve as a means of communicating findings in fields outside the creative arts, as in poetic inquiry. Key examples include a/r/tography (living inquiry through the artist/researcher/teacher relationship), body mapping, choreographic inquiry, poetic inquiry, and videography.

### *Non-representational process-based methods*

Non-representational methods turn around the conventional definition of method itself. What is listed here might be better described as a "sense" of research rather than a procedure: data is not a given but created. These methods prioritise the doing, the be(com)ing, and the happenings: the experimentation, record keeping, and journeys of discovery are primary. Steps of thinking, doing, making, and finding function together simultaneously rather than sequentially.

Three key aspects of what Beth Greenhough et al. call "more-than-human and more-than-representational methods" are: "a focus on bodies and their affective capacities", "emphasis on experiment and play", and being "committed not to shaping futures so much as leaving them open" (2025, 70–71). These characteristics lead to methods that are sensorily driven, purposely messy, and open-ended, and that value discovery over predetermined findings. Examples include deep mapping, diarising, experimentation and play, and inefficient mapping.

### *Agential realism/new materialism methods*

Methods emerging from agential realism are configured by the principle that entities, time, processes, and roles cannot be separated in any event. Throughout *Meeting the Universe Halfway*, Karen Barad develops their concept of "mattering" as a way of attending to the world that refuses to isolate researcher, subject, and object (2007). Agency extends to all matter and living things in this framework as "more-than-human".[3] Key methods include apparatus analysis, diffractive analysis, entanglement, intra-action, and intra-active interviewing.

### *Cultural analysis*

Cultural analysis methods stem from Mieke Bal's five principles: interdisciplinarity, social relevance, detailed analysis, the object as subject, and a dialogue between current and historical elements (2007). What translates these principles into method is flexibility in thought, and a capacity to treat the unknown, not understood, or conflicting as productive rather than problematic. Bal explains:

> You do not apply one method; you conduct a meeting between several, a meeting in which the object participates so that, together, object and methods can become a new, not firmly delineated, field. This is where travel becomes the unstable ground of cultural analysis.
>
> *(1)*

In her informative and quirky "Lexicon for Cultural Analysis", Bal reveals: "It takes a lot of persuasion to tell a struggling PhD candidate that one only knows what one is looking for when one is writing and finding? that glaring gap staring at you" (2013, 69; question mark in original). Bal synthesizes notions of object agency, flexibility, the positivity of doubt, and the significance of the journey in research. Key methods include concept-based analysis, concepts as tools, dialogue with the object, differentiation, and listening.

This list is a starting point rather than a complete map. For a representative list of methods for each framework, see Appendix B.

## 7 Categorising methods by activity

The approaches discussed so far have organised methods by research tradition: qualitative, quantitative, mixed, performative, and emergent. Anna Juliane Heinrich et al. propose a different organising principle: grouping methods by the activity they involve (2024).

Their four categories are "conversing and storytelling" (methods of interviewing and narrative); "observing and experiencing" (observation, ethnography, and physical or virtual site exploration); "drawing and visualizing" (mapmaking, drawing, photography, and other visual methods); and "reading and reflecting" (qualitative analysis, interpretation, and multimodal discursive practices) (Heinrich et al. 2024, 11–14).

What makes this framework valuable for creative arts researchers is that it reverses the conventional selection process. Rather than starting with methodology and working towards method, you start with what you are already doing or what feels most natural to your practice, and work outward towards a methodological framework. For a practitioner whose research process begins in the studio or on location, asking "what am I doing?" before "what methodology am I using?" can generate a more organic and practice-aligned methodology. This technique offers a valid alternative to the top-down sequence rather than a contradiction of it. For those who find the paradigm-to-practice sequence counterintuitive, it offers a genuine entry point into method selection, though it won't suit every researcher.

## 8 Post-qualitative inquiry

Post-qualitative inquiry (PQI) is a mode of research thinking that moves away not only from conventional methods but from the construct of methodology itself. It isn't added on top of an existing qualitative approach; research must begin with this position and remain committed to it throughout.

Elizabeth Adams St. Pierre developed this concept after realising that no existing methodology (mode of inquiry) could accommodate post-structuralist thought, whose philosophers "refused pre-existing methods and methodologies" (2020, 14). PQI begins onto-epistemologically rather than methodologically, allowing inquiry to develop naturally around a research question rather than being predetermined by a framework. Each PQI thesis is therefore structured differently from another, invented for its specific inquiry (St. Pierre 2020, 17–18). St. Pierre describes it as "concerned not with what *is* but what is *not yet, to come*" (2021, 163; emphasis in original). Carol A. Taylor and Vivienne Bozalek characterise it as an inquiry that "entangles affective alliances of the human and nonhuman; it becomes a joyful unfolding of that which is and which might become" (2022, 89).

Several of the emergent methods discussed here, particularly non-representational and agential realism/new materialism, have contributed to or arisen alongside PQI, and their methods align naturally with this mode of inquiry. Whether PQI constitutes a genuinely distinct approach or an extension of experimental qualitative research remains debated. For creative arts research, the distinction is arguably already moot: this mode of inquiry is being adopted and developed regardless of whether the debate is resolved.

One critical distinction must be clearly stated: decolonising methodologies should not be conflated with or subsumed under PQI. They have separate origins. Decolonising methodologies emerge from First Nations sovereignty and anti-colonial struggle; PQI emerges from Western post-structuralist thought. What they share is a commitment to reinvention and a refusal of imposed frameworks. That connection is worth acknowledging; the difference in origin and epistemological commitment demands respect.

## 9 Determining your methods

Having explored the range of methods available, the practical question remains: how do you actually determine which methods to use? Three sound paths exist for creative arts researchers: drawing on established methods within your field, borrowing from other disciplines, and developing methods specific to your own inquiry. Most creative arts researchers will use some combination of all three.

The following steps pull together points made throughout this decalogue and offer a framework for this process, while acknowledging that in practice it is rarely linear.

**Begin with your research question**. Ask yourself: What kind of material or evidence do I need to answer this question? If the answer involves exploring meanings, experiences, or interpretations, qualitative methods will likely serve you. If it involves measuring, counting, or comparing data, quantitative or mixed methods may be relevant. If the act of making is itself a means of knowing, performative or arts-based methods may be most appropriate. Your research question is your most reliable guide.

**Let the methodology narrow the field**. Methodology acts as a filter: once your methodological framework is in place, the range of possible methods narrows considerably. Review the methods associated with your methodology. You don't need every method available within a given approach; you need those that best serve your specific question.

**Consider your research activities**. Heinrich et al.'s (2024) activity-based framework offers a useful check at this stage. What will you actually be doing? Conducting interviews? Analysing films or artworks? Making work? Documenting process? Match your activities to methods and verify that those methods are consistent with your methodology.

**Borrow deliberately**. Creative arts research draws methods from other disciplines. If a method from sociology, geography, education, or elsewhere serves your inquiry, use it. Be explicit about this borrowing in your methodology chapter: explain where the method originates and why it serves your research question.

**Consider developing your own**. The determination of methods is itself a creative act. If no existing method adequately captures what your research requires, you may opt to develop your own. This approach is not unconventional in creative arts; it is one of its defining characteristics.

**Document your reasoning**. Whatever methods you select, be able to articulate why. Your methodology chapter will need to explain not just which methods you used but how they emerged from your methodology and why they were the most appropriate tools for your inquiry.

## 10 Maintaining flexibility

The methods you identify at the beginning of your research may not be the methods you end up using. This consequence is not a problem; it is the research process working as it should.

Methods evolve for many reasons. Your research question may sharpen in ways that make some methods redundant and others newly relevant. Your engagement with materials, participants, or practice may reveal needs you couldn't have anticipated. A method you planned to use may prove impractical, ethically complicated, or less generative than you hoped. A method you hadn't considered may suggest itself through the literature or through your supervisor's feedback.

This flexibility is not methodological inconsistency; it is again an unfolding through engagement (Lincoln and Guba 1985). As Hübner observes, it is important to leave "time and space in the planning of a research project for the unexpected and emergent" (2024, 134). Build that space into your plan from the outset.

What matters is not that your methods remain constant but that they remain coherent. At every stage, ensure you can explain why your chosen methods serve your research question and how they emerge from your methodological framework. That coherence, rather than rigid adherence to an original plan, is what your examiners will be looking for.

The methods that surprise you are often the ones that take your research somewhere you couldn't have reached by following your initial plan alone. Trust the process, remain attentive to what your research is telling you, and be prepared and motivated to adjust.

## Notes

1 See Donna Mertens (2023).
2 See Gallagher (2022).
3 This phrase was coined by David Abram in *The Spell of the Sensuous: Perception and Language in a More-Than-Human World* (1996). A description of this key characteristic recurs throughout new materialism and agential realism literature. For this particular contextual wording, see Phillip Vannini (2015) and Katve-Kaisa Kontturi (2025, 161).

## References

### *Cited works*


Abram, David. 1996. *The Spell of the Sensuous: Perception and Language in a More-Than-Human World*. Random House.

Bal, Mieke. 2007. "Working with Concepts" In *Conceptual Odysseys: Passages to Cultural Analysis*, edited by Griselda Pollock. I. B. Tauris.

Bal, Mieke. 2013. "Lexicon for Cultural Analysis." In *Die Lust an der Kultur/Theorie. Transdisziplinäre Interventionen Für Wolfgang Müller-Funk*, edited by Anna Babka, Daniela Finzi, and Clemens Ruthner. Turia + Kant Verlag.

Barad, Karin. 2007. *Meeting the Universe Halfway: Quantum Physics and the Entanglement of Matter and Meaning*. Duke University Press.

Cahill, Helen. 2020. "Foreword." In *Global Youth Citizenry and Radical Hope: Enacting Community-Engaged Research through Performative Methodologies*, edited by Kathleen Gallagher, Dirk J. Rodricks, and Kelsey Jacobson. Springer Nature.

De Santolo, Jason. 2022. "The Emergence of *Yarnbar Jarngkurr* from Indigenous Homelands: A Creative Indigenous Methodology." In *Decolonizing Research: Indigenous Storywork as Methodology*, edited by Jo-ann Archibald Q'um Q'um Xiiem, Jenny Bol Lee-Morgan, and Jason De Santolo. Bloomsbury Academic.

De Santolo, Jason. 2022. "Indigenous Storywork in Australia." In *Decolonizing Research: Indigenous Storywork as Methodology*, edited by Jo-ann Archibald Q'um Q'um Xiiem, Jenny Bol Lee-Morgan, and Jason De Santolo. Bloomsbury Academic.

Denzin, Norman K. 2001. "The Reflexive Interview." *Qualitative Research* 1 (1): 23–46. https://doi.org/10.1177/146879410100100102

Gallagher, Kathleen. 2022. *Hope in A Collapsing World: Youth, Theatre, and Listening as a Political Alternative*. University of Toronto Press.

Ghemmour, Riadh. 2024. "Reimagining Research Methods Curriculum in Education Otherwise: A Decolonial Turn." In *Creative Ruptions for Emergent Educational Futures*, edited by Kerry Chappell, Chris Turner, and Heather Wren. Palgrave Macmillan.

Greenhough, Beth, Jamie Lorimer, Joshua Evans, and Oscar Hartman Davies. 2025. "More-than-representational Methods for Encountering Viruses, Bacteria, and Other Microbes." In *Non-Representational and More-Than-Human Research: Vitalist Methodologies for the End of Data*, edited by Phillip Vannini. Routledge.

Haseman, Brad. 2006. "A Manifesto for Performative Research." *Media International Australia, Incorporating Culture and Policy* 118 (1): 98–106. https://doi.org/10.1177/1329878X0611800113

Heinrich, Anna Juliane, Séverine Marguin, Angela Million, and Jörg Stollmann. 2024. "Introduction: Spatial Research from an Interdisciplinary Perspective." In *Handbook of Qualitative and Visual Methods in Spatial Research*, edited by Anna Juliane Heinrich, Séverine Marguin, Angela Million, and Jörg Stollmann. transcript Verlag. https://doi.org/10.14361/9783839467343

Hübner, Falk. 2024. *Method, Methodology and Research Design in Artistic Research: Between Solid Routes and Emergent Pathways*. Routledge.

Johnson, R. Burke, Anthony J. Onwuegbuzie, and Lisa A. Turner. 2007. "Towards a Definition of Mixed Methods Research." *Journal of Mixed Methods Research* 1 (2): 112–113. https://doi.org/10.1177/1558689806298224

Kara, Helen. 2020. *Creative Research Methods: A Practical Guide*, 2nd ed. Bristol University Press.

Kershaw, Baz, and Helen Nicholson. 2011. "Introduction: Doing Methods Creatively." In *Research Methods in Theatre and Performance*, edited by Baz Kershaw and Helen Nichoson. Edinburgh University Press.

Kontturi, Katve-Kaisa. 2025. "Following Table-Work: Affirming More-than-Human Agency in Art-based Workshops." In *New Materialist Affirmations: Creative Research Interventions in Methods and Practice*, edited by Anna Hickey-Moody, Suvi Pihkala, Gretchen Coombs, and Marissa Willcox. Edinburgh University Press.

Kovach, Margaret. 2005. "Emerging From the Margins: Indigenous Methodologies." In *Research As Resistance: Critical, Indigenous, and Anti-oppressive Approaches*, edited by Leslie Brown and Susan Strega. Canadian Scholars' Press. [Please note, the second edition of this book is also listed in "Decalogue IV: Ten Methodology Things" suggested readings as it contains different content].

Lincoln, Yvonna S., and Egon G. Guba. 1985. *Naturalistic Inquiry*. SAGE Publications.

Mertens, Donna M. 2023. *Mixed Methods Research: Research Methods*. Bloomsbury Academic.

Neale, Margot. 2020. "The Last Song." In *Songlines: Power and Promise*, edited by Margot Neale and Lynne Kelly. Thames and Hudson Australia.

Rose, Gillian. 2023. *Visual Methodologies: An Introduction to Researching with Visual Materials*. Sage Publications.
St. Pierre, Elizabeth Adams. 2020. "Post Qualitative Inquiry, the Refusal of Method, and the Risk of the New." In *Qualitative Inquiry and the Politics of Resistance: Possibilities, Performances, and Praxis*, edited by Norman K. Denzin and Michael D. Giardina. Routledge.
St. Pierre, Elizabeth Adams. 2021. "Why Post Qualitative Inquiry?" *Qualitative Inquiry* 27 (2): 163–166. https://doi.org/10.1177/1077800420931142
Steffensen, Victor. 2022. "Putting the People Back into the Country." In *Decolonizing Research: Indigenous Storywork as Methodology*, edited by Jo-ann Archibald Q'um Q'um Xiiem, Jenny Bol Lee-Morgan, and Jason De Santolo. Bloomsbury Academic.
Tashakkori, Abbas, and Charles Teddlie. 2010. *Sage Handbook of Mixed Methods in Social and Behavioral Research*, 2nd ed. SAGE Publications.
Taylor, Carol A., and Vivienne Bozalek. 2022. "Method." In *A Glossary for Doing Postqualitative, New Materialist and Critical Posthumanist Research Across Disciplines*, edited by Karin Murris, 88–89. Routledge. https://doi.org/10.4324/9781003041153-44
Tsinnajinnie, Leola Roberta Rainbow, Robin Starr Zape-tah-hol-ah Minthorn, and Tiffany S. Lee. 2019. "K'é and Tdayp-tday-gaw: Embodying Indigenous Relationality in Research Methods." In *Applying Indigenous Research Methods: Storying with Peoples and Communities*, edited by Sweeney Windchief and Timothy San Pedro. Taylor and Francis.
Vacchelli, Elena. 2018. "Embodiment in Qualitative Research: Collage Making with Migrant, Refugee and Asylum Seeking Women." *Qualitative Research* 18 (2): 117–190. https://doi.org/10.1177/1468794117708008
Vannini, Phillip. 2015. "Non-Representational Research Methodologies: An Introduction." In *Non-Representational Methodologies: Re-Envisioning Research*, edited by Phillip Vannini. Routledge.

## *Suggested reading*

Absolon, Kathy, and Cam Willett. 2005. "Putting Ourselves Forward: Location in Aboriginal Research." In *Research As Resistance: Critical, Indigenous, and Anti-oppressive Approaches*, edited by Leslie Brown and Susan Strega. Canadian Scholars' Press.
Aidley, Daniela. 2019. *Introducing Quantitative Methods: A Practical Guide*. Red Globe Press.
Archibald Q'um Q'um Xiiem, Jo-ann, and Amy Parent Nox Ayaaw̓ilt. 2019. "Hands Back, Hands Forward for Indigenous Storywork as Methodology." In *Applying Indigenous Research Methods: Storying with Peoples and Communities*, edited by Sweeney Windchief and Timothy San Pedro. Taylor and Francis.
Bal, Mieke. 2025. "Cultural Analysis: Critical Encounters in Time, Space, and Thought." In *The Future of Cultural Analysis: A Critical Inquiry*, edited by Murat Ayemir, Noa Roei, and Aylin Kuryel. Routledge. https://doi.org/10.5117/9789048559794

Barad, Karen. 2014. "Diffracting Diffraction: Cutting Together-Apart." *Parallax* 20 (3): 168–187. https://doi.org/10.1080/13534645.2014.927623

Bayley, Annouchka. 2023. "Entanglements and the Many-Worlded Doing of Research-Based Practice, Practice-Based Research, Practice-as-Research, and Postqualitative Inquiry in the Academy." In *Diffracting New Materialisms: Emerging Methods in Artistic Research and Higher Education*, edited by Annouchka Bayley and J. J. Chan. Palgrave Macmillan. https://doi.org/10.1007/978-3-031-18607-3

Boydell, Katherine M. 2021. "Introduction." In *Applying Body Mapping in Research: An Arts-Based Method*, edited by Katherine M. Boydell. Routledge.

Candy, Linda, Ernest Edmonds, and Craig Vear. 2022. "Method." In *The Routledge International Handbook of Practice-Based Research*, edited by Craig Vear. Routledge.

Denzin, Norman K., and Yvonna S. Lincoln, eds. 2018. *The Sage Handbook of Qualitative Research*, 5th ed. Sage Publications.

Edwardes, Christian. 2025. "On Becoming Intimate with Scorched Earth: Research-Creation and Infrathin Data." In *Non-Representational and More-Than-Human Research: Vitalist Methodologies for the End of Data*, edited by Phillip Vannini. Routledge.

Given, Lisa M., ed. 2008. *The SAGE Encyclopedia of Qualitative Research Methods*, vols. 1 and 2. SAGE Publications.

Kirkness, Verna J., and Ray Rarnhardt 1991. "First Nations and Higher Education: The Four R's – Respect, Relevance, Reciprocity, Responsibility." *Journal of American Indian Education* 30 (3): 1–15. https://www.jstor.org/stable/24397980

Knight, Linda. 2021. *Inefficient Mapping: A Protocol for Attuning to Phenomena*. Punctum Books. (See chap. 2, "Chaosgraphics.")

Kovach, Margaret. 2021. *Indigenous Methodologies: Characteristics, Conversations, and Contexts*, 2nd ed. University of Toronto Press.

Leavy, Patricia. 2016. *Essentials of Transdisciplinary Research: Using Problem-Centered Methodologies*. Routledge. (See chap. 5, "Arts-Based Research Practices: Designing Research that Is Useful for the Public.")

Leavy, Patricia. 2017. *Research Design: Quantitative, Qualitative, Mixed Methods, Arts-Based, and Community-Based Participatory Research Approaches*. The Guilford Press.

Leavy, Patricia. 2020. *Method Meets Art: Arts-based Research Practice*, 3rd ed. The Guilford Press.

Murris, Karin, ed. 2022. *A Glossary for Doing Postqualitative, New Materialist and Critical Posthumanist Research Across Disciplines*. Routledge.

Nabigon, Herb, Rebecca Hagey, Schuyler Webster, and Robert Mackay. 1999. "The Learning Circle as a Research Method: The Trickster and Windigo in Research." *Native Social Work Journal* 2 (1):113–137. https://laurentian.scholaris.ca/handle/10219/461

Nelson, Robin. 2022. *Practice as Research in the Arts and Beyond: Principles, Processes, Context, Achievements*, 2nd ed. Palgrave MacMillian. (See chap. 6, "PaR Doctorates: A Guideline/*Clew* to a

Successful Outcome for All (Candidates, Examiners, Supervisors, Administrators, Regulators).")

Newhart, Michelle, and Mildred L. Patten. 2023. *Understanding Research Methods: An Overview of the Essentials*, 11th ed. Routledge.

O'Dwyer, Laura M., and James A. Bernauer. 2014. *Quantitative Research for the Qualitative Researcher*. SAGE Publications. (See chap. 3, "Research in the Quantitative Tradition.")

Seppälä, Tiina, Melanie Sarantou, and Satu Miettinen, eds. 2021. *Arts-Based Methods for Decolonising Participatory Research*. Routledge.

Tashakkori, Abbas, and Charles Teddlie. 1998. *Mixed Methodology: Combining Qualitative and Quantitative Approaches*. SAGE Publications.

Teddlie, Charles, and Abbas Tashakkori. 2011. "Mixed methods: Contemporary Issues in an Emerging Field." In *The SAGE Handbook of Qualitative Research*, 4th ed., edited by Norman K. Denzin and Yvonna S. Lincoln. SAGE Publications.

Tempone-Wiltshire, Julien, and Tyson Yunkaporta. 2025. "Contributions From Aboriginal Australian Psychology: Songlines, Memory, and Relational Knowledge Systems." *Psychotherapy and Counselling Journal of Australia* 13 (2). https://doi.org/10.59158/001c.143975

Tuck, Eve, and Marcia McKenzie. 2015. *Place in Research: Theory, Methodology, and Methods*. Routledge. (See chap. 6, "Indigenous Methods of Critical Place Inquiry.")

Windchief, Sweeney, and Timothy San Pedro, eds. 2019. *Applying Indigenous Research Methods: Storying with Peoples and Communities*. Taylor and Francis.

not standing still
VI

# Decalogue VI

## TEN PRACTICE THINGS

This decalogue examines practice not as creative output alone but as a research process, foregrounding reflection, documentation, and decision-making. If methods are the specific tools and techniques used to implement and enact your research, practice is the art of doing (analysing, writing, and making) and of sustaining the doing. The focus here is on the conditions that support these creative processes.

Let's address the factors that make practice possible: collaborative relationships (supervisor, peers, and institutional support), research habits (reflection, documentation, and reading strategies), and milestones (presentations and submission protocols). These are the foundations within which your creative and analytical work can take shape and sustain emotion.

### 1 Finding your supervisor

The PhD supervisor relationship is arguably the most significant collaboration of your thesis.[1] How do you go about finding the right supervisor? If you are moving directly from a bachelor's or master's degree to a PhD programme in the same university, it may be clear whom to approach as a supervisor. In fact, they may contact you to suggest you continue your studies by enrolling in a PhD. If you have prior connections to the research sector, you may also have ideas about potential supervisors. On the other hand, if you are embarking on a PhD after a break in academic learning, as I did, or are coming from a practitioner background, you may not know where to begin.

If your research requires that you be in the same city or town as your university, then location will limit your supervisor options, unlike conducting research as a distance or online student. Begin by identifying universities that have a research programme in your field and academics available to supervise PhD students. Of these potential supervisors, look

DOI: 10.4324/9781003584209-7

for a scholar researching or practising in your area of study. You may already be aware of an academic or teaching practitioner whose focus aligns with yours, in which case you can contact them directly to ask whether they would consider supervising your project before exploring universities more broadly. If they agree, this information can be included on your application, and they may advocate for you with the research office, which can strengthen your application.

Your selection of a supervisor (and their selection of you) is of primary significance, more so than your choice of university. That said, some universities prefer or require that students apply before approaching a supervisor, which allows them to clarify how their work may align with the programme. You will typically also have a co-supervisor or associate supervisor. This role is generally appointed by your primary supervisor, a colleague whose knowledge, skills, or focus complements their own.

Once enrolled, if you find that your supervisor is not a good fit (unavailable, unethical, or mismatched in approach), speak with your research office about changing supervisors. The university may also have reason to change a student's supervisor. Perhaps your supervisor is taking an extended academic leave or finds that you are not a good fit for them. Or, as in my case, my supervisor was promoted and announced one day that there was another academic at the university whose expertise was more aligned with my research. This was an emotional moment. I took a deep breath, met with the new supervisor, and refocused. This new supervisor's expertise in cinema and some of the themes I was exploring in magical realism meshed. We didn't start over, but overviewed things afresh. Changing supervisors can be destabilising, but this move typically occurs for sound reasons and doesn't need to cause a crisis.[2] The opportunity to see your thesis from a new point of view can often have a positive and beneficial impact.

## 2 The artefact and exegesis spiral

As discussed, there is an ongoing debate about whether a creative artefact thesis requires an accompanying conventional text, [3] and if so, whether the exegesis should be written as analysis after the artefact is created or follow a more integrated approach.

The relationship between theory and practice in your thesis requires careful reflection. Evaluate how your approach is aligned with your creative practice and the expectations of your supervisor and research department. If an unconventional relationship of artefact and exegesis (including the complete absence of a written exegesis) is critical to your thesis, you will need to explore this fundamental component as part of your proposal prior to committing to a specific programme.

As noted throughout these decalogues, the spiral process is defined by movement back and forth, or in and out and through writing, not only reflective, but also analytic and process notes; the exegesis continually forms before, during, and after periods of creative practice. This iterative cycle allows reflection and analysis to shape the next stage of artefact making, which in turn provides insight incorporated into the next exegesis draft. Through this practice, the boundary between artefact and exegesis diminishes; the exegesis no longer appears as a chore tacked onto artwork that simply answers to academia.

As in a written thesis, the creative artefact argument evolves through research, contributing to and forming the final communication of knowledge. The making of the artefact is part of this research and therefore informs the exegesis. When following a spiral process, both the written work and creative artefact follow essentially the same progression. Elements include research, a subject/object, and inquiry, though the methods differ.

Several academics support this interdependent relationship between artefact and exegesis. Sean Lowry argues that an integrated process is critical since creative artefact research is "often bound up in processes of becoming rather than found in fixed and immovable destinations" (2014, 349). Nigel Krauth describes the value of "woven forms" that "use nonlinear fragmented structures and blended creative/scholarly strategies" (2018, 9). These ideas reinforce the effectiveness of a spiral research process rather than a linear, forward-only journey. Details of the exegesis writing practice are further addressed in the writing decalogue.

## 3 Reading strategically

One area that receives limited attention in research is how to read strategically. If you are about to enrol, or have enrolled in a PhD programme, you know how to read. However, what is your reading strategy when conducting text-based research? How do you balance time efficiency while remaining intellectually productive enough to thoughtfully absorb critical information and reflect on ideas? And how do you record these thoughts and details while reading?

The next decalogue explores academic tools for note-taking, but here I focus on reading strategies and recording what you encounter in your sources (how to read, what to note, and when to make notes).

In your research process, read and view written, film-based, or object-based texts to discover ideas, direction, and information. Read in stages: first for inspiration and broad ideas, noting responses and further resources; second to formally record supporting information and quotations; third to revisit sources with your concretised research question in mind. Katherine Firth indicates another reading stage, "pre-research", which I would suggest runs alongside stage I. She describes this practice as orienting your research, providing "the lay of the land in a new field before you jump into a deeper literature review" (2024, 30). This reading gives an overview of conversations in your field and frames your general knowledge base.

Reading often and reading widely is critical at all points in your research. However, reading is arguably most significant in the messy beginning stage. At this point, you open yourself to theories, ideas, and inspiration that will energise you to advance your ideas. Elizabeth Adams St. Pierre advises "students to read hard, write hard, and think hard because all that reading, writing, and thinking gives them expertise and confidence and will very likely point them toward something 'to do'" (2020, 19). Only by being constantly exposed to texts can your original knowledge emerge.

Keep track not only of sources, but of ideas, theories, inspiration, connections, realisations, data, authors, and practitioners who may become relevant through the natural snowballing of research. It is your responsibility to analyse as you go, and to consider what types of ideas, information, or data are critical to record. The most efficient software in the world offers a system of note-taking, but will not tell you what is most significant to document. Visual methods such as mind maps, charts, or sketches, whether created by hand or digitally, can support this process.

Prior to reading (via words, sounds, visuals, or experiences), consider how you will distinguish the range of information in your notes. Categorise files by name or location, use colour coding within documents, or employ note-taking software with sidebar panels. You may prefer to use a spreadsheet to contain this information. There are endless strategies. What matters most is choosing a method early that works for you and is easily searchable as your research grows. This approach can then be adapted as you move through stages of research. Experiment with different organisational processes before your research becomes too complex to manage efficiently and you suddenly find yourself surrounded (physically or digitally) by scraps of ungraspable, illegible, and unsearchable documents.

It is easy, while in the act of reading, to lose track of significant ideas if you do not record them. Reading is for inspiration, gaining knowledge, and understanding information; however, most critically, it allows your research and questions to evolve and mature. For this effect to occur, reading also requires remembering and the ability to return to the source.

## 4 Document everything

Documentation of your creative artefact is not merely good practice; for examination purposes, it is essential. Examiners evaluate your work based on what they can access, and for ephemeral, performative, or installation-based work, documentation may be the primary means through which they engage with your process. A performance cannot be re-staged for an examiner in another country; a site-specific installation cannot be reconstructed. What you document, and how carefully you document it, may directly affect how your research is assessed.

Consider documentation at two levels: process and outcome. Process documentation captures the development of your work: inspirations, technical decisions, material experiments, iterations, dead ends, and breakthroughs. This document acts as a key resource in your creative process, enabling you to refer back as your research question and aims develop. Knowing where you have been can inform where you are striving to go, and how you will get there.

Outcome documentation captures the final work itself, whether through photography, video, audio recording, notation, or other means. Both are necessary. Process documentation provides evidence of the research journey; outcome documentation provides evidence of the research result.

Creative decisions often arise intuitively and may go unrecorded. Although creative artefact research may enable the practitioner to reach creative insight and generative moments in the formation of the work, its design can help the researcher find a way to analyse and record this process in support of defending the research question. By designing methods that enable creation, solutions, and new directions to emerge unexpectedly, these moments can still be captured and documented for later analysis.

The technical quality of your documentation matters. Blurred photographs, inaudible recordings, or incomplete video documentation will not serve your examination adequately. Plan your documentation approach as part of your research methodology, not as an afterthought. Include significant documentation within your exegesis to provide direct evidence for the arguments you are making about your practice.

## 5 Start your reflection journal early

Reflective analysis of the research process is beneficial for all theses, though it may be particularly applicable to creative artefact PhDs. This practice informs the development of your artefact and will certainly contribute to your exegesis. Stephen Scrivener identifies reflective practice and problem-solving as two critical research strategies in creative arts research (2011, 321), noting that while the problem-solver tests ideas against theory, "the reflective practitioner solves the problem in practice and may not even feel the need to theorise" (320). Here, I focus on reflective practice: the least prescribed of the two strategies, and the one most directly tied to the creative arts PhD.

A reflection journal is distinct from the reading strategy of note-taking described earlier. These entries are different in function and mode, though they may be housed in the same document or file. What matters is finding a system that works for you: one that keeps your reflections accessible and your developing research coherent.

Many research scholars draw on Donald Schön's foundational work on reflective practice, which remains central to professional and research education. His key concept, "reflection-in-action" describes reflection "triggered by features of the practice situation, undertaken on the spot, and immediately linked to action [...] Here the exchange between research and practice is immediate" ([1983] 2016, 308–309). For creative arts researchers, this in-the-moment reflection often takes the form of diarising: notes made at the moment of making, thinking, or creating.

Schön distinguishes "reflection-in-action" from "reflection-on-action" ([1983] 2016). He explains that "[w]hen practitioners reflect-in-action, they describe their own intuitive understandings" (276). Reflection-on-action, by contrast, allows for considered review without interrupting the creative process. As Schön suggests, a potential "gap between artistry and its description need not obstruct reflection-in-action" (276). For creative arts researchers, this is a significant reassurance.

Linda Candy explains that "Schön showed that practitioners are capable of bringing tacit understandings to solving problems" (2020, 17). Reflection-in-action enables a practitioner to also be a researcher (235). This concept is the foundation of reflective practice as a research strategy: it gives the creative arts practitioner both the means to record thoughts and processes in the moment of making, and the capacity to respond to emerging ideas in ways that actively shape the work.

This routine of reflective practice, as Carole Gray and Julian Malins describe, "attempts to unite research and practice, thought and action into a framework for inquiry which involves practice, and which acknowledges the particular and special knowledge of the practitioner" (2016, 22). This uniting of thought and action is what gives reflective practice its research legitimacy and, as aligned with the spiral nature of research, its particular value for creative arts PhD students.

In written theses, reflective practice can track the evolution of your thinking: revealing connections between texts and your research question, recording decisions, and documenting the shifts that shape your final work.

## 6 You will collaborate

Alongside these individual habits of practice, your research is also shaped by the people and communities around you. Even if you are conducting a written thesis or producing a creative artefact as a solitary act, you are still collaborating. Your university, your supervisor, your librarian, your research office, and potentially your fellow candidates all contribute to your research environment. This colleague interaction may not resemble collaboration in the traditional artistic practice sense, but all these people are acting as a sounding board, providing advice and feedback. The most significant person in this collaboration is your supervisor; arguably, without their input, your work would not be research.

You may be creating a project that involves collaboration with other arts practitioners. An interdisciplinary topic that includes a scientific component may entail working with others in a laboratory. An interactive artefact may necessitate collaboration with an audience experiencing an installation. Collaboration in the making of a creative artefact will be addressed in greater detail in the artefact decalogue.

If you are feeling isolated, reach out to communicate with other PhD students, groups, and organisations in your university, or attend conferences. Whether you present at a conference or visit exhibitions of other researchers' work, it will encourage you to feel part of a community and part of a collaboration. Colleen Ryan describes communities of practice (CoP) as a "form of practice development" (2019, 103). A community can be established formally or informally and evolve over time. They may include colleagues who participate regularly as well as those who attend infrequently. Such a group enables regular feedback and advice that may not occur with casual colleague interaction.

As a creative arts PhD researcher, you are never working completely on your own.

## 7 The title will change

The title is a tool, and its function is to communicate the contents of your thesis effectively. As part of the thesis apparatus, the title also plays a crucial role in allowing your thesis to be easily discoverable, both online and in libraries. Readers and researchers looking for work in your area will often search for key terms, so your title should contain words that articulate the central ideas of your research. Therefore, when formulating your title, identify the primary concepts of your thesis and ensure that they appear in clear and recognisable terms.

The typical structure for a thesis title contains a main phrase followed by a sub-phrase separated by a colon. This format allows you to present the most significant concept in the main phrase, which catches a potential reader's attention. The second part describes additional details of the research content, elaborating on your idea and providing more searchable terms. Construct a title that uses words and phrases that avoid unnecessary complexity and succinctly capture the essence of your thesis.

The initial title of your thesis is not static; it is fluid and most probably will evolve as your work progresses. Its primary function at the proposal stage is to communicate your intended topic clearly; however, that working title will most probably shift as your research develops. When your thesis is submitted, your title should reflect both your topic and your specific findings, and may incorporate nuanced terms that capture what you have discovered. In this sense, the changing nature of your title reflects the evolution of your research.

## 8 Editing, copyediting, proofreading: what each does

There is a difference between editing, copyediting, and proofreading. Many of you may be thinking: "of course there is!" However, as an arts practitioner, I lumped these three activities together, using the terms interchangeably without thought.

If you are uncertain about the distinction, it may help to imagine these activities as related tiers. An editor examines ideas, content, and structure; identifies issues, gaps, inconsistencies, and lack of clarity; and suggests structural or conceptual changes, while leaving solutions to you. A copyeditor focuses on consistency and language, and may also flag broader clarity issues. A proofreader addresses errors in grammar, spelling, and format.

Your supervisor is your primary editor. They may also provide feedback on copyediting and proofreading issues for each draft, depending on their supervisory approach and the time they have available. Typically, universities don't expect, and in most cases don't permit, you to engage an external primary editor for your thesis or exegesis, as that is the responsibility of your supervisors.

Copyediting and proofreading, however, are often completed by a professional outside the university. This professional is engaged as a paid practitioner experienced in PhD theses and exegeses, and typically, one person undertakes both roles. Generally, they will review the work only when a final draft is complete. Some copyeditors will accept chapters one by one, allowing final chapter drafts to be submitted as completed. The issue with individual chapter submissions is that less can be achieved within the time allocated. For instance, the copyeditor will not be able to check for inconsistencies throughout the work until all chapters are received, by which point, they will already have completed that work within each chapter.

Many candidates decide to save money by proofreading their own bibliography. I decided to do this, but my generous copyeditor cross-checked bibliography entries against citations, flagging missing and inaccurate information. If I had paid for my bibliography to be fully proofread, he would have checked through the entire bibliography with meticulous accuracy, saving me valuable time. The small sum saved, in my opinion, is a false economy. Instead, your mind should be focused on revising critical content requiring greater clarity.

## 9 Sharing your work

Throughout your PhD study, you may be required to submit a range of work outside of drafts (both written and artefact-based) to acknowledge milestones in your research, formally marking the stages of your PhD process. This section discusses three common forms of dissemination: presentations, interim papers, and publishing.

### *Presentations*

Certain milestones need to be met during your studies to ensure your research is on course. These progress moments include candidature confirmation during the first year of your study and an annual review, which confirms satisfactory progress. These two waypoints typically require written work to be submitted.[4]

Your university may also require work-in-progress presentations. For creative artefact research, this waypoint may be in the form of a studio visit, a presentation, or submission of work progress. A creative arts researcher submitting a written thesis may compile a visual presentation, showing any visual texts investigated in their research.

These presentations give you an opportunity to speak to your work using visual communication in the articulation of your ideas. Using images alongside spoken explanation can reduce reliance on written text and prompt you to see your research from a new perspective. This clarity may indicate strengths and weaknesses in your research unseen previously. This type of presentation satisfies a milestone, but also, it builds confidence. The academic tool decalogue considers strategies for designing appropriate and effective visual presentations.

### *Interim papers*

Common in scientific and medical theses, interim papers based on individual chapters may be submitted to a journal during your PhD. This mode is uncommon in creative arts theses since results often emerge more gradually than in quantitative work. However, if you are investigating a process as part of your research question, for instance, you may have preliminary findings suitable for publishing.

Prior to submission of the final artefact, you may also want to explore possibilities of publishing individual creative writing, exhibiting visual works, or presenting performances, as produced during your study. This early sharing of your work may provide valuable feedback on your ongoing research and contribute to the exposure of your artistic practice.

### *Publishing*

Further to the above, you may aim to publish on an aspect of your thesis or a parallel topic prior to the start of your PhD or during your studies. A publication may be in the context of a journal, edited collection, or conference proceeding. This ideally includes a process of peer review where your submitted work is rigorously assessed by experts in the field, which will substantiate the publication of your thesis.

You may opt to produce your PhD by publication. In this case, your thesis is submitted in the form of a published book. Not all disciplines or universities allow this mode of submission, and it is not suitable for every project. The expectations of scholarly publications do not always align with the structure and language required in a thesis; confirm whether this pathway is appropriate and permitted.

Following the awarding of your PhD following the awarding of your PhD you may aim to publish in a journal article or book chapter, or you may propose a book based on your theories, artefact(s), and findings. This possibility may seem distant and need not affect your current research practice, but it is worth keeping in mind.

## 10 Submission

Every university has its own requirements for submission; therefore, to prepare for this final step, review the policy and procedure guidelines. In addition to known due dates, expected thesis format, and elements required for submission, you also need to determine what content is preferred, accepted, and required. Submission is not only a procedural process, but a moment of synthesis and consolidation; the point at which your research coheres into its final form.

Creative arts research, whether submitted as a written thesis or as an artefact and exegesis, may require a unique form to explore questions concerning artistic works. Departures from established norms, however, are not always straightforward to navigate. Only you, with advice from your supervisor, can decide whether arguing for an unconventional format is necessary or worth the effort. In the creative arts, particularly, proposing new approaches can be critical when they align with your topic and genuinely advance the articulation of new knowledge, though such innovative forms are not always welcomed.

### *Written work: thesis and exegesis*

Drafts are typically submitted chapter by chapter to allow you to work on the next chapter while your supervisor generates feedback on the work already submitted. When a full draft is completed, your supervisor will then read and respond to the thesis as a whole. In the management decalogue, I outline what a thesis timetable might look like, including a schedule with multiple draft submission deadlines. These dates include drafts to your supervisor, submission to your associate supervisor, the copyeditor/proofreader, revised drafts back to your supervisor, and finally submission to the thesis committee for assessment. Between each stage, you will be responding to feedback and feeding your input and revisions into the next draft. These intervals require intense focus, simultaneously appraising content, structure, and writing technicalities.

Finally comes the time to press the button on the submission page. Before that moment, reread the policies and procedures one last time and check your document thoroughly. Are you uploading the correct draft? Has every page been formatted correctly? Does the file name follow institutional conventions, and is the size of the file acceptable? Make a checklist. This is not a moment for assumptions.

### *Creative artefact*

Creative artefact PhDs often have additional submission requirements that need planning well in advance. As discussed in Section Four, thorough documentation is essential preparation for this stage, and the nature of your artefact will determine the complexity of arrangements required.

If your work is distributable, submission follows a similar process to a written thesis, with the artefact included digitally or in print alongside the exegesis. Consider how you will reference and reproduce your work within the exegesis, and ensure that any permissions required for reproduction are secured before submission.

If your work is non-distributable, as mentioned, specialised planning is required. Performative, interactive, ephemeral, or installation-based work exists in the moment of its presentation. Your submission schedule will need to include the presentation of the artefact to your thesis committee and examiners, which raises significant logistical questions.

Where will the work be staged or exhibited? What technical requirements does the space need to meet? If examiners are based in another city or country, can they travel to see your work? If they cannot, is it acceptable to all parties to film the performance or document the installation so they can engage with it remotely? A recording transforms an ephemeral work into something documented and repeatable: does this affect the authenticity of the work and therefore its evaluation? These are not questions with universal answers. These are questions to work through with your supervisor, who may in turn consult your thesis chair and research office.

The key principle is simple: begin these conversations as early as your work starts to take form, not at the point of submission. As soon as the mode of presentation becomes clear, a dialogue can begin on the most appropriate approach. Leaving these arrangements until the final stages of your candidature risks your submission timeline being shaped by logistical constraints rather than by the needs of your research.

### *Oral examination*

The requirements for an oral component to the PhD submission vary greatly across countries and universities. Across the world, this presentation may be referred to as the *viva voce* or *viva* (UK, Latin for "living voice"), the dissertation defence (US), the thesis defence (Canada), *disputation* (Germany), *soutenance* (France), and many other geographical variations. In Japan, by contrast, the doctoral examination is typically a public and celebratory occasion. In Australia, an oral examination is extremely uncommon, though some universities may include it as an optional component or in cases where examiners disagree.

My own PhD was conducted in Australia, where no oral examination was required, though one of my milestone reviews was presented orally to my thesis chair, supervisors, and internal academics not associated with my thesis. This oral and visual presentation provided a valuable opportunity to experience presenting at this level. For students facing oral examinations, the preparation and stakes are of a different order entirely.

The oral examination typically includes two examiners and an independent chair who introduces the thesis and an overview of the university's guidelines. Estelle M. Phillips and Colin G. Johnson explain the aim of an oral examination: "to demonstrate that you are a fully professional researcher, who is, on this topic, the equal of your examiners" (2022, 192). This remains a useful benchmark for your submission, whether it includes an oral examination or not.

A typical oral examination consists of a series of questions from the very broad ("how does your thesis contribute to research in your field?") to the specific ("why did you relate this particular theory of a given source to your artefact?"). The questions may require you to rephrase your abstract, describe your analysis while specifically citing the relevance of two sources, or answer what your creative intention was with an aspect of your artefact.

To prepare for this presentation and questioning, create a summary document of your thesis for your own reference that includes critical ideas from each chapter, a list of points to raise, and perhaps a reminder of key topics and sources. Allow time for practice sessions, which will help you anticipate examiner questions and feel more confident with the process.

The examiners come to this meeting having read your thesis and seen, heard, read, or experienced your artefact. They use this time as an opportunity for you to expand on and illuminate aspects of the thesis. Typically, the examiners meet prior to your presentation to gain an understanding of each other's point of view, and after the oral examination to agree on an outcome.

Natalie Hills, whose coordination of higher degree examinations informs her research, outlines the advantages and disadvantages of oral examination systems. Oral presentations provide students an opportunity to practice presenting their work and support transparency regarding authorship, knowledge, and examiner recommendations (Hills 2020, 121). These benefits are particularly relevant to creative artefact research as "a moment of multimodality" (121). Hills describes an advantage of systems without a mandatory oral defence: Without the need for examiners to be physically present, the "thesis can be tested on an international scale with a greater number of examiners available to choose from, in turn decreasing the possibility of conflicts of interest" (124).

Although I recognise the benefits of the *viva voce*, I admit I was relieved not to present my thesis orally. My dread was peculiar given that I was, already at that time, an experienced lecturer teaching without notes. Yet the oral examination is unnerving for a good reason. You are proving your argument and the value of your new knowledge directly to those who matter most. However, while the oral examination can be an empowering moment, the focus on my written work afforded me greater time to elevate my final submission to a higher level. The Australian system had a further advantage: my thesis was examined by international scholars who were foundational to my research, and removed any concern of internal institutional bias.

## *Revisions*

As noted, nearly every submitted thesis requires revision stemming from examiner feedback. Feedback is typically first reviewed and considered with your supervisor. Together, you determine which feedback is relevant and necessitates revision, and which feedback cannot, at this stage, be incorporated into your thesis.

All examiner comments, whether leading to revision or not, require acknowledgement as a documented response. In all cases where corrections or revisions are requested, you will receive detailed feedback from examiners indicating the required changes. Understand the timeline for making corrections and revisions and resubmitting. Keep a record of corrections in a revision table that lists each examiner's comment, your response, and either the page number where the change was made or an explanation of why the revision was not made. This table is submitted alongside your revised thesis as a guide for your supervisor, the examiners, and the thesis committee. This systematic approach demonstrates professionalism and ensures all examiner concerns are addressed thoroughly.

If possible, start making revisions immediately. The thesis will be clear in your mind, and other life events will not yet be distractions. You have reached this point. Don't stop now. When the revised thesis is approved by your supervisor, submit it again. This time, hopefully for the last time.

## Notes

1 Different terms are used internationally for the role overseeing your academic study. I use the term supervisor, as common in Australia and the UK. The US tends to use advisor and some European countries use, as translated into English, director or promotor. In many Asian countries, doctoral advisor is used, originating from a term meaning master or guiding teacher. The literal definition of director, as used in Germany, is doctor father/doctor mother. This translation reflects the primal significance of this relationship. See Génisis Guarimata-Salinas et al. (2024).

2 The supervisor-supervisee relationship itself, and its challenges, are discussed in the emotion decalogue. Critical supervisor issues are covered in the wellbeing decalogue.

3 For an overview of this extensive debate, see Tara Brabazon et al. (2020), Louise Ravelli et al. (2014), Sian Vaughan (2022), and Brad Haseman and Daniel Mafe (2009).

4 Gordon Rugg and Marion Petre prefer the term "waypoint" as the commonly used milestone has been adopted for use in particular bureaucratic processes (2020, 19).

## References

### *Cited works*

Brabazon, Tara, Tiffany Lyndall-Knight, and Natalie Hills. 2020. *The Creative PhD: Challenges, Opportunities, Reflection*. Emerald Publishing.

Candy, Linda. 2020. *The Creative Reflective Practitioner*. Routledge.

Firth, Katherine. 2024. *Writing Well and Being Well for Your PhD and Beyond: How to Cultivate a Strong and Sustainable Writing Practice for Life*. Routledge.

Gray, Carole, and Julian Malins. 2016. *Visualizing Research: A Guide to the Research Process in Art and Design*. Routledge.

Guarimata-Salinas Génisis, Joan Josep Carajal, and M. Dolores Jiménez López. 2024. "Redefining the Role of Doctoral Supervisors: a Multicultural

Examination of Labels and Functions in Contemporary Doctoral Education." *Higher Education* 88(4): 1305–1330. https://doi.org/10.1007/s10734-023-01171-0

Haseman, Brad, and Daniel Mafe. 2009. "Acquiring Know-How: Research Training for Practice-led Researchers." In *Practice-led Research, Research-led Practice in the Creative Arts*, edited by Hazel Smith and Roger T. Dean. Edinburgh Press.

Hills, Natalie. 2020. "Creative Examinations and the Administrator's Perspective." In *The Creative PhD: Challenges, Opportunities, Reflection*, edited by Tara Brabazon, Tiffany Lyndall-Knight, and Natalie Hills. Emerald Publishing.

Krauth, Nigel. 2018. "Exegesis and Artefact as a Woven Work: Problems of Examination." *TEXT* 22 (1): 1–12. https://doi.org/10.52086/001c.25111

Lowry, Sean. 2014. "Strategies for Artists Becoming Writers: Tackling the Written Component of Practice-Based Research in the Creative and Performing Arts (a Report from the Regions)." In *Doctoral Writing in the Creative and Performing Arts*, edited by Louise Ravelli, Brian Paltridge, and Sue Starfield. Libri Publishing.

Phillips, Estelle M., and Colin G. Johnson. 2022. "The Examination System." In *How to Get a PhD: A Handbook for Students and their Supervisors*, 7th ed. McGraw Hill Open University Press.

Ravelli, Louise, Brian Paltridge, and Sue Starfield, eds. 2014. *Doctoral Writing in the Creative and Performing Arts*. Libri Publishing.

Rugg, Gordon, and Marian Petre. 2020. *The Unwritten Rules of PhD Research*, 3rd ed. McGraw-Hill Open University Press.

Ryan, Colleen. 2019. "Developing Communities of Practice." In *The Doctoral Experience: Student Stories from the Creative Arts and Humanities*, edited by Donna L. Brien, Craig Batty, Elizabeth Elison, and Alison Owens. Palgrave Macmillan.

Schön, Donald. (1983) 2016. *The Reflective Practitioner: How Professionals Think in Action*. Routledge.

Scrivener, Stephen. 2011. "Reflections on Interactive Art and Practitioner Research: 2 Interpretation." In *Interacting: Art, Research and the Creative Practitioner*, edited by Linda Candy and Ernest Edmonds. Libri Publishing Ltd.

St. Pierre, Elizabeth Adams. 2020. "Post Qualitative Inquiry, the Refusal of Method, and the Risk of the New." In *Qualitative Inquiry and the Politics of Resistance: Possibilities, Performances, and Praxis*, edited by Norman K. Denzin and Michael D. Giardina. Routledge.

Vaughan, Sian. 2022. "Understanding Doctoral Communities in Practice-Based Research." In *The Routledge International Handbook of Practice-Based Research*, edited by Craig Vear. Routledge.

## *Suggested reading*

Bedwell, Stacey, and Isabelle Butcher. 2022. *How to Excel in Your Doctoral Viva*. Palgrave Macmillan.

Borgdorff, Henk. 2012. In *The Conflict of the Faculties: Perspectives on Artistic Research and Academia*. Leiden University Press. (See chap. 9, "Artistic Practices and Epistemic Things.")

Cassuto, Leonard, and James M. Van Wyck. 2021. "The PhD Adviser-Advisee Relationship Reimagined for the Twenty-First Century." In *The Reimagined PhD: Navigating 21st Century Humanities Education*, edited by Leanne M. Horinko, Jordan M. Reed, and James M. Van Wyck. Rutgers University Press.

Firth, Katherine, Liam Connell, and Peta Freestone. 2020. In *Your PhD Survival Guide: Planning, Writing and Succeeding in Your Final Year*. Routledge. (See chap. 8, "Working with Your Supervisor.")

Goddard, Stephen. 2007. "A Correspondence Between Practices." In *Practice as Research: Approaches to Creative Arts Enquiry*, edited by Estelle Barrett and Barbara Bolt. I. B. Tauris.

Grant, Cynthia, and Daniel R. Tomal. 2013. *How to Finish and Defend your Dissertation*. Rowman and Littlefield Education.

Kamler, Barbara, and Pat Thomson. 2014. In *Helping Doctoral Students Write*, 2nd ed. Routledge. (See chap. 8, "Publishing Out of the Thesis.")

McCormack, Jon, Alon Ilsar, Tom Chandler et al. 2022. "Practice-based Research at Sensilab." In *The Routledge International Handbook of Practice-Based Research*, edited by Craig Vear. Routledge.

Owens, Alison. 2019. "Understanding Issues of 'Truth' and Integrity in Doctoral Research." In *The Doctoral Experience: Student Stories from the Creative Arts and Humanities*, edited by Donna Lee Brien, Craig Batty, Elizabeth Ellison, and Alison Owens. Palgrave Macmillan.

Remenyi, Dan. 2019. "Never Smile at a Crocodile: A Bad Viva Voce by the Rule Book." *The Electronic Journal of Business Research Methods* 17(2): 67–73. https://doi.org/10.34190/JBRM.17.2.02

Smith, Peter. 2014. *The PhD Viva: How to Prepare for Your Oral Examination*. Palgrave Macmillan.

Smith, Susan. 2015. *PhD by Published Work: A Practical Guide for Success*. Palgrave.

van der Gaast, Koen, Laura Koenders, and Ger Post. 2019. "Research Practice." In *Academic Skills for Interdisciplinary Studies*, revised ed. Amsterdam University Press.

Vukov, Joseph. 2021. "Building Professional Connections in Graduate School." In *The Reimagined PhD: Navigating 21st Century Humanities Education*, edited by Leanne M. Horinko, Jordan M. Reed, and James M. Van Wyck. Rutgers University Press.

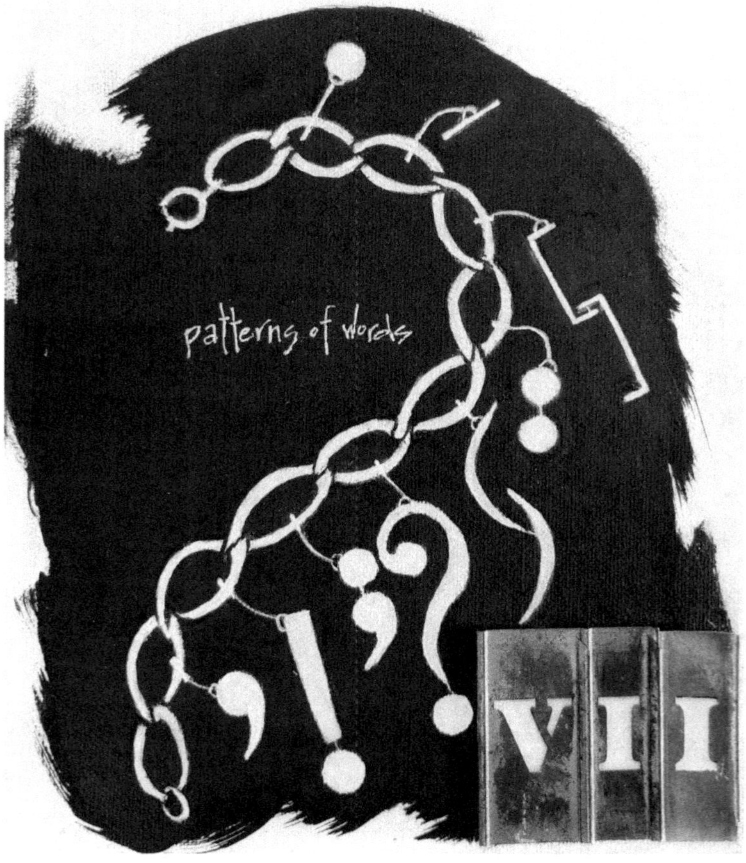
patterns of words
VII

# Decalogue VII

## TEN ACADEMIC TOOL THINGS

This decalogue addresses practical tools that support efficient and effective academic research, from foundational elements like formatting and reference systems to rapidly evolving artificial intelligence (AI) tools. The landscape of academic software has expanded dramatically: reference managers, writing applications, citation generators, note-taking platforms, and collaborative tools now offer unprecedented support for researchers. Yet this abundance creates its own challenge: which tools serve your specific needs?

Instead of giving prescriptive advice that insists on specific software or systems, this decalogue provides a framework for your decision-making. What mode of reference system suits your discipline and your visual literacy? Which type of writing software supports your process? How do you establish clear boundaries around the use of AI while taking advantage of its possibilities?

Building on the management decalogue, this list addresses the tools and conventions that support academic work: format, grammar, tense use, and citation systems. It also covers the broader work of communicating research through presentations, networking, social media, and building an online presence.

### 1 You are a scholar, and you are also a manager

Time and project management are critical responsibilities as a PhD candidate. Effective management relies on the feasibility and comprehensiveness of the timetable you design, as discussed earlier. Develop tools to manage the minutiae of each working day to ensure you effectively implement your timetable.

Schedule time every day to work on your thesis. This suggestion may sound impossible if you care for family, have a demanding job, or have other commitments. However, even 15 minutes at the start of the day

DOI: 10.4324/9781003584209-8

maintains cognitive continuity. Jotting down ideas or listing follow-up tasks prevents the work from feeling stagnant or detached. When leaving my thesis untouched for several days, returning to it was difficult. Once I committed to a minimum of 15 minutes daily, even on busy days, returning became effortless.

Keep your timetable easily accessible. I used both a digital calendar and a gridded whiteboard with Post-it notes for individual tasks, which I could move around as needed. These tools sound simplistic, but making the process easy ensures your timetable stays visible and current.

Track what you discuss, agree to, and action with your supervisor by taking detailed notes or recording meetings (with approval). Recording is often the most accurate option: seemingly minor points may become significant later, and you won't be distracted while taking notes. Immediately after each meeting, write a summary with action points for both you and your supervisor, revise your timetable, and email both documents promptly. This practice keeps the next steps clear and allows your supervisor to manage their time efficiently. Remember, you're unlikely to be their only PhD candidate; maintaining current information is your responsibility.

## 2 Format early

Format your document before you begin the first kernel of your draft. This includes margins, spacing, indents, and page number location. Your university will provide a document with details for thesis submission, specifying the required or preferred font, margins, and line spacing. If your document is formatted as required from the outset, you won't face the laborious process of reformatting later, and you will be free to concentrate on the non-technical aspects of your thesis without distraction. However, as your thesis has a foundation in the creative arts, you may have formatting ideas that fall outside of guidelines. If an unusual format or font is critical for your thesis, confirm that the proposed variation is acceptable before proceeding.

Clean initial formatting prevents irregularities like line spacing variations or stray section markers. In most writing software, discovering why your document behaves unexpectedly can be time-consuming. These hidden issues can affect preparation of your final draft. When combining chapter documents and inserting page breaks, software may renumber pages, include hidden spaces, or shift figures if irregularities exist.

Most universities suggest several font options rather than requiring a single choice. For advice, see the font selection guide in Appendix C.

## 3 Choosing your reference system

It is critical to establish a bibliographic system early. Select your reference system after thorough investigation and agreement by your supervisor, then commit to it as soon as possible. You don't want to get partway through your research and change reference systems, which would require the reformatting of all your references, a laborious process that is prone to error. Learn everything you can about the system, including how to efficiently utilise its style guide.

What factors contribute to this decision-making process? You may make the choice based on common usage within your discipline, your supervisor's preferred system, or your university's prescribed option. Beyond these factors, you will also consider other logistical features such as whether references appear in-text, in footnotes, or as endnotes. Make choices that align with your logical approach and visual literacy, including matters such as grammatical conventions and whether the system uses an initial or full name for an author's given name.

Speak to the university's librarian or research department, or look online to determine which system is typically used in your discipline. Discuss your choice with your supervisor, as their approval is critical. If you select a system that they do not support, it may constantly distract them when they see it in your documents, which is counterproductive.

Of the large range of reference systems, the most commonly used in the humanities and the creative arts include: APA (American Psychological Association), Chicago (Author-Date), Chicago (Notes-Bibliography), Harvard, and MLA (Modern Language Association). Additionally, the MHRA (Modern Humanities Research Association) and Oxford referencing style are commonly used, but almost exclusively in the UK. There are also many other reference styles that are commonly used in non-English-speaking countries. See Appendix D for a reference systems comparison chart.

I originally used the Harvard style for my thesis; however, I found the citation style clunky for films, my field of study. So, I changed to Chicago (Author-Date) with little discussion with my supervisors. Initially, they were not pleased, as Harvard and APA were the most commonly used systems in my university and in my field. I argued that I was drawn to Chicago (Author-Date) for its logic and clarity, and I also found it less rigid. I prefer using the full first name of the author/creator, rather than initials only, and Chicago (Author-Date) does not note the year parenthetically in the reference list, giving the citation a more streamlined look. It also gave me the opportunity to combine in-text referencing with explanatory footnotes, which lent an immediacy to its presentation.

My preferred reference system was reluctantly approved, and I am still partial to Chicago (Author-Date).[1]

When you have committed to a reference system, make sure to have 24/7 access to the style guide, usually available digitally through your library. Use your selected system from the outset when building your reference lists, since this simple habit will save you significant time at the final draft stage, while familiarising you with the system. Ensure you are consulting the most up-to-date version of the reference style guide since requirements, systems, and conventions in writing can change with each update, such as when APA revised their advice to ascribe a page number to a paraphrased passage, a practice that Chicago has long followed (Friedman 2014, 255).

To save time, develop strategies for managing the numerous anomalies that may arise in any reference system. Keep your own list of matters that you check frequently. It's surprising how often you return to the same unusual point, such as punctuation or formatting of titles in languages other than English, and then forget it again the next time the same question arises. Some issues are not easily found in the style guides; if you find it once, you won't need to search again; you can simply check your notes.

Ken Friedman developed a list, which his students refer to as "Friedman's Ten Commandments" (2014, 257). Two of my favourite standard rules are: "Never use second-hand references from other authors. Always check cited sources first hand" and "Each item cited in the text must appear in the reference list. Every item in the reference list must appear in the text" (2014, 257). His list is essential reading; each rule is simple, yet often overlooked or left unchecked.

## 4 Writing and reference software

I didn't discover until late that valuable word processing alternatives to Microsoft Word existed. I had manipulated Word to function like more sophisticated process-based writing software: adding notes in comments and footnotes, highlighting passages needing revision, using a second document as a sidebar for sudden ideas. These applications existed during my own PhD, but I was entirely Word-centric and failed to consider them. I wish I had explored alternatives earlier, as they're designed specifically for the kind of process-based writing I was improvising in Word.

For *CAPC*, I tested Scrivener, which proved freeing despite requiring some adjustment.[2] This and similar applications allow you to view chapters individually or search the whole text. Their "corkboard view" displays chapter headings and top-level text like a Post-it note grid, exactly what I set up with my whiteboard. I adopted a combined approach: using Scrivener alongside Word by exporting drafts while maintaining the Scrivener file for reference, which allowed me to search through all documents as a whole to locate content or resources.

Investigate available options for bibliographic management and note-taking software, selecting tools that suit your workflow and discipline conventions. Reference software accuracy is improving; however, always verify entries, particularly for unique sources. Keep one of your "future ideas" files for references that may be of interest for future projects and set up your system early, since renaming and relocating materials mid-research is time-consuming and disruptive. Reference management and note-taking software allows you to keep notes, references, images, and files together in a single holistic structure where even loosely organised material can be located if it is labelled. Discover which software works best for your process.

## 5 Quoting and paraphrasing

While the requirement to accurately cite every quoted passage is well known, paraphrasing carries its own obligations. To adequately paraphrase, you must refer to the source and alter the articulation of ideas so that the wording is genuinely your own voice and cannot be judged to be plagiarism.

Your selected reference system will instruct you how to cite your source, whether in-text, as a footnote, or as an endnote. Whichever system you use, you will communicate some combination of author name, text title, year of publication, and page number. And remember Friedman's rule: "Treat direct quotations, indirect quotations, and paraphrases the same way" (2014, 257).

A note on digital formats. PDFs and ePubs generally maintain fixed pagination, and many digital formats now maintain stable page numbers. However, some proprietary e-reader formats present texts without page numbers, instead using location numbers. These locators are unreliable for identifying the precise placement of selected text; reference systems, therefore, typically request the page number from a hard copy of the source. If a physical version is not accessible, some style guides accept chapter or section headings for e-books without page numbers. For digital journal articles or webpages without page numbers, indicate the location of the passage by providing a paragraph number counted from the start of the piece. Confirm this advice with the requirements of your selected reference system.

Verify the correct punctuation and format for citations within your selected reference system and remain absolutely consistent throughout. Triple-check that all direct quotations are exact. Consistency and accuracy are not merely procedural obligations; they make reading and accessing your thesis as streamlined as possible for your thesis committee and examiners.

## 6 Grammar and style conventions

You probably don't want to think about grammar before beginning research; however, this area is critical. The most brilliant idea loses impact if readers must wade through inconsistent or unclear grammar. What seems perfectly clear to you may confuse readers if grammar or punctuation is inconsistent.

### *Following conventions*

Following grammatical rules and formal guidelines in your thesis and exegesis is essential. There are accepted conventions that may exist geographically, per university, or at the discretion of your supervisor. Some of these expectations may not become clear until you receive feedback on your first draft; however, determining them before writing will put you several steps ahead.

Review verb tenses, word order, and pronoun use before drafting so you can begin your first draft with accuracy and consistency top of mind; the most automated and natural tendencies often produce errors. Re-examine colons, semicolons, hyphens, commas, dashes, and parentheses. Even small details can be unclear. For example, punctuation goes inside the closing parenthesis if the parenthetical statement is a complete sentence, outside if it's a phrase within a sentence, or if the parenthetical sentence is embedded within another sentence. This is a convention I thought I knew.

Eric Hayot, a supporter of parenthetical composition, offers a warning on the correct use of the em dash: "don't confuse the use of material between long dashes—which usually has a parenthetical function—with the use of a single long dash for emphasis. The latter replaces a comma—and highlights an upcoming clause by delaying its appearance" (2014, 183). This distinction is especially significant now, given the current prolific use of em dashes in AI-generated text. As a result, while em dashes remain entirely legitimate in academic prose, their use can lead some readers to question whether a section has been produced by AI.[3] Therefore, if you do choose to use this particular punctuation mark, do so sparingly and correctly. Hayot's chapter offers detailed guidance on the correct use of this alternative to parentheses.

Some rules of the English language grammar are fixed, while other areas allow for individual choice. Variations depend on the country where you are studying, generational change, the language norms of your university, or the rules of your reference system. Differences include spelling conventions, such as the British and American use of S/Z and ou/o (organise/organize; favour/favor), the use of one space or two at the end of a sentence after a full stop/period (typewriter era—two spaces; computer era—one space), and the style of inverted commas/quotation marks.[4] Some rules, such as when to capitalise words in a resource title, will usually be dictated by your reference system.

More significant than what convention you choose is the consistency with which you apply it. Follow advice, rules, and conventions as required and be consistent throughout your thesis and exegesis. By determining these rules in advance, you can develop an efficient writing process that minimises the need for constant revisions and adjustments.

### *Habitual errors*

As you type quickly, you may notice that you make recurring errors. If the error involves incorrect word usage rather than a misspelling, spell check won't detect it. Similarly, if you make a grammatical error that is permissible but not preferred or stylistically weak, Grammar Check won't flag it.

I make two constant habitual errors. One is typing "form" instead of "from". Another is typing two spaces following a full stop when the convention I am following requires one space. I am from the typewriter generation, and breaking this mind-to-finger habit has taken time. I search for both these errors after completing each draft.

To combat your own habitual errors, build a list of them as a separate document (or sidebar); then periodically search throughout your work to clean up these particular issues. My list also included words such as "however" and "therefore", which are acceptable, though I tend to overuse them. Learn the patterns of your writing; keep track of your common errors and repeated words; then search for and correct grammatical errors, overused terms, and punctuation issues before a final edit.

Study grammatical rules and conventions, make choices in line with your country, university, and reference system, and above all, be consistent. These practices will streamline your writing process and, ultimately, make your thesis a more pleasurable read for your examiners.

## 7 Grammar and style expectations

In addition to grammatical and spelling rules and choices, there are expectations that apply to your style of writing. These principles may arise through your supervisor, university, or field.

### *Beware of repetition*

A common but unofficial expectation is to avoid repeating the same word in sequential sentences, or within a paragraph or section. Doubling up on a word may make a passage feel dull and cause the reader to lose their place in the text as they sense they have read the same phrasing already. Head to the thesaurus, or consider this one of the tasks where AI-powered writing tools prove genuinely useful.

You can also go too far in searching for other words to mean the same thing. Using multiple terms for the same concept can feel confusing or annoying to readers, or simply pretentious.[5] Hayot makes a case that some repetition is appropriate in allowing for the expansion of ideas, suggesting that this technique allows the writer to "manage its contours, and build toward a final expression that the reader will chunk and walk away with" (2014, 188). This power of repeating terms in building an argument aids the reader in absorbing complex notions. Again, a convention is just that: preferred but not always appropriate in context.

### *Understand tense use*

Broader expectations, such as tense use, are not necessarily universally adopted, and many universities have no prescribed conventions. Creative arts theses often have more flexibility than other disciplines, and some researchers may view tense guidelines as formulaic or unnecessarily traditional, a perspective that is often valid in creative arts contexts.

I was given this advice for my thesis as per my supervisor and the university's tense conventions (unfortunately, I discovered these expectations after my first drafts):

- **Introduction**: present and future tense, as appropriate
- **Body Chapters**: present, future, and past tenses, as appropriate
- **Conclusion**: past perfect and simple past tenses, as appropriate

Examples of tense conventions and a refresher on English tense description are provided in Appendix E. Where conventions do apply, attending to tense builds consistency into your writing and supports the reader's comprehension of complex ideas rather than imposing unnecessary standardisation.[6]

## 8 Building your presence

Talk to people about your thesis. If you can afford the time and cost, attend conferences. Be in touch with other candidates or recent graduates whose research relates to your area and ask for advice on resources.

Take their advice and look at all the references they recommend. Don't respond "thanks, but I think I have enough resources on that point" (as one candidate said to me). If another researcher has taken the time to recommend a reference, just look at it. Always be open to strengthening your research; you don't know what you will find.

Consider establishing a social media presence. Select a platform type that is flexible rather than static, and that is used by others in academia.[7] Consider how you will use the platform. Are you documenting your research process, communicating your reflective thinking, sharing your research progress, or looking for a vehicle through which to post surveys or other types of questionnaires in order to gather data?

In addition to social media platforms, you may want to create a professional website where you can curate your work, ideas, and reflections. Social media is dynamic, but it is also platform-dependent (controlled by algorithm changes, platform policies, and potential termination). A website is more stable and under your control. It allows you to present your research focus, post your CV/résumé, share published articles and works, and link to your active social media platforms.

An online presence may be a vehicle to test ideas throughout the PhD. However, before committing to a platform, consider:

- **Why maintain one?** (By extending networks and creating research exposure, you are ensuring collaborators and future employers can find your work.)
- **Will you update it regularly?** (An inactive presence is worse than none.)
- **Will posting thesis content or information online create conflicts?** (Consider self-plagiarism, IP complications, and examination implications.)
- **Will it generate a valuable community?** (Effective titles and search terms help reach your audience.)

Before posting online any information pertaining to your thesis, obtain technical, legal, and institutional guidance. Research which platforms provide the best service for your needs, and commit to engaging with your online community regularly.

## 9 AI as a research tool

The conversation addressing AI use in academia is rapidly evolving. *CAPC* explores the current state of engagement for PhD candidates with a disclaimer that this information will likely be outdated by the time this section is published. Two recent books, Bron Eager's *AI-Powered Scholar* (2025) and Mark Carrigan's *Generative AI for Academics* (2025) provide useful discussions on AI.

I focus here on large language models (LLMs) rather than generative AI more broadly.[8] Creative arts researchers may also engage with AI tools for visual generation, music composition, or audio analysis. The ethical and methodological considerations discussed below apply across these modalities. Image and sound generation raise additional questions specific to creative artefact research, particularly around authorship, originality, and whether AI-generated elements constitute creative practice or research tools. For an extended discussion, I recommend Emily K. Johnson and Anastasia Salter's *Critical Making in the Age of AI* (2025). Supplement any resources with current guidance as policies and tools continue to evolve.

Eager emphasises the significance of "translational thinking" in your AI interaction with written text. In general, you are reliant on words alone for your prompts; therefore, you need to develop a technique of using precise and unambiguous language. Eager explains that effective use "requires a bit of a micro shift, wherein we break down our larger goals and complex ideas into logically sequenced, precise, and unambiguous instructions that AI can interpret and execute" (2025, 34). You can practice this approach before applying it in your PhD to ensure you receive relevant advice.

Carrigan suggests that academics interact with relevant AI software "as interlocutors in the sense of participants in a dialogue", and as "conversational agents" (2025, 17–18). He explains an ethos that views "GenAI as *tools for thinking* rather than *substitutes for thought*" (18; emphasis in original). I agree with Carrigan's suggestion to trial multiple AI platforms to test how each behaves.[9] By giving them identical prompts, the quality of this "collaboration" and relevance of advice to your thesis topic will quickly become apparent.

I did not use AI for my PhD. I completed it in mid-2023, just as AI was becoming widely accessible in academic contexts, and I wasn't completely aware of its implications. As AI wasn't incorporated into my practice, and I was wary of it, I simply disregarded its possibilities. Some universities consider any AI editing, even minimal use, to be an academic integrity violation, while others view it as equivalent to using grammar-checking software.

After completing my thesis, I started experimenting with ChatGPT and then moved to Claude. At the time of writing, I found Claude to be more nuanced in exchanges regarding the creative arts and more responsive to my analytical and interpretive questioning.

As an experiment and as research, I used Claude in the preparation for *CAPC*. My four approaches functioned as "tools for thinking" in the following capacities:

- **Thesaurus**: to find alternative, or more specific, words and terms. If initial suggestions don't fit, request options that are more tailored to your needs.
- **Copy-editor/proofreader**: when directed, to check for clarity, grammar and spelling, to reduce word count, and to maintain voice.
- **Encyclopedia**: to explain complex theories and information, simplifying ideas that, though clear to me, were a challenge to explain simply in their essence.
- **Literature review**: to search comprehensively. Claude's natural snowball method leads to a wide net of new resources. However, always verify sources suggested by AI, as it can "hallucinate" (generate plausible but non-existent) citations or suggest outdated references.[10]

An additional unintended tool was endorsement. Even knowing an AI "friend" was helping me, I felt joy reading Claude's encouraging responses like "the text is coming together well—you're doing good work distilling complex ideas while maintaining accuracy!" (2025; em dash in original). Claude even suggested I take a break when I really need one. These comments can be useful wellbeing tools, but remember, Claude doesn't actually know you. Responses designed to encourage can feel helpful, but they are not genuine assessments of your work.

I didn't use Claude to create original writing. I reviewed every suggested edit and submitted only short sections at a time rather than a full manuscript. Before proceeding, I disclosed my intentions to my editor and publisher, who agreed to this experimental trial.

While these tools proved valuable, it's essential to recognise AI's limitations and risks. Consider the following:

- **Bias**: LLMs can perpetuate biases present in their training data, significant for creative arts research where representation and diverse voices are critical.
- **Data privacy**: Never input confidential material (participant data, interview transcripts, proprietary information). Most platforms retain your inputs for training purposes.

- **Academic integrity**: Maintain clear boundaries about what constitutes your intellectual work. Using AI to generate arguments, structure chapters, or produce substantial content may violate academic integrity policies.
- **Authorship in creative artefacts**: For visual, sonic, or interactive work, AI generation tools raise questions about whether AI-generated elements constitute your creative practice. Discuss any use of these tools with your supervisor early, particularly if considering incorporating AI-generated content into your artefact itself.

Policies concerning the use of AI vary significantly between institutions, with some prohibiting AI use entirely, others allowing it with disclosure, and some having no policy yet. Finally, whether required or not, it is best practice to include a note outlining how you used AI. For example: "Claude AI was used to check grammar and suggest alternative terminology. All content and ideas are the author's own". AI isn't going anywhere, so Carrigan's approach of thoughtful engagement, when permissible, is a sensible strategy (2025, 49–51).

## 10 Visual documentation

In this section, I refer to visual documentation outside of your creative practice, which is relevant for all creative arts theses. You may generate visual images for figures that appear in your text, as a plate section, or in an appendix. You may also create visual presentations for milestones or conferences, or incorporate images in a reflective journal that later becomes part of your thesis or exegesis. Developing a visual language for your thesis is critical across the process, presentation, and submission of your thesis. This section addresses practical considerations for creating, formatting, and integrating visual materials.

### *Figures*

Figures included in your thesis/exegesis may include tables, graphs, diagrams, artwork, photographs, film stills, and any other images. I discuss permissions required for third-party material in the management decalogue. Here, the focus is on the selection or generation of images. Whether you use material created by others or by yourself, the goal of each figure is to support your argument in a clear and visually engaging manner.

Refer to all figures within the text and direct the reader to their location. In your discussion of each figure, inform the reader why this image or table is significant and what details it adds to your discussion. Practices in labelling vary, such as using "Fig." or "Figure". Figure numbers may include the chapter (such as Figure 1.1: caption), or the numbering may continue from chapter to chapter sequentially throughout the entire thesis. Label all figures consistently in the format your reference system advises.

If you place figures within the text, position them after the end of the paragraph in which you first refer to them. If you group figures in a plate section, check whether your discipline or university has guidelines for their position. Alternatively, depending on the relationship of image to text, figures may be best included as an appendix. This approach is effective if you are providing additional information that is tangential to the main aim of the text.

## *Visual presentations*

Creating effective visual presentations requires transforming notes into articulate and concise slides. Slides accompanying a talk may serve as support for a milestone during your PhD, or may be presented at a conference. Slides may also play a role in your artefact.

The visuals in a slide presentation primarily support your spoken component, unless the visual material stands alone without an accompanying verbal lecture. The slides support not only your ideas but also your delivery by reminding you of key points. Visuals need to be engaging and exemplify the points you are making, but they should not distract from what you are saying. Don't put your audience in a position to choose whether to listen to you or read the slides.

As creative arts researchers, you will likely bring an astute design sense to your presentations. This can be both an asset and a challenge: slide presentation is a hybrid form combining visual design with verbal communication, and the difficulty lies not in visual skill but in adapting that ability to presentation constraints, where clarity and simplicity must take precedence over artistic expression. Even the most visually sophisticated researchers struggle with this balance.

See Appendix F for a presentation design checklist that overviews common mistakes and design principles.

## *Reflective journal*

A reflective process journal is extremely personal. Initially, words, diagrams, sketches, and visual references need only make sense to you. While some entries may eventually find their way into your thesis or exegesis, I don't recommend keeping that end use constantly in mind, as it may compromise the authenticity and accuracy of your record. That said, having some basic principles in mind from the start, such as consistent dating, legible notation, and varied documentation modes, may make the journal more useful when you return to it later.

As discussed in the practice decalogue, reflective practice, particularly Donald Schön's concepts of reflection-in-action and reflection-on-action, provides the theoretical foundation for keeping a process journal. Your visual journal entries serve as evidence of this reflective practice, capturing tacit knowledge and documenting the iterative development of your creative work. Rachel Gannon and Mireille Fauchon suggest that "Illustrative strategies can be used to bring together different bodies of knowledge in order to present and communicate multifaceted perspectives surrounding a particular subject matter or concern" (2021, 176). In this way, a visual record can surface connections between ideas and theories as your thesis develops.

### Practical considerations for journal entries:

- **Include dated entries** to track the evolution of your thinking.
- **Use clear visual organisation** to later identify significant moments.
- **Note context briefly:** What problem are you solving? What have you just read or made? What are you thinking about and inspired by?
- **Consider legibility** without over-polishing; authenticity matters more than perfection.
- **Photograph or scan regularly** if using physical journals as backup and for potential digital submission.

When curating journal entries for your thesis, select excerpts that illustrate key turning points, demonstrate iterative thinking, or provide visual evidence of your methodology, methods, and practice in action. These visual entries may be integrated within chapters to support your argument or compiled in an appendix as a chronological record of the process. In either case, your visual journal is not supplementary material; it is evidence of your research thinking made visible.

## Notes

1 Each reference system has an available style guide. Become familiar with your selected resource, such as *The Chicago Manual of Style*, 18th ed. (2024).

2 Some of Scrivener's functionality is clunky and may be resolved in future versions.

3 This AI preference has attracted media attention; see, for example, Nitsuh Abebe (2025).
4 Benjamin Dreyer's "66 Assorted Things to Do (and not to do) with Punctuation" (2019, 20–61) covers full-stops and other detailed advice.
5 See David Evans et al. (2014, 32).
6 For further information on tense conventions, see Evans et al. (2014, 29–30) and William Strunk Jr. and E. B. White (2005, 49–52).
7 Given how quickly platforms emerge and disappear, I offer a typology rather than specific names: newsletter/long-form, visual/short-form, microblogging/discussion, professional networking, and academic-specific.
8 LLMs are a class of AI systems used to analyse, edit and generate text.
9 Consider the following: quality and relevance of responses, ease of iterative dialogue, handling of specialised terminology in your field, source citation capabilities. Investigate platform behaviours, but prioritise your own testing to determine what best serves your specific needs.
10 For more information on AI hallucinations, see Carrigan (2025, 47) and Eager (2025, 91).

## References

### *Cited works*

Abebe, Nitsuh. 2025. "With the Em Dash, A.I. Embraces a Fading Tradition." *The New York Times Magazine*, September 18. https://www.nytimes.com/2025/09/18/magazine/chatgpt-dash-hyphen-writing-communication.html

Carrigan, Mark. 2025. *Generative AI for Academics*. Sage.

Dreyer, Benjamin. 2019. *Dreyer's English: An Utterly Correct Guide to Clarity and Style, The UK Edition*. Century.

Eager, Bron. 2025. *AI-Powered Scholar: A Beginner's Guide to Artificial Intelligence for Academic Writing and Research*. Routledge.

Evans, David, Paul Gruba, and Justin Zobel. 2014. *How to Write a Better Thesis*, 3rd ed. Springer.

Friedman, Ken. 2014. "Now that We're Different, What's Still the Same?" In *Doctoral Writing in the Creative and Performing Arts*, edited by Louise Ravelli, Brian Paltridge, and Sue Starfield. Libri Publishing.

Gannon, Rachel and Mireille Fauchon. 2021. *Illustration Research Methods*. Bloomsbury Visual Arts.

Hayot, Eric. 2014. *The Elements of Academic Style*. Columbia University Press.

Johnson, Emily K., and Anastasia Salter. 2025. *Critical Making in the Age of AI*. Amherst College Press.

Strunk Jr, William, and E. B. White. 2005. *The Elements of Style Illustrated*. Illustrated by Maira Kalman. Penguin Press.

## *Suggested reading*

Carrigan, Mark. 2019. *Social Media for Academics*, 2nd ed. Sage.

Cook, Margaret. 2019. "Building Confidence About the Academic Journey." In *The Doctoral Experience: Student Stories from the Creative Arts and Humanities*, edited by Donna Lee Brien, Craig Batty, and Alison Owens. Palgrave Macmillan.

Duarte, Nancy. 2010. *Resonate: Present Visual Stories that Transform Audiences*. Wiley.

Frost, Charlotte. 2018. "Going from PhD to Platform." In *The Digital Academic: Critical Perspectives on Digital Technologies in Higher Education*, edited by Deborah Lupton, Inger Mewburn, and Pat Thomson. Routledge.

Holosko, Michael J., and Bruce A. Thyer. 2011. *Pocket Glossary for Commonly Used Research Terms*. Sage Publications. https://doi.org/10.4135/9781452269917

Huizingh, Eelko K. R. E. 2023. *Unlocking PhD Success: How to Acquire Crucial PhD Skills*. Springer. (See chap. 5, "Presentation Skills.")

Kamler, Barbara, and Pat Thomson. 2014. *Helping Doctoral Students Write*, 2nd ed. Routledge. (See chap. 6, "A Linguistic Tool for Supervisors.")

Lucan, Tinca. 2023. "A Journey from Researcher to Influencer: TikTok as a Methodological Tool." *Elephant in the Lab*. https://doi.org/10.5281/zenodo.10404739

Mewburn, Inger. 2013. "Doing Your Dissertation with Microsoft Word: A Book Review." https://thesiswhisperer.com/2013/10/09/doing-your-dissertation-with-microsoft-word-a-book-review/

Mewburn, Inger, Katherine Firth, and Shaun Lehmann. 2019. *How to Fix your Academic Writing Trouble: A Practical Guide*. McGraw-Hill Education.(See chap 4, "Your Writing doesn't Flow: Making Your Text Coherent and Fluent.")

Mewburn, Inger, and Pat Thomson. 2018. "Towards an Academic Self? Blogging during the Doctorate." In *The Digital Academic: Critical Perspectives on Digital Technologies in Higher Education*, edited by Deborah Lupton, Inger Mewburn, and Pat Thomson. Routledge.

Pears, Richard, and Graham Shields. 2025. *Cite Them Right: The Essential Referencing Guide*, 13th ed. Bloomsbury Academic. https://www.citethemrightonline.com/

Reynolds, Garr. 2020. *Presentation Zen: Simple Ideas on Presentation Design and Delivery*, 3rd ed. New Riders.

Rose, Gillian. 2023. *Visual Methodologies: An Introduction to Researching with Visual Materials*. Sage Publications. (See chap. 6, "How to Find, Format, Reference and Reproduce images.")

Salmons, Janet, and Helen Kara. 2020. *Publishing From Your Doctoral Research: Create and Use a Publication Strategy*. Routledge. (See chap. 11, "Why, When, and How Should I Contribute to a Blog?")

Sheldon, Julie, and Victoria Sheppard, eds. 2022. *Online Communities for Doctoral Researchers and Their Supervisors: Building Engagement with Social Media*. Routledge.

Skillin, Marjorie E., and Robert M. Gay. 1974. *Words into Type*, 3rd ed. Prentice-Hall.

Sword, Helen. 2012. *Stylish Academic Writing*. Harvard University Press. (See chap. 12, "Points of Reference.")

Thomson, Pat. "Starting the PhD – Learning New Vocabulary." *Patter: Research Education, Academic Writing, Public Engagement, Funding, Other Eccentricities* (blog). January 28, 2019. https://patthomson.net/

Trevethan, Robert, and Michela Betta. 2017. "Academic Referencing on University Library Websites: A Call for Clear, Coherent and Correct Categorisation." *Journal of the Australian Library and Information Association* 66 (1): 50–67. https://doi.org/10.1080/00049670.2017.1281371

*The Chicago Manual of Style*. 2024. 18th ed. The University of Chicago Press.

van der Gaast, Koen, Laura Koenders, and Ger Post. 2019. *Academic Skills for Interdisciplinary Studies*, revised ed. Amsterdam University Press. (See chap. 8, "Research Practice.")

van der Tuin, Iris, and Nanna Verhoeff. 2022. *Critical Concepts for the Creative Humanities*. Rowman and Littlefield.

Williams, Joseph M., and Joseph Bizup. 2021. *Style: Lessons in Clarity and Grace*, 13th ed. Pearson Education.

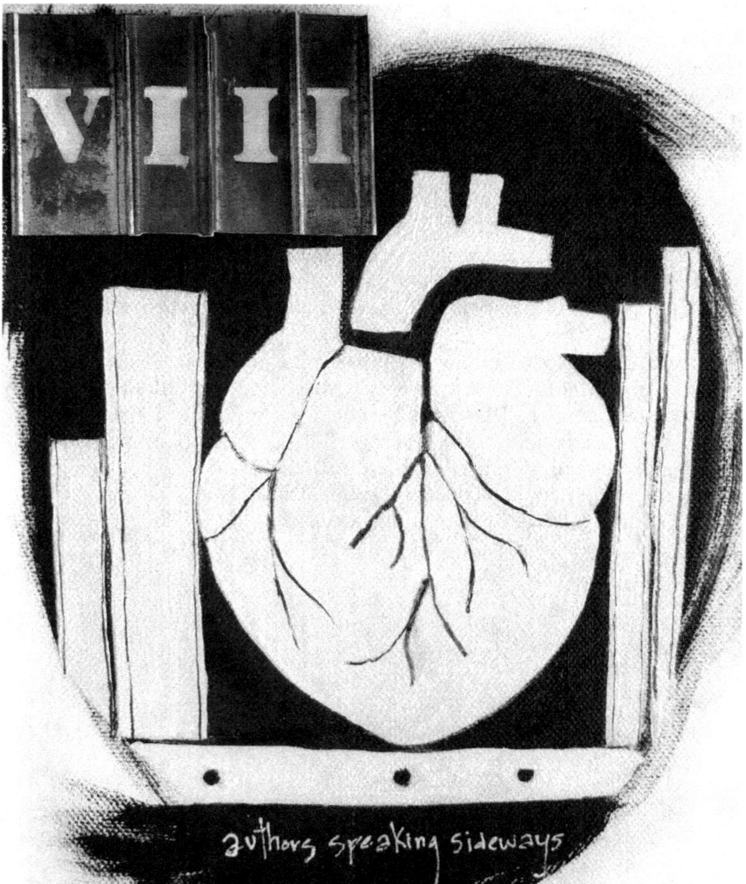
VIII
authors speaking sideways

# Decalogue VIII

## TEN EMOTION THINGS

This decalogue addresses the emotional dimension of doctoral research as a generative force within the research process itself, not as a matter of wellbeing or mental health.[1] In research, and particularly in the creative arts, passion and emotional engagement shape motivation, interpretation, and decision-making. This decalogue recognises emotion as one of the conditions through which rigorous research becomes possible, meaningful, and sustainable.

I didn't expect to feel a flutter when reading a passage that connected my disparate ideas, or have tears welling up while concepts validated my thinking through seemingly divergent texts. I didn't expect to fall in love with authors, films, and filmmakers, or feel wonder as challenging theories became clear. But these feelings drove my research, pushing me from text to text, eventually shaping my research question and findings.

This decalogue celebrates that emotional dimension: embracing ideas, resources, and creative work that move you, and acknowledging the emotional demands of each stage of research.

### 1 Love your topic

Love has a natural alignment with this academic pursuit. Philosophy, as it appears in the title Doctor of Philosophy, refers not to the academic discipline but to a "special sort of love, viz. the love of wisdom" (Sermamoglou-Soulmaidi and Keeling 2021, xii). This joining of love and wisdom serves as a foundation for your studies.

Whether you complete your thesis as a full-time student in three years or as a part-time student over the maximum period your university allows, you will be immersed intensely in your topic. You may be interested in the ideas, curious about the concepts, or obsessed with the questions that arise. However, if you don't fall in love with your topic, disinterest,

DOI: 10.4324/9781003584209-9

boredom, or even anger may set in. Completing a PhD is challenging academically, mentally, and emotionally, and without this attachment, stopping or refocusing may be the wiser path.

What do I mean when I say love? For me, this love showed up unexpectedly: thinking of my topic as I fell asleep, searching endlessly online for others equally obsessed. For me, intellectual love drove deep curiosity, sustained engagement, and intrinsic motivation.[2] In creative artefact research, it manifests through both analysis and making.

Love can also overwhelm, distracting you from your main focus. I developed a practice of stepping back from divergent paths. When three sources deep into a tangent, I'd pause: "Does this connect to my research question, or am I just drawn to the ideas?" If pure fascination, I'd note sources in my "future ideas" file and return to my main topic. Sometimes those tangents proved essential; other times they remained absorbing detours.

Elliot Eisner observes: "If the arts are about anything, they are about emotion, and emotion has to do with the ways in which we feel. Becoming aware of our capacity to feel is a way of discovering our humanity" (2008, 11). His observation speaks to the breadth of human emotion explored through creative arts research. Artistic expression, underpinned by emotion, is shaped by dimensions of selfhood, including identity, views, and values. Acknowledging love's role allows the intuitive nature of making to become a legitimate and generative part of your research.

This practice might involve creating your painting, poem, or composition intuitively, then stepping back to analyse its emotional effect. Your reflection might reveal something unexpected. Perhaps the work evokes melancholy when you felt joy, or creates tension you didn't intend. With this awareness, you can make deliberate choices: try a different approach, lean into the unexpected emotion, or investigate why the work resists your intentions. Recognising how emotion operates in your creative work, both in the making and in your response to it, is essential to understanding how love can function as part of your research process.

Intellectual love enables you to invest deeply in your topic. Recent scholars have explored this terrain: Rayann Alves-Bryan frames love as "a researcher's wider reflexive framework that encompasses intimacy and vulnerability" (2025, 82); Laura T. Crystal uses the phrase "intimate inquirer" to describe researchers invested in the emotional landscape of their process (2016, 218); and Kathleen Gallagher proposes "a three-fold construct: love as a feeling, an intellectual struggle, and an action" (2018, 93). Love as a reflexive framework may involve engaging with feeling, responding to sensorial experience, and understanding lived experience as part of the research process (Alves-Bryan 2025). This approach legitimises subjectivity in research. Rather than passively feeling love for your topic, you can treat that attachment as part of how you notice, interpret, and pursue inquiry; your emotions become tools rather than obstacles to overcome.

These ideas of emotion in research may come as a surprise. They certainly did for me. After all, the PhD thesis is just an assignment, right? And what if I don't feel this love? Passion can be cultivated over time. There may be periods when you feel loathing for your topic. Pay attention since this feeling provides significant information about temporary exhaustion, a misalignment between your topic and your research trajectory, or the need to reconsider your direction. Umberto Eco concludes his classic PhD guide with emotion: "your thesis is like your first love: it will be difficult to forget. In the end, it will represent your first serious and rigorous academic work, and this is no small thing" ([1977] 2015, 223). Intellectual love transforms research from obligation into sustained and meaningful inquiry.

## 2 Love your sources

I never thought I would hug a book, stare longingly at a book icon on my Kindle, or gaze at a file in a folder. However, I have, and the significance of this feeling is inspiring. If you experience this sensation, you are passionate about your research. Some resources are straightforward and some technical, but others reach into your mind, your heart, and your research, altering your thinking or even your understanding of the world. A resource may be the single prompt that causes previously incomprehensible, convoluted, overly complex, unwieldy, fuzzy, and impenetrable ideas to come together and solidify before your eyes.

The text may describe an affect, clarify or introduce a theory, make a connection, or simply provide a word or an elegant thought. This is the source I hug, physically or digitally. Artist Carrie Mae Weems echoes this emotion by referring to her books as "my playmates, my best friends, my running buddies, my partners in crime, my solace, and my occasional lover" (as interviewed by Steffens and Neumann 2017, 148).[3] Pay close attention to this feeling—it is significant. This love can also make your body tingle. It is a form of love that is not romantic or familial, but one of intellectual intimacy: deep respect, profound gratitude, and the sense that this author understands something you have been trying to articulate. The source may become a critical research reference, or it may remain a personal reference that graces the pages of your thesis or exegesis. Even so, you know that you love it and that it has played a huge role in shaping your research.

I would feel the flutter I described when my intuition was justified in leading me to a significant source. When I discovered a writer or film-maker whose work illuminated my questions, I didn't stop at one book or one film; I sought out every article, every film, every interview, and every scholarly analysis of their work. I'd find myself following tangential leads, reading texts that weren't completely relevant. This wasn't driven by discipline but by love. I was compelled to discover where the perfect kernel of information lay.

I organised my books so they could support each other and sense each other's presence, arranging them on a shelf to trace my thesis's interdisciplinary direction.

I know this may sound absurd, even childish, yet I felt validated when reading a passage in Eco's *The Name of the Rose*. Two characters discuss how to determine which book contained words they had read before. They suddenly grasp that by reading one book, another may be revealed, leading to the source they sought. At this realisation, one character responds: "Until then I had thought each book spoke of the things, human or divine, that lie outside books. Now I realized that not infrequently books speak of books: it is as if they spoke among themselves" (Eco 1986, 168). For me, imagining the authors speaking sideways with one another kept me company through isolating times. Relationships with texts and their authors can become as real as relationships with living colleagues. Your resources are your constant friends.

That companionship is more than a metaphor. Rather than separating the artist and the audience in research, Gallagher suggests considering both roles as "witnesses to each other" (2018, 98). I am witness to my sources' ideas; they are witnesses to my development. Linda Tuhiwai Smith captures this relationship with authors perfectly: "I see many of these scholars as 'my friends and mentors' […] They gave me a language, a way to imagine something I could not voice in education, a way to see my own reality through a different lens" (2019, vii). These words express what I hope you'll experience: sources that come alive in your mind, become friends and mentors, and give you language for what you cannot yet voice.

## 3 Feel the words

When you read text, you read words. When you write, you use words. Simple? Yes.

Before embarking on my PhD, I thought I had a strong vocabulary. I certainly did in my area of expertise and in everyday life, but my mastery of language associated with philosophy, theoretical perspectives, and methodology grew exponentially throughout my time as a PhD candidate. Because I discovered this gap while alone, I experienced no intellectual ignominy, only shock at how much I didn't know. When I read Elizabeth Adams St. Pierre's description, I felt a real kinship. She reflects:

> I know some word or phrase on the page will send me spinning down a rabbit hole and tear apart whatever comfort I've made for myself. But I've learned over the years that the terrifying discomfort of being unmoored and lost is what I most desire.
>
> *(2020, 19)*

St. Pierre's simultaneous feelings of alienation and exhilaration echo exactly what I mean by feeling the words and desiring more.

I realised that there was not only significant language that I had never encountered, but also words that I thought I knew, but couldn't formally define. Some of the words I had never heard of included *concatenation* and *adequation* (linked together; the act of equalising). Some of the words I wouldn't have been able to explain to others included *phenomenology* and *epistemology*, which seems incredible now.

When I recovered from my horror of having so much to learn, I revelled in my newly discovered language. Some terms were so essential to academic research in general, or to my topic, that I adopted them quickly into my vocabulary. Other new words that weren't necessarily relevant intrigued me in their meaning, sound, or origin. For these words, I created a list (another personal sidebar) to ensure I remembered them and put them in my "future ideas" folder.

You might be wondering: what does "feel the words" even mean? I was surprised to experience great pleasure when finding a word that perfectly described a concept I had been circling. I definitely had a physical sense of gratification when I encountered the precision of adding the perfect word to my sentence.

The joy in feeling a word is not only about a perfect meaning; the sound or rhythm of a new word can also be exciting, comforting, or empowering. Vocabulary, like tools, can propel you forward through previously messy or unclear territory in your thinking or writing. These tools can help you comprehend new ideas and communicate them. Words that become your friends open pathways to new knowledge. As with your source friends, you develop love for a word as it supports your research journey.

My most significant word moment came from discovering not an unknown term, but its application. Reading *thingness* in Bill Brown's writing on thing theory sounded so non-academic, so familiar, so tangible (2015, 2004). Heidegger uses this word as a way to answer "what determines a thing as such to be a thing" (1967, 11). Brown builds on this notion, exploring how thingness emerges when a thing ceases to function or transforms: moments when objects suddenly assert their own agency. This word started me on a long philosophical and cultural study of objects, things, props, and *thingness*.

When this word and its theories clicked, I felt a weight lift and a warm flush in my face. I had turned a corner in connecting production design and thing theory. I suddenly felt intimately linked to a word that had once felt entirely foreign to me.

In creative arts, new images, sounds, or mediums can also stimulate sensory friendship; language, in this sense, refers to more than words. James Elkins suggests that "[e]very smear of paint works to communicate *something*, whatever it might be" (1996, 185; emphasis in original). The effect of that smear can be as enlightening as an unknown word.

As a creative artist entering academia, you're navigating between evocative and precise language, translating embodied experience into scholarly discourse. Kerstin Mey describes this exploration: "Each language has its own atmosphere, it is a biotope, a cultural universe in itself" (2006, 206). Newfound theoretical vocabulary, which sometimes feels constraining, can open frameworks for discussing work that resists verbal description.

Enfold yourself in new words. Let yourself feel their precision, their power, the way they unlock ideas you couldn't previously articulate. These moments are among the unexpected joys of doctoral study.

## 4 Embrace this place of focus

Creating a dedicated space for research is more than practical; a focused working space supports focused work.[4] When you surround yourself with objects that inspire and anchor, you're creating an environment that holds and centres your intellectual work. I put a standing unit on top of my desk. Not only was it healthy to alternately stand and sit, but the centralised space for my laptop, second screen, keyboard, and mouse helped me to sustain focus.

Next to my computer, I had a framed family photograph, a bowl that belonged to my mother filled with Post-it page markers, and a red stone heart with white dots that my son gave me. A Danish wooden monkey with a smile on his face sat on my laptop stand, and he made me laugh when my eyes wandered or filled with tears. When I reached my desk each day, these items were there to greet me. They reminded me why I was doing this work and who I was doing it for. The qualities of the space, including objects around you, engender a feeling of purpose; you are returning to the place of study.

It may not be possible for you to set up a separate space for writing or creating. You may live in a small apartment; there may be children running around, housemates, and partners filling the space. Virginia Woolf famously argued for "a room of one's own" as essential for intellectual work (1929/2020), but she was writing from a position of relative privilege. Your "room" may be the dining table, and all traces of research may need to be put away at the end of the day or night. Even so, think about what small things you can keep close by to inspire: a paperweight, a book, a special pen, or a photograph. The space, even if impermanent, is your space for intellectual inquiry.

When Stephen King's books started selling, he moved from his small desk tucked in the eaves of his house to an enormous desk in a large room, but found he couldn't work there. He returned to a small desk in a small space: "put your desk in the corner, and every time you sit down there to write, remind yourself why it isn't in the middle of the room. Life isn't a support-system for art. It's the other way around" (King [2000] 2020, 112). What you think you need as a working space may not best sustain your research.

Throughout your process, you may want to move around, using a couple of spaces that suit different activities or moods. Outside your home, this place may be the university library, workshop, studio, community library, or wherever you create your artefact. As my research was writing-based, I remained at my desk. I was near my books, and I felt connected to the life of the house. When I reached my final drafting stage, however, rather than feeling supported by the sounds of family, I suddenly found myself easily distracted. I set up an area in a more secluded part of the house, and the change in environment signalled that I was no longer in the phase of formulating ideas; I was now in the doing phase. I looked at my small objects, which moved with me, to remind me of my journey thus far.

Your digital space deserves the same attention as your physical one. Keeping research files organised is not only practically useful but also emotionally stabilising. As with a chaotic physical environment, files scattered all over your screen can be overwhelming; you may feel lost in your own work. Your digital space will go through messy periods when sources and files end up everywhere. Take the time each week to tidy and file, and incorporate something personal, such as new wallpaper, to make you smile.

A sense of personal connection to your space, both physical and digital, is what King's return to his snug space captures. His retreat reminds me of Gaston Bachelard's observation that the comforting support of a bird's nest reflects the effect of intimate space on profound thought ([1964] 2014, 123). Connect your working space to your own sense of home, including qualities and elements that enrich your experience, because as Bachelard points out, "Being starts with well-being" (123). Enjoy your space as a place set aside for deep thinking.

## 5 Rituals and routines

Maintaining focus is not only guided by physical space, but by boundaries in time. Dedicated research time signals to yourself and others that this work matters.

As a creative arts researcher, you understand the significance of rituals and routines. Don't adopt someone else's perfect routine. Get to know yourself. Reflect on which habits have supported or hampered your work in the past.

PhD research differs from creative practice: deadlines, academic requirements, and formal structures demand different rhythms. Mason Currey asks: "are comfort and creativity incompatible, or is the opposite true: Is finding a basic level of daily comfort a prerequisite for sustained creative work?" (2013, xiv). This question matters particularly if you have considerable commitments outside your doctoral study.

You may need to add a level of ritual to your routine in order to invite inspiration, a little like the presence of my wooden monkey. Rituals also aid focus. If you feel lost in the process, a ritual may remind you of what you're doing and why you chose this path.

In the early years of my research, I didn't establish a plan. I would fit research into gaps, which was reactive rather than intentional. Time vanished.

This changed when I started researching full-time during my last year. I'd work straight through with only breaks for food and tea. This punishing approach caused isolation and loss of confidence. I suddenly realised how unhealthy it was to block out life until dinner. I changed two things: morning dog walks before work, and afternoon tea in a comfortable chair, reading thesis-related books. These small changes broke the pattern and restored my inspiration and confidence.

I didn't think I had any rituals, though looking back, I did say hello to my books every morning and brought my tea to the desk in the yellow mug. It had to be the yellow one. Other rituals may include starting each session by reviewing yesterday's work, lighting incense, listening to a particular song, using a special pen to jot down notes, or establishing a moment of meditation. You might decide to end each day by writing down your next task. Your ritual doesn't need to be elaborate; the point is simply to signal a transition into focused work.

Know your most effective work habits and put a plan in place. Choreographer Twyla Tharp describes her approach to planning as "the scaffolding", explaining that it must "be sufficiently thoughtful and solid to get the work up and standing straight, but it cannot take over as you toil away on the interior guts of a piece" (2003, 119). Create a balance between plan and flexibility. Most crucially, remain attentive to what sustains you and what depletes you and adjust accordingly.

## 6 Unexpected inspiration

Surprises, when welcomed, enrich research in unexpected ways. Embrace them.

Develop awareness, curiosity, and openness. Notice when seemingly disconnected ideas come together, images resonate unexpectedly, or chance encounters illuminate your research.

You may visit a museum intending to take a break. Yet while researching intensely, questions rarely stay away. You walk through the rooms, turn the corner. There it is. Your heart makes itself known. Your eyes tear up. Someone has put into paint the themes you've been attempting to articulate. It's Elkins' "smear of paint" (1996, 185).

It can happen at any time. Maybe you're reading a novel and encounter a metaphor that perfectly captures what you've been trying to articulate. These "smear" moments of unexpected resonance are inspiration in action. Pause when this happens, make notes to add to your journal later, take a photo or make an audio record, and most importantly, remember this feeling when you return to your desk or studio.

These emotional responses trigger forward movement in your research. Be aware of these moments and allow them to inspire you.

Sara Ahmed stresses the significance of thinking about "what the materials are 'doing', how they work through emotions to generate effects" (2014, 19). These emotions aren't properties of the artwork itself but emerge through engagement, the "doing" of making or analysing. Awareness of emotion can actively shape your research direction.

Jot down moments of inspiration to hold onto them. A reflective journal tracks both process and emotion. Judith M. Meloy explains the significance of this practice: "That we do not always 'know' or appreciate now does not mean we will not come to understand later" (1994, 67). These moments don't always arrive at convenient times. When they do—and they will, as discussed earlier—capture them immediately: voice memo, photo, phone note, or napkin sketch. Don't trust memory. The detailed reflection can wait; the spark needs immediate capture. Revisiting these notes during difficult phases can help break through confusion.

## 7 Let go of beautiful ideas

My supervisor would listen to my new, amazing (my word) theories, connections, or ideas, pause, and say: "Save that for the book". I may have had an earth-shatteringly original thought, but the question remains: "Does it support your research question, or is it, alas, tangential to your argument?" This is tough: letting go. The idea may not make it into your thesis, but it may land somewhere else. I kept track of ideas as a sidebar, some of which became the book you are reading right now.

Why is letting go difficult? A tangential idea often feels like your most original contribution; a brilliant connection no one else has made. The tangent may even seem more interesting than your actual research question. These are typical feelings. Every researcher falls in love with ideas that don't serve the thesis. This is not only an academic tension. Filmmakers are constantly confronted with this notion of letting go of their favourite scenes because when they come to the edit, they simply don't serve the story. Creative arts researchers **will** likely have experienced or observed this firsthand. You may already know the challenge in distinguishing between relevant expansion that creates interdisciplinary contribution and tangential distraction, particularly when you're emotionally attached to the idea. This notion is deceptively simple but genuinely difficult to follow.

Ask yourself these questions: Does this idea answer my research question, or does it raise a different question? If I removed this section entirely, would my argument still stand? (If the answer is yes, it's probably tangential). Am I including this idea because it serves the thesis, or because I'm proud of discovering it? Be honest in your answers. If the idea doesn't serve your thesis, it doesn't belong, no matter how brilliant it is. A peripheral idea excluded from your thesis **may** yet set in motion a chain of thinking that leads to something vital.

Document these ideas while they're fresh in your mind. Make a note of your thinking, key sources, and why it's significant. You're not abandoning these thoughts; you're postponing them. They may belong elsewhere, in footnotes (if they contextualise your argument), in appendices (if they're supporting material), as journal articles (tangents often make excellent **standalone** publications), or in a future project. The thesis is not the only opportunity to share your thinking.

Remember from the first decalogue: your thesis is fundamentally an assignment. Knowing what to remove from your thesis is nearly as important as determining what to include. Stay focused on your end goal, practice restraint, and when necessary, detach emotionally from particular ideas, which is the exception to this decalogue's broader encouragement of emotion. Know when to move on, and when to keep a sidebar for the future.

## 8 Accept yourself as a scholar

You are embarking on high-level academic research that demands deep thinking. Your acceptance into a PhD programme confirms you are a scholar in your field of inquiry. This is no small thing. Close your eyes and consider this notion if you begin to feel like you cannot possibly be a PhD candidate. If imposter syndrome creeps in, remember: your candidature is not a folly. These academics saw sufficient promise in your work to admit you to the programme.

You are a scholar now, not someone merely becoming one.

Remind yourself that this opportunity to study, practice deep thought, and explore ideas for a concentrated period of time is a luxury. You may be pursuing your PhD as a qualification for your work; in that sense, it may feel less like a luxury and more like a requirement. However, even when your aim is to fulfil a professional goal, research at this level of intensity is a privilege, and both an intellectual and personal honour that forms part of your identity.

If your research seems meaningless, confused, or dull, resist pushing through mindlessly. Try these strategies: take a genuine rest; return to a source that first excited you; read something completely new; write something exploratory; connect to bigger questions; focus on one tiny aspect; explain why your research matters to someone outside your field. Shifting direction often reminds you that this work is enriching and invigorating. If you still question the significance of your research, consider this statistic: only one per cent of the population of European Union (EU) member and associated countries holds a PhD.[5]

There is much to learn, but when you feel overwhelmed recall what you already know. Your research typically begins in your area of expertise, in which you already have a significant voice. To acknowledge this, make a list of your areas of knowledge and practitioner experience. Trust this base, this jumping-off point into the unknown: your research.

## 9 Do you respect your supervisor?

Eco states that students "must also intuitively feel some sense of trust and respect toward the professor" ([1977] 2015, 44). Ask yourself: Do you respect your supervisor? Do you feel professional affection for them? Are you excited to engage with their work and pleased to see them at meetings?

Professional affection doesn't necessarily mean friendship. Rather, I refer here to genuine regard for your supervisor as scholar and person; interest in their perspective; appreciation for their investment in your development; pleasure in working towards shared goals. This warmth, even combined with nervousness or disagreement, sustains the relationship through challenging years.

Can you cultivate these characteristics of a healthy relationship? Half the responsibility is in your hands. You can cultivate respect and affection by being prepared for meetings and submissions, communicating regularly, and remaining receptive to feedback. The professional affection I describe is different from that for a peer; I pair it with respect, as affection carries a quality of esteem and gratitude that respect alone does not necessarily hold.

Not every supervisor relationship feels like professional affection. Some are intellectually electric, others quietly supportive, still others merely adequate. All can work. Key here is mutual respect, reliable feedback, and genuine support for your development.

Professional affection enriches the experience but isn't required. Respect and support are required. Everything else is a bonus. If these basics exist, the relationship works. If not, it's time to seek change.

If you work with associate supervisors or a committee, these principles apply across all relationships, and you may have a stronger connection with one supervisor than others, which is natural. What matters is professional respect across your entire team while cultivating at least one relationship characterised by genuine warmth.

You may feel petrified at the sound of your supervisor's voice if unprepared, yet within that fear should remain respect. This quality, as the basis of a strong supervisor-supervisee relationship, enables you to absorb feedback, sort through its relevance, and apply it effectively.

If fear stems from your supervisor's treatment of you, such as disinterest, dishonesty, or bullying, the relationship is fundamentally compromised. If you are being treated unfairly, find someone else.[6]

## 10 Celebrate each step achieved

Celebration isn't frivolous; it's essential. Pausing to acknowledge achievements energises your research and reminds you why this work matters. Eelko K.R.E. Huizingh notes: "Celebrations give energy, which you can then use to overcome problems" (2023, 137). Marking these moments helps you recognise the value of what you are building.

Many moments throughout your PhD deserve celebration: developing an initial thesis argument, completing your first draft, delivering a milestone presentation, sending your final draft to the copyeditor, and, of course, your final submission and successful examination, not to mention graduation.

Take time with your supervisor, friends, family, and yourself to celebrate these moments and pause to acknowledge your achievements. Some of these moments may seem small, such as suddenly understanding a complex theory, discovering an artistic process that unlocks your project, or recognising a pattern across your research. If you rush past these magical moments, you miss a powerful tool for motivation and encouragement: *celebrating yourself*. Consider developing a personal ritual that you return to each time you reach a milestone, whether that involves champagne, chocolate, a walk or swim, meditation, playing with children or pets, reading a book of fiction, or whatever feels celebratory to you.

Although celebration creates energy, it can also reveal its absence. If celebrating feels hollow or you can't access joy, this reaction may signal deeper exhaustion or self-doubt. Be gentle with yourself, and consider seeking support. Even then, a simple acknowledgement, such as a day of rest or marking it quietly as a milestone, recognises you've moved forward.

Research, like the poet's attention to objects, is sustained by care; care for your ideas, your process, and yourself. Bachelard describes the generative power of this attention: "When a dreamer can reconstruct the world from an object that he transforms magically through his care of it, we become convinced that everything in the life of a poet is germinal" ([1964] 2014, 90). Celebrating your achievements is one expression of that care; a moment of attention to what you have built and who you are becoming through the process.

## Notes

1 For discussions on this perspective see the well-being decalogue.

2 The phrase "intellectual love" draws on 17th-century philosopher Baruch Spinoza's concept of the intellectual love of God (for Spinoza, "God" signifies nature and the world). In his framework, love represents the highest form of human knowledge and emotion: rational apprehension arising from deep understanding rather than fleeting passion. While Spinoza's metaphysics differ from the concerns of contemporary research, his insight remains relevant: profound understanding can generate a form of love that bridges reason and emotion. My use adapts this philosophical tradition to describe the passionate engagement that sustains scholarly inquiry. (For more about Spinoza's conception of intellectual love and its significance in research, see Stephen Rowland 2008.)

3 This anthology, *Unpacking My Library: Artists and Their* Books (2017), takes its title from Walter Benjamin's well-known essay "Unpacking My Library: A Talk about Book Collections" (1955/2007) which also serves as an introduction to the first book in Steffens' series (2009). The book's epigraph, "Books share fate with their readers" (2017, vii), is by Eco.

bell hooks' *Art on My Mind: Visual Politics* (1995), in which she speaks with Weems about her art, extends this conversation further.

4 Significant resources adding to this conversation include Cal Newport on productivity (2016), Pat Thomson and Barbara Kamler on doctoral research (2016, 45–49), and Mihaly Csikszentmihalyi on creativity (1996).

5 This statistic includes European Union (EU) countries (excepting Romania), three EU candidate countries (Serbia, North Macedonia, and Turkey) and four EFTA/Schengen area countries (Iceland, Liechtenstein, Norway, and Switzerland). As of 2023, Slovenia and Switzerland top the list with 3 per cent of their populations holding a PhD. See World Population Review (2026). Statistics for the UK can be found at Higher Education Statistics Agency (2026); statistics for the US can be found at National Science Foundation (2024); and for Australia at Australian Bureau of Statistics (2025).

6 See the practice decalogue for guidance on finding or changing supervisors, and the well-being decalogue for further discussion on urgent well-being issues.

## References

### *Cited works*

Ahmed, Sara. 2014. "Introduction: Feel Your Way." In *The Cultural Politics of Emotion*, 2nd ed. Edinburgh University Press.

Alves-Bryan, Rayann. 2025. "Doing Love in Research." In *Creative Disruption: Psychosocial Scholarship as Praxis*, edited by Guilaine Kinouani, Hannah Reeves, and Clau Di Gianfranesco. Palgrave Macmillan. https://doi.org/10.1007/978-3-031-63661-5_5

Australian Bureau of Statistics. 2025. "Education and Work, Australia." Accessed April 8, 2026. https://www.abs.gov.au/statistics/people/education/education-and-work-australia/may-2025

Bachelard, Gaston. (1964) 2014. *The Poetics of Space*. Translated by Maria Jolas. Penguin Classics.

Benjamin, Walter. (1955) 2007. "Unpacking My Library: A Talk about Book Collections." In *Illuminations: Essays and Reflections*. Translated by Harry Zohn. Schocken Books.

Brown, Bill. 2004. "Thing Theory." In *Things*, edited by Bill Brown. The University of Chicago Press.

Brown, Bill. 2015. *Other Things*. The University of Chicago Press.

Crystal, Laura, T. 2016. "Intimate Inquiry: A Love-Based Approach to Qualitative Research." *Critical Questions in Education* 7(3): 215–231. EBSCOhost Education Research Complete.

Csikszentmihalyi, Mihaly. 1996. *Creativity: Flow and the Psychology of Discovery and Invention*. Harper Collins.

Currey, Mason. 2013. *Daily Rituals: How Artists Work*. Alfred A. Knopf.

Eco, Umberto. 1986. *The Name of the Rose*. Translated by William Weaver. Warner Books.

Eco, Umberto. (1977) 2015. *How to Write a Thesis*. Translated by Caterina Mongiat Farina and Geoff Farina. MIT Press.
Eisner, Elliot. 2008. "Art and Knowledge." In *Handbook of the Arts in Qualitative Research: Perspectives, Methodologies, Examples, and Issues*, edited by J. Gary Knowles and Ardra L. Cole. SAGE Publications.
Elkins, James. 1996. *The Object Stares Back: On the Nature of Seeing*. Simon and Schuster.
Gallagher, Kathleen. 2018. "Love, Time, Reflexivity, and the Methodological Imaginary." In *The Methodological Dilemma Revisited: Creative, Critical and Collaborative Approaches to Qualitative Research for a New Era*, edited by Kathleen Gallagher. Routledge.
Heidegger, Martin 1967. *What is a Thing?* Translated by W.B. Barton, Jr. and Vera Deutsch. Henry Regnery Company.
Higher Education Statistics Agency (HESA). 2026. "What Are HE Students' Progression Rates and Qualifications?" Accessed April 8. https://www.hesa.ac.uk/data-and-analysis/students/outcomes
hooks, bell. 1995. *Art on My Mind: Visual Politics*. Penguin Random House. (See "Talking Art with Carrie Mae Weems," 93–116.)
Huizingh, Eelko K.R.E. 2023. *Unlocking PhD Success: How to Acquire Crucial PhD Skills*. Springer Nature.
King, Stephen. (2000) 2020. *On Writing: A Memoir of the Craft*. Hodder and Stoughton.
Meloy, Judith M. 1994. *Writing the Qualitative Dissertation: Understanding by Doing*. Lawrence Erlbaum Associates.
Mey Kerstin. 2006. "The Gesture of Writing." In *Thinking Through Art: Reflections on Art As Research*, edited by Katy Macleod and Lin Holdridge. Routledge.
National Science Foundation (NSF). 2024. "Doctorate Recipients from U.S. Universities." Accessed April 8, 2026. https://ncses.nsf.gov/pubs/nsf26315/
Newport, Cal. 2016. *Deep Work: Rules for Focused Success in a Distracted World*. Hachette.
Rowland, Stephen. 2008. "Collegiality and Intellectual Love." *British Journal of Sociology of Education* 29(3): 353–360. https://doi.org/10.1080/01425690801966493
St. Pierre, Elizabeth Adams. 2020. "Post Qualitative Inquiry, the Refusal of Method, and the Risk of the New." In *Qualitative Inquiry and the Politics of Resistance: Possibilities, Performances, and Praxis*, edited by Norman K. Denzin and Michael D. Giardina. Routledge.
Steffens, Jo, ed. 2009. *Unpacking My Library: Architects and Their Books*. Yale University Press.
Steffens, Jo, and Matthias Neumann, eds. 2017. *Unpacking My Library: Artists and Their Books*. Yale University Press.
Sermamoglou-Soulmaidi, Georgia, and Evan Robert Keeling, eds. 2021. *Wisdom, Love, and Friendship in Ancient Greek Philosophy: Essays in Honor of Daniel Devereux*. de Gruyter.
Tharp, Twyla. 2003. *The Creative Habit: Learn it and Use it For Life: A Practical Guide*. Simon and Schuster.

Thomson, Pat, and Barbara Kamler. 2016. *Detox Your Writing: Strategies for Doctoral Researchers*. Routledge.
Tuhiwai Smith, Linda. 2019. "Foreword." In *Decolonizing Interpretive Research: A Subaltern Methodology for Social Change*, edited by Antonia Darder. Routledge.
Woolf, Virginia. (1929) 2020. *A Room of One's Own*. Penguin Classics.
World Population Review. 2026. "PhD Percentage per Country 2026." Accessed March 13. https://worldpopulationreview.com/country-rankings/phd-percentage-by-country

## *Suggested reading*

Brown, Bill. 2025. "Afterword: Upheavals of Matter." In *Virginia Woolf – Objects, Things, Matter*, edited by Laci Mattison. Edinburgh University Press.
Evans, Kate. 2013. *Pathways Through Writing Blocks in the Academic Environment*. Sense Publishers. (See chap. 6, "Creative Academic Writing: How 'Creative' Techniques Can Facilitate Academic Writing.")
Fraser, Mariam, and Nirmal Puwar. 2008. "Introduction: Intimacy in Research." *History of the Human Sciences* 21(4): 1–16. https://doi.org/10.1177/0952695108095508
Kelly, Frances. 2017. *The Idea of the PhD: The Doctorate in the Twenty-First Century Imagination*. Routledge. (See chap. 4, "The Spaces of Doctoral Research.")
Kiriakos, Carol Marie, and Janne Tienari. 2018. "Academics as Love." *Management Learning* 49(3): 263–277. https://doi.org/10.1177/1350507617753560
McLaughlin, Colleen. 2003. "The Feeling of Finding Out: the Role of Emotions in Research." *Educational Action Research* 11(1): 65–78. https://doi.org/10.1080/09650790300200205
Meloy, Judith M. 2012. *Twenty-first Century Learned by Doing*. Sense Publishers.
Milroy, A. K. 2019. "Making Time (and Space) for the Journey." In *The Doctoral Experience: Student Stories from the Creative Arts and Humanities*, edited by Donna Lee Brien, Craig Batty, Elizabeth Ellison, and Alison Owens. Palgrave Macmillan.
Sword, Helen. 2017. *Air & Light & Time & Space: How Successful Academics Write*. Harvard University Press. (See chap. 10, "The Pleasure Principle.")
Williams, Alison, Derek Jones and Judy Robertson, eds. 2014. *Bite: Recipes for Remarkable Research*. Sense Publishers.

IX
the unfolding of thought

# Decalogue IX

## TEN WRITING THINGS

This decalogue considers writing as a scholarly practice, focusing on both the written thesis and the exegesis, rather than on creative artefact production. I explore the nature of the written thesis and exegesis, their components, and critical elements: structure, style, and process. I also consider whether and how conventional thesis formats can be challenged.[1]

Writing a PhD thesis or exegesis is simultaneously technical and creative, a hybrid practice that many students find disorienting. The technical demands are real: thesis structure follows conventions, citation requires precision, and academic voice maintains formal tone. Yet writing is also where research happens. As you synthesise sources, articulate arguments, and revise structure, you generate insights unavailable through reading or making alone. Writing is the unfolding of thought.

For creative practitioners, the formal requirements of academic writing can feel incompatible with artistic practice. The prescribed structure, referenced content, and analytical tone may seem to contradict the intuitive, embodied, or experimental qualities of creative work. Building on the earlier reframing of writing as integral to research, rather than a bureaucratic requirement, this decalogue addresses that tension practically, framing writing itself as a creative act. Once recognised, thesis writing and your research subject become mutually reinforcing rather than at odds.

This perspective particularly matters for creative artefact researchers as they often struggle with exegesis writing, seeing it as explaining or justifying their artefact rather than as a parallel inquiry. Understanding writing as research rather than merely documenting or justifying transforms the process. The exegesis becomes not a chore tacked onto artwork but a site where knowledge emerges through articulation, revision, and synthesis. The following sections address how to make that reframing practical: how to structure arguments, develop a scholarly voice, achieve clarity, and use revision as a research tool rather than merely a corrective one.

DOI: 10.4324/9781003584209-10

## 1 What is a thesis? What is an exegesis?

I have explored definitional answers to these two questions, and here extend that discussion to consider practical applications of the thesis and exegesis as a written form.

In the broadest sense, the written thesis and creative artefact thesis (comprising exegesis and artefact) serve as vessels for communicating research. The written elements demonstrate your skill as a researcher and convey your contribution to knowledge.

In both the conventional thesis and exegesis, the written text articulates research through question, exploration, description, and argument. However, in the creative artefact thesis, this content is communicated through the combined contribution of an academic written text and artistic work. The exegesis, therefore, differs from the written thesis in that it does not stand alone but exists in a symbiotic relationship with the artefact. These two components function together; they are interdependent regardless of the form either takes.

Both the written thesis and the exegesis are typically supplemented by images, tables, graphs, or other illustrations. The exegesis may include images of the artefact in progress and in final form, and of other related works.

As an arts practitioner, you may be deciding whether to pursue a creative artefact thesis or a written thesis. Both approaches are sound research pathways. The decision lies in what framework most effectively explores your area of questioning. In a creative artefact thesis, focus is shared between making and writing, while a creative arts written thesis entails a more sustained engagement with the work of others. Consider which methodology works best for your questions, topic, and aims.

## 2 "You must write a thesis that you are able to write"

Umberto Eco offers essential guidance: "You must write a thesis that you are able to write" ([1977] 2015, 8).

Eco's guidance is deceptively practical. Before committing to a thesis structure or scope, assess honestly what you are currently capable of writing. Consider what you can sustain over the length of a doctoral candidature rather than what you aspire to write or what you imagine a PhD thesis should look like. This means considering the complexity of your argument, the breadth of your methodology, and the volume of material you can realistically synthesise. Overreaching risks incoherence; working within your capacity allows depth and originality to develop. Knowing what you are able to write is not a limitation; it is the foundation from which the creativity of writing can emerge.

You may feel dissonance between thesis writing and your topic research. This tension can be particularly acute in creative fields, where the formal process, referenced content, and structure of academic writing often appear incompatible with the creative works you study or produce. Yet this relationship can become not just compatible, but generative.

When you love your topic, the distance between you and your thesis dissolves, allowing creativity to become part of the academic process. Once writing itself becomes a passion rather than a perfunctory task, and is approached with the same creative investment as your artistic practice or research, you claim ownership of it.

Research is a creative act, as established earlier. Academic writing, like research itself, is a creative act. Once you embrace this concept, writing and subject (or artefact) begin to support each other rather than competing for your energy.

I discovered the creativity of academic writing while analysing film scenes and objects. Weaving my interpretations with those of other scholars revealed the intricacies and unexpected joy of the process. When a point crystallises through an original linking of ideas, you feel it. Pat Thomson and Barbara Kamler capture this well: "The writing is research" (2016, 211). Once recognised, your academic writing and subject matter become inseparable.

Karen Barad describes writing as an "intra-active" relationship where writing and thinking mutually form each other, "an iterative and mutually constitutive working out, and reworking" (2007, x). These moments are where creativity is most acutely felt, when a revised sentence crystallises an idea or a restructured paragraph reveals previously unseen connections.

Revision can both surface new connections and reveal what needs to be cut. As discussed in the previous decalogue, the creativity of academic writing as an iterative process also involves the practice of restraint: knowing what to remove. Deletion doesn't mean wasted time; restraint itself is a creative act.

## 3 The exegesis as parallel text

The exegesis, from the Greek meaning explanation, has special characteristics worth considering. Here, I examine what makes the exegesis distinctive as a form of scholarly writing.

Caroline Durré offers an illuminating perspective on the relationship between exegesis and artefact. She explains that:

> As partners in allegory, each text in the research setting is allowed its own destiny and integrity in a dynamic of mutual interpenetration or co-interpretation. Each side of the equation allegorises the other; neither necessarily has subsidiary or master status. The model is rhizomatic, not hierarchical.
>
> *(2014, 195)*

Durré's framework is liberating: the exegesis does not simply function to justify your creative work, but contributes knowledge alongside your artefact in a different register, with neither serving the other. The exegesis "is deeply connected to the creative process and can also stand alone without compromise" (196). This framing frees the exegesis from the assumed role of obligatory addendum and positions it instead as a creative endeavour in its own right.

The notion of parallel texts (one is making, the other is analysis and reflection) supports "a differently ordered form of enquiry; neither is subordinate, and the deadening demand to 'theorise the work' can be elided" (Durré 2014, 195). This perspective presents the exegesis as an equal and creative part of the thesis. Rather than writing to explain your artefact, your writing explores ideas and knowledge that emerge alongside the making.

## 4 Thesis components

This section outlines the key conventional components of both the written thesis and the exegesis. Although the exegesis is typically shorter and distributes research content across both writing and artefact, these general requirements apply to both forms.

Thesis components fall into three organisational parts: front matter, the body, and back matter. The components listed below reflect what is generally required and are presented in the order in which they are typically compiled.

**Front matter**: elements that appear before the body

**The title page** is the first encounter the examiners have with your thesis. An effective title balances specificity with accessibility, identifying your topic and approach without using jargon or unnecessary complexity. An expressive title may be paired with a descriptive subtitle. The title page typically includes your name, ORCID number, faculty, supervisor's name(s), and submission date.

**The acknowledgements page** expresses gratitude to supervisors, colleagues, family, funding bodies, and anyone else who supported your research journey. This page can include a First Nations acknowledgement.

**The copyright statement** (or declaration) confirms the work is your own original research, not submitted elsewhere, and documents any copyright permissions for reproduced material or prior publications.

**The ethics statement** confirms that your research complies with the university's ethical guidelines.

**The abstract** summarises your thesis in 250–500 words (this count varies), covering argument, methodology, aims, and findings in a self-contained form.[2]

**The table of contents** lists front matter pages, body chapter titles, back matter elements, and corresponding page numbers.

**List of figures** identifies all illustrations (photographs, tables, graphs, charts, artwork, artefact documentation, and process images) throughout your thesis with corresponding page numbers.

**Body**: elements that comprise all substantive chapters[3]

**The introduction** orients readers to your research. It typically includes your research question and establishes your central argument or thesis statement. It encompasses the claims built throughout the thesis and demonstrates their validity, significance, and contribution to new knowledge. This overview maps the scope of the research by stating aims and objectives and clarifying expectations. Some exegeses include both a preface (framing personal and artistic aims) and an introduction (focusing on research framing).[4]

**The literature review** positions your research and "'adds value' by mapping the territory" (Rugg and Petre 2020, 135). The literature review may be included in the introduction, as a standalone chapter, or, less commonly, be integrated throughout the thesis. Its objective is not simply to describe and recount your references, but to provide critical "analysis and sense-making" (135). In creative arts theses, the literature review often includes both scholarly works and creative works. For creative artefact theses, the literature review should address how these works inform the practice.[5]

**The middle chapters** include all those between the introduction and the conclusion. These chapters typically cover your theoretical perspective and methodology, your analyses, and findings (presentation and interpretation of your research). For the exegesis, these chapters also include analysis of the artefact, process documentation, and images of work in progress and final form.

**The conclusion** synthesises your work, addresses implications and limitations, and suggests future research directions.[6] It is not the place to introduce new arguments or evidence.

**Back matter**: elements that appear following the body

**The bibliography** (or references) includes only resources explicitly cited in the thesis or exegesis, not everything you read during research. This list includes all written text and artwork, films, music, and other creative work cited.

**Notes formatted as endnotes** (if your citation style uses them) appear here in sequential order. Footnotes are often preferred as they keep reference information immediately visible to the reader.

**Appendices** may include additional images, interview transcripts, data, illustration copyright permissions, a glossary, or process information (for creative artefact theses). Not all theses have appendices. Include them only if you have relevant material too detailed for body chapters. Don't hide critical research in appendices.

The introduction and conclusion remain among the most consistent in their function, bookending the research. However, resist the temptation to draft the introduction before completing your main chapters. Given the fluid nature of doctoral research and its many unknowns, an introduction written before findings are established rarely reflects the research you will actually have completed.

These components provide the structural architecture of your thesis. Understanding each function allows you to make informed decisions about how to organise and present your research, and where creative departures from convention might be appropriate.

## 5 Planning and discovering structure

Whether your thesis or exegesis follows conventional form or takes an innovative approach, its form must serve your argument and fulfil institutional requirements. This section explores structural conventions and addresses a key tension: Do you plan structure before writing, or discover it through writing?

### *Conventional structural approaches*

A common structural approach uses mirroring at every level. Just as the thesis body has a structure of introduction-middle-conclusion, each chapter follows the same pattern, and each section within a chapter mirrors this structure. This form creates consistency: Readers always know where they are and where you are going. Following the same pattern, your thesis argument appears in the general introduction, each chapter's argument appears in that chapter's introduction, and each section begins with a topic statement. This mirroring structure functions as a synecdoche, where the part reflects the whole, providing clarity and a thesis map for your reader.

Another conventional approach is signposting (or top-and-tailing), which guides readers by explicitly noting connections: "as discussed in Chapter Two" or "the next section explores". Traditional academic writing relies heavily on these phrases to help readers navigate. Current trends, however, lean away from overt signposting, as many now consider it unnecessarily repetitive. You can signpost effectively through consistent terminology, strategic citation, clear topic sentences, and thoughtful transitions that bridge ideas conceptually rather than mechanically. Determining your approach early helps avoid extensive revision later.

### *Planning versus discovery*

When should you determine structure? Two approaches exist, and they can work together. If you plan early by establishing a consistent organisation before substantial writing begins, you minimise extensive restructuring later. This scaffolding approach provides a framework that guides your writing. If you discover structure through writing, as Thomson and Kamler suggest, your drafts written in "chunks" rather than predetermined chapters allow structure to develop along with your argument (2016, 134). This method allows a framework to emerge organically.

These two approaches aren't mutually exclusive. You can begin with a provisional structure while remaining flexible as your writing reveals what shape your argument needs.

### *Writing as research*

Thomson and Kamler argue that writing itself discovers structure: "Writing is your biggest research friend. Writing provides the opportunity to be innovative and insightful—to explore meanings and possibilities, rather than close them off prematurely" (2016, 131). The process of writing uncovers connections and findings in your research that might otherwise remain hidden.

My own experience, writing three methodology chapters before understanding that one belonged within another, as described in the method decalogue, demonstrates this directly. The writing didn't document the discovery; it produced it. Start writing before you feel ready.

Don't wait until research is complete to start writing. Only through synthesis can you discover your thesis statement and the structure your argument requires. Remain flexible. Structure serves your argument, not the other way around.

## 6 Voice

Let's consider your academic voice. Reading published theses in your field is one of the most efficient ways to explore different tones. Clarify whether your university has a preferred academic tone: are there strong views on the presence of the first-person voice?

Academic writing uses a formal tone to facilitate a clear presentation of findings that support your thesis argument. Yet the research process, and the manner in which it is documented, is also personal; you develop a unique topic and research question, pursue investigation, and discover ideas and findings that lead to original knowledge. Your personal and scholarly tone can be developed through your positioning as a researcher and practitioner.

### *First person or third person*

The choice of grammatical person (first, second, or third) is one of the most significant decisions you will make about your academic voice.[7] The aim of maintaining a position of objectivity in research is commonly supported through the use of the third person, still the prominent choice in academic writing. In contemporary practice, however, the first person is increasingly acceptable and often preferable, particularly in the creative arts. Both approaches are academically valid.

The key to an effective scholarly voice is creating a balance between academic authority and personal engagement. The sometimes mechanised tone of the third person can be elevated through use of a more conversational style, and the sometimes intimate sound of first person can be balanced by an expert tone.

The distinction between tone and authority can be illustrated through comparison. For example, using the third person:

- **Mechanised** (stripped of voice): "Prop agency in specific film genres demonstrates magical characteristics that influence narrative progression".
- **Personal** (tone): "Although objects in any cinematic mode can be significant in driving the narrative, in some types of film, the agency of a prop does appear to induce a magical nature" (Stollman 2023, 3).

And the sometimes emotive tone of the first person can be elevated through evidence of expert opinion. For example:

- **Emotive** (personal reaction): "I am fascinated by how objects in film can be so significant. In some movies, I feel like the props themselves have this incredible, almost magical power that really draws me in and makes the narrative so much more compelling and exciting to watch".
- **Expert** (analytical): "I would argue that although objects in any cinematic mode can be significant in driving the narrative, in certain films props possess an agency that I interpret as magical in nature".

You may decide to use first person only in relevant front matter, your general introduction, and conclusion. Using "I" sparingly is an effective approach to maintaining that scholar/intimate balance. As an exercise, Katherine Firth et al. suggest you write a chapter draft in first person and then revise it without the "I". Some of your personal tone will inevitably remain in the third-person version, keeping the tone from sounding mechanised (2021, 165).

### *Multiple voices*

In a creative artefact thesis I copyedited, the PhD candidate used dual voices in their exegesis: third-person formal tone for theoretical analyses and first-person auto-ethnographic voice when analysing their artefact and creative process.[8] This approach created a powerful effect of twin voices weaving between theory and practice. As a reader, this seamless shift allowed both intimacy and scholarly authority while never losing sight of the research question.

This method requires careful integration to ensure the reader doesn't feel like they are reading two different exegeses. Jillian Hamilton describes the effective articulation through this "multi-perspectival" approach in negotiating the roles of researcher and practitioner throughout the exegesis. She suggests that such a text "establishes that the author is the practitioner and the driver of the innovation at the heart of the thesis" (2014, 386). This technique, which entwines the practitioner and the researcher's voices together, serves to unify artefact and exegesis.

### *Active and passive voice*

Passive voice is a sentence structure that creates distance and is generally not conducive to clear and concise writing. Benjamin Dreyer explains: "A sentence written in the passive voice is one whose subject would, in a sentence constructed in the active voice, be its object" (2019, 15). In the passive voice, responsibility may be missing ("The thesis was written") or, as Dreyer untangles, "the thing that is acted upon is front-loaded, and the thing doing the acting comes at the end" (15). This sentence structure can often be found by searching for the words "have been". Passive voice is often used by default rather than by choice; its tone can suggest a lack of commitment.

Compare these two sentences:

- **Passive voice**: "The notions of objects becoming things, the thingness of an object, and the object's acquisition of agency have been related to the process of a prop becoming magical" (Stollman 2023, 49–50).
- **Active voice**: "The process of a prop becoming magical is related to the notions of objects becoming things, the thingness of an object, and the object's acquisition of agency".

Both sentences are grammatically acceptable; however, the active voice version foregrounds the prop. This structure creates an upward movement in the sentence, which projects a more grounded, confident, and positive statement. When I read the passive version aloud, I can feel my voice descending and almost mumbling the name of the most important actor: the prop. Unfortunately, I included the passive version, as you can see from the citation above, in my thesis.

Passive voice has its uses: when identity needs to be removed ("the manuscript was damaged during transport"), when giving instructions ("images are to be captured using an SLR camera"), or when describing a method ("data were obtained by testing ten materials").
Using active voice lends a clarity and accessibility that passive voice doesn't allow. In general, passive voice gives the writing a distant feel, requires many more words, and can be convoluted; therefore, making it a challenge to read and comprehend. Don't fall back into it by default.

## 7 Clarity

Clarity in language and sentence structure ensures that you communicate your points and argument effectively, allowing readers to move effortlessly through your thesis. Your content may be complex, but the prose should be clear, creating that effortless reading experience. Dreyer posits: "If words are the flesh, muscle, and bone of prose, punctuation is the breath" (2019, 20). Punctuation, like breath, gives prose its rhythm and pace; without it, even clear ideas are a challenge to follow.

### *What not to do: "Thesiese"*

David Evans et al. coined the term "thesiese" to describe language that appears to be academic but obfuscates, complicates expression, and undermines any clarity and critical thinking (2014a, 26). The language issues characterising this flaw include run-on sentences, overlapping paragraphs, clichés, meaningless adjectives, unnecessary qualifiers, needlessly complex wording, repetition, and passive voice. David Evans et al. point out that "[u]sing eight words where three did the job very well is one of the building blocks of thesiese" (28). "Thesiese" typically develops when students misguidedly use seemingly academic language that hides their ideas.

Creative arts research engages with complex ideas, including those of phenomenology, materiality, and embodied knowledge. These concepts are inherently challenging. Your aim as a writer is to make them as clear as possible, not to add unnecessary linguistic complexity. Don't make complicated ideas more complicated by wrapping them in pretentious language.

The following deliberately exaggerated example illustrates how meaning can be buried under performative scholarly language. First, here is my revised sentence from the previous section, without passive voice, which clearly communicates a complex idea:

> The process of a prop becoming magical is related to the notions of objects becoming things, the thingness of an object, and the object's acquisition of agency.

Here is what happens when elements of "thesiese" are layered throughout:

> It can be argued that there exists a paradigmatic relationship vis-à-vis objects transitioning into things within the liminal space of material discourse, which problematises the hegemonic understanding of props in conjunction with the transformational process whereby props become imbued with magical characteristics within the nexus of cinematic representation.

Your eyes likely glazed over. This extreme version exemplifies the problem of writing to sound scholarly rather than to communicate.

When communicating complex ideas, clarity is a form of respect for your reader. Write as simply as your ideas allow. No simpler, but certainly no more complicated.[9]

### *What to do instead*

**Be concrete, not abstract**. Abstract language is vague: "The work explores themes of identity" tells readers little. Concrete language is specific: "The film foregrounds documents and photographs to suggest the disruption of self-perception through migration" gives readers something tangible.

**Use precision in your word choices**. Select language that conveys exactly what you mean. Replace vague evaluations such as "interesting" with specific claims such as "contradictory" or "unexpected". Replace umbrella descriptors like "aspect" with the more precise "characteristic" or "quality".

**Use jargon purposefully**. Technical terms are appropriate when they convey a precise meaning that everyday language cannot. Jargon becomes a barrier when complex words replace simple ones: "utilise" instead of "use", "prior to" instead of "before", "elucidate" instead of "clarify". Ask yourself: Does this word add precision, or am I trying to sound scholarly?

**Eliminate repetition and redundancy**. Some repetition (words and ideas) is natural as you present your argument in different contexts, but excessive repetition confuses and fatigues readers. Don't restate the same point, hoping at least one version will be clear. Say it once, say it well, move on.

Repetition is a challenge at the word level as well. Verbs such as describe, discuss, explain, explore, and suggest are easily overused. Develop your own list of preferred alternatives rather than repeatedly consulting the thesaurus. Select the most precise word for each context rather than altering simply for variety's sake.[10]

**Create flow through strategic transitions**. Your sentences, paragraphs, sections, and chapters should connect logically. Avoid mechanical transitions such as "furthermore" or "moreover". These terms signal connection without creating one. Instead, use conceptual bridges by repeating key terms, showing cause-and-effect relationships, and posing questions you'll answer in the next section.

### *Define practice-specific terms*

As a creative practitioner, you may develop your own vocabulary to describe your practice, process, and artistic intent. These terms may not exist in standard academic discourse, but they are not jargon: they provide precision about your creative work. Define these terms clearly when you first use them, and apply them consistently throughout your exegesis, allowing readers to recognise and engage with your language as established scholarly terminology.

## 8 Revising your work

In basic terms, revision follows a process of reading, assessment, and editing. An effective revision method divides supervisor feedback into two steps. First, correct all straightforward revisions: grammar, word choice, punctuation, and minor sentence restructuring. Second, address comments requiring deeper thought: lack of clarity, insufficient evidence, major structural reorganisation, and need for additional research. In other words, fix technical issues quickly, then tackle substantive revisions.

This two-step approach may already be instinctive; if it's not, it's worth adopting consciously. By following this process, your brain concentrates on similar tasks without constantly shifting attention between removing a comma, finding a better word, and re-examining phenomenology. After completing this two-step drafting process in response to feedback, I suggest a third step: working with a hard copy.

This third step uses paper and, therefore, is not environmentally friendly, but it is effective. Print out the chapter or section (single-sided so you can see all pages at once) and lay the pages out on a large table. As mentioned earlier, reading your writing aloud helps to determine what lacks clarity, what doesn't work structurally, what you don't need, or what doesn't sound right. When you read the same pages repeatedly, especially on screen, familiarity can dull your attention. Reading aloud raises your concentration because it's an unfamiliar mode, compelling you to listen to every word. You perceive ideas differently and uncover previously unseen issues. If someone you know is willing, have them read your work aloud to free you up to simply listen and make notes.

Physical paper enables a large-scale evaluation of structure, repeated words or ideas, paragraph length, and information distribution. When I completed my final draft, I printed out my entire thesis and went through it chapter by chapter. The process was painstaking but allowed me to polish the writing comprehensively in a way that, for me, was more effective than scrolling through my screen.[11]

When your final draft is complete, arrange professional copyediting if possible. Apply the same revision process to their feedback, assessing each suggestion rather than accepting it uncritically.

After incorporating supervisor feedback, copyeditor feedback, and your own checks, read your thesis again. When you think you can't read it again, take a break and then read it once more. You will always find something, and that is not a failure; it is the nature of writing.

## 9 Responding to supervisor feedback

Receiving supervisor feedback on your writing is one of the most significant steps in the PhD process, and one of the least discussed in practical terms. This section focuses on the craft question: once you have the feedback in front of you, how do you use it effectively?

The first and most important step is to read all feedback before responding to any of it. Resist the urge to begin correcting immediately. Reading the complete response first allows you to understand the overall direction your supervisor is pointing towards, rather than assessing individual issues in isolation. A comment on page three may resolve a question raised on page one. A structural suggestion late in the feedback may make several earlier corrections unnecessary.

Once you have read everything, apply the two-step approach from the previous section: technical corrections first, followed by substantive revisions.

When you encounter feedback you disagree with, resist the immediate impulse to dismiss or defend. Sit with the comment long enough to understand what prompted it. A supervisor who notes that an argument is unclear is almost always right that something isn't working, even if their suggested solution isn't the one you would choose. The problem they identify is usually genuine; the approach is yours to find.

Some feedback will require you to return to your research rather than simply to your writing. If your supervisor identifies a gap in your argument, an underdeveloped theoretical framework, or insufficient evidence, the revision is both a research task and a writing task. Recognising this distinction early saves time and frustration.

Keep a record of repeated issues across drafts, such as overuse of passive voice, insufficient signposting, or too much signposting, and add them to your "habitual errors" list. One recurring note from my supervisor was not to leave "this" hanging without a noun, as in "this book examined..." I added "this" to my list. These targeted searches catch common mistakes your eyes might miss. Supervisory feedback, accumulated over your candidature, is one of the most precise writing development tools available.

## 10 Challenging conventional forms

Some creative practitioners question whether the exegesis must be a conventional written text. They regard a separate linear reflective text as contradicting their artistic practice. Others believe their artefact already expresses everything the exegesis would say. If viewing the exegesis and the artefact as parallel or interwoven texts, as discussed in Section Three, still doesn't resolve your concerns, can you innovate within academic constraints? In most institutional contexts, an artefact alone does not satisfy doctoral research requirements without an accompanying exegesis to articulate research aims, context, and contribution. Therefore, if you are interested in developing an innovative alternative, strategise, don't simply rebel.

### *Models of the exegesis*

James Elkins describes three approaches to the exegesis. In the first, research informs the art practice, functioning as art history, theory, or criticism. In the second, the exegesis is equivalent to the artefact: "research and artwork comprise a new interdisciplinary field", or remain "wholly separate projects" (2014b, 309). In the third, the exegesis and the artefact are one and the same: the exegesis "is intended to be read as art, and the visual practice as research", or there is no separation: "The research and visual art are fused" (309). The effective exegesis described in this decalogue aligns most closely with Elkins' second model. The third represents the kind of innovation this section addresses.

### *Institutional considerations*

Before attempting innovation, confirm your university will support a different exegesis form. Examine previous creative artefact theses, especially those from universities known for innovative PhDs, to find precedents. Then develop your rationale clearly.

Innovation is worth pursuing when your methodology genuinely requires an unconventional structure, when your creative artefact research aligns more closely with experiment-based fields than with theory-driven formats, or when your research question interrogates the scholarly or conventional forms themselves. It may not be worth pursuing when institutional constraints make approval unlikely, when innovation risks distracting from content, or when you haven't yet mastered the conventions you're proposing to challenge. Consider your post-PhD trajectory: an experimental thesis may limit journal publication options while opening others.

If you have sound methodological reasons to proceed, obtain written approval from your research department and supervisor, document all conversations, and ensure you can transfer your exegesis to a more conventional form if needed. Your thesis must still demonstrate literature engagement, methodological rigour, critical analysis, and original knowledge. Innovation changes how you present research, not whether you meet scholarly standards.

### *Examples of innovation*

Structural innovation might involve chapters organised thematically rather than conventionally, or written reflection woven throughout the documentation of making in a photo-essay format, creating a dialogue between making and analysis. Voice innovation might involve the dual-voice exegesis I described in Section Six, combining third-person theoretical analysis with first-person autoethnographic reflection.

Visual or material innovation might involve a thesis on textile materiality printed on handmade paper, where presentation choices themselves support an argument.

These innovations must still serve a scholarly purpose. Tara Brabazon uses the metaphor of throwing a pebble into a pond: "the goal of the exegesis [...] to connect the shoreline—the limitations of knowledge—with the object thrown in advance of knowledge" (2020, 44–45). As artefact (pebble) and exegesis (ripples) meet, "knowledge moves forward in interesting and unpredictable ways" (45). Again, the artefact alone is not research.

Anne-Marie Forbes identifies two extreme modes that impede an exegesis's success: an exegesis so personal it becomes memoir, or so independent from the artefact it appears to be a separate thesis (2014, 276–277). The exegesis, she argues, "makes explicit the implicit decision-making that has attended the creative act of performance and establishes the originality of the endeavour, the generation of new knowledge and contributions to the field—the very hallmarks of doctoral research" (278). When approached strategically, innovation in form enables you to find the balance between exegesis and artefact while still meeting doctoral research standards.[12]

## Notes

1. For strategies addressing writer's block, see the well-being decalogue and Appendix H.
2. See Carole Gray and Julian Malins (2016, 172–174) for innovative approaches to writing your abstract.
3. Note on terminology: "body" and "core content", or "core", are used inconsistently across PhD guides. These terms sometimes refer to all substantive chapters and sometimes only the middle analytical chapters. In *CAPC*, the "body" includes introduction through conclusion, while the "middle chapters" refer specifically to analytical/findings chapters.
4. Introduction length varies (typically 10–15 per cent of the total word count). For a written thesis, expect 8,000–12,000 words; for an exegesis, 2,000–6,000 words. These are guidelines, not rules. Your introduction should be as long as it needs to be to orient readers effectively.

5 See Kamler and Thomson for a unique and enabling perspective on the literature review (2014, 30–38).
6 Conclusion length guidelines vary (typically 5–10 per cent of the full word count). For a written thesis, expect 3,000–8,000 words; for an exegesis, 1,000–4,000 words. Your conclusion should be as long as needed to reflect on your research effectively.
7 I found a technical term for this aspect of voice: "grammatical person" or "person" (neither term in common usage). This term describes the forms of first, second, and third persons, indicating "the three relations in which a subject stands with respect to a verb, referring severally to the person speaking, the person spoken to, and the person spoken of" (Skillin and Gay 1974, 400).
8 See Mahsa Makki Alamdari (2025).
9 This phrasing echoes a sentiment commonly attributed to Albert Einstein: "Everything should be made as simple as possible, but no simpler". This widely cited formulation appears to be a condensed version of Einstein's statement: "It can scarcely be denied that the supreme goal of all theory is to make the irreducible basic elements as simple and as few as possible without having to surrender the adequate representation of a single datum of experience" (1934, 165). The simpler formulation is the one that has passed into common usage.
10 Examples of overused verbs and alternatives: describe (articulate, delineate, depict, explain, portray), discuss (analyse, address, consider, engage with, review), explain (demonstrate, exhibit, illustrate, reveal, show), explore (examine, interrogate, investigate, review, trace), suggest (convey, indicate, point out, state).
11 Patrick Dunleavy also discusses the practice of printing out written work ([2003] 2022, 138). On drafting practices, see Thomson and Kamler (2016, 169); on maintaining working documents, see Eco ([1977] 2015, 112) and Thomson and Kamler (2016, 144–146).
12 For examples of varied approaches to creative artefact exegeses, see Elkins (2014a), Louise Ravelli, Brian Paltridge, and Sue Starfield (2014), Hazel Smith and Roger T. Dean (2009), and Laurene Vaughan (2017). Also consult *Text: Journal of Writing and Writing Courses* for current articles, and digital repositories at universities known for their creative arts PhDs for recent examples.

## References

### *Cited works*

Alamdari, Mahsa Makki. 2025. "Trying Identity Through Illustrating; an Autoethnographic Acculturation Journey." PhD diss., University of South Australia. UniSA Creative. https://doi.org/10.13140/RG.2.2.11299.31523

Barad, Karen. 2007. *Meeting the Universe Halfway: Quantum Physics and the Entanglement of Matter and Meaning*. Duke University Press.

Brabazon, Tara. 2020. "The Specificity of Creative-Led Theses." In *The Creative PhD: Challenges, Opportunities, Reflection*, edited by Tara Brabazon, Tiffany Lyndall-Knight, and Natalie Hills. Emerald Publishing.

Dreyer, Benjamin. 2019. *Dreyer's English: An Utterly Correct Guide to Clarity and Style, The UK Edition*. Century.

Dunleavy, Patrick. (2003) 2022. *Authoring a PhD: How to Plan, Draft, Write and Finish A Doctoral Thesis or Dissertation*. Bloomsbury Academic.

Durré, Caroline. 2014. "Poetics of the Studio: The Allegorical Impulse." In *Doctoral Writing in the Creative and Performing Arts*, edited by Louise Ravelli, Brian Paltridge, and Sue Starfield. Libri Publishing.

Eco, Umberto. (1977) 2015. *How to Write a Thesis*. Translated by Caterina Mongiat Farina and Geoff Farina. MIT Press.

Einstein, Albert. 1934. "On the Method of Theoretical Physics." *Philosophy of Science*, 1 (2): 163–169. https://www.jstor.org/stable/184387

Elkins, James, ed. 2014a. *Artists with PhDs: On the New Doctoral Degree in Studio Art*, 2nd definitive ed. New Academia Publishing.

Elkins, James. 2014b. "Positive Ideas for PhD Programs." In *Artists with PhDs: On the New Doctoral Degree in Studio Art*, 2nd definitive ed., edited by James Elkins. New Academia Publishing.

Evans, David, Paul Gruba, and Justin Zobel. 2014a. *How to Write a Better Thesis*, 3rd ed. Springer.

Firth, Katherine, Liam Connell, and Peta Freestone. 2021. *Your PhD Survival Guide: Planning, Writing, and Succeeding in Your Final Year*. Routledge.

Forbes, Anne-Marie. 2014. "Doctoral Research Through Music Performance: The Role of the Exegesis." In *Doctoral Writing in the Creative and Performing Arts*, edited by Louise Ravelli, Brian Paltridge, and Sue Starfield. Libri Publishing.

Gray, Carole, and Julian Malins. 2016. *Visualizing Research: A Guide to the Research Process in Art and Design*. Routledge.

Hamilton, Jillian. 2014. "The Voices of the Exegesis: Composing the Speech Genres of the Practitioner–Researcher into a Connective Thesis." In *Doctoral Writing in the Creative and Performing Arts*, edited by Louise Ravelli, Brian Paltridge, and Sue Starfield. Libri Publishing.

Kamler, Barbara, and Pat Thomson. 2014. *Helping Doctoral Students Write*, 2nd ed. Routledge.

Ravelli, Louise, Brian Paltridge, and Sue Starfield, eds. 2014. *Doctoral Writing in the Creative and Performing Arts*. Libri Publishing.

Rugg, Gordon, and Marian Petre. 2020. *The Unwritten Rules of PhD Research*, 3rd ed. Open University Press.

Skillin, Marjorie E., and Robert M. Gay. 1974. *Words into Type*, 3rd ed. Prentice-Hall.

Smith, Hazel, and Roger T. Dean, eds. 2009. *Practice-led Research, Research-led Practice in the Creative Arts.* Edinburgh University Press. (See part 2, "Case Histories.")

Stollman, Sarah Ellen. 2023. "Magical Props: The Cinematic Object and Narrative Magic in Poetic Realist, Surrealist and Magical Realist Film." PhD diss., Curtin University School of Media, Creative Arts and Social Inquiry. https://hdl.handle.net/20.500.11937/94397

*Text: Journal of Writing and Writing Courses*. https://textjournal.scholasticahq.com/

Thomson, Pat, and Barbara Kamler. 2016. *Detox Your Writing: Strategies for Doctoral Researchers*. Routledge.

Vaughan, Laurene. 2017. *Practice-based Design Research*. Bloomsbury Academic.

## Suggested reading

Bacon, Eugen. 2014. "Journaling – a Path to Exegesis in Creative Research." *Text*, 18 (2): 1–8. https://doi.org/10.52086/001c.27310

Bacon, Eugen. 2017. "The Scholarly Exegesis as a Memoir." *New Writing*, 14 (3): 386–397. https://doi.org/10.1080/14790726.2017.1284245

Barrett, Estelle. 2007a. "Appendix: Developing and Writing Creative Arts Practice Research: A Guide." In *Practice as Research: Approaches to Creative Arts Enquiry*, edited by Estelle Barrett and Barbara Bolt. I. B. Tauris.

Barrett, Estelle. 2007b. "The Exegesis as Meme." In *Practice as Research: Approaches to Creative Arts Enquiry*, edited by Estelle Barrett and Barbara Bolt. I. B. Tauris.

Beattie, Annalea. 2014. "How Artists Write in a Doctoral Writing Circle." In *Doctoral Writing in the Creative and Performing Arts*, edited by Louise Ravelli, Brian Paltridge, and Sue Starfield. Libri Publishing.

Bolker, Joan. 1998. *Writing your Dissertation in Fifteen Minutes a Day: A Guide to Starting, Revising, and Finishing your Doctoral Thesis*. Holt Paperbacks.

Bottery, Mike, Nigel Wright, and Mark A. Fabrizi. 2023. *Writing a Watertight Thesis: Structure, Demystification and Defence*, 2nd ed. Bloomsbury Academic.

Brien, Donna Lee, Jen Webb, and Sandra Burr. 2014. "Examining Doctoral Writing in the Creative Arts." In *Doctoral Writing in the Creative and Performing Arts*, edited by Louise Ravelli, Brian Paltridge, and Sue Starfield. Libri Publishing.

Edmonds, Ernest. 2020. "The Practice-Based PhD: Some Practical Considerations." In *The Routledge International Handbook of Practice-based Research*, edited by Craig Vear. Routledge.

Evans, David, Paul Gruba, and Justin Zobel. 2014b. *How to Write a Better Thesis*, 3rd ed. Springer. (See chap. 3, "Mechanics of Writing.")

Faulkner, Sandra L. 2020. *Poetic Inquiry: Craft, Method and Practice*, 2nd ed. Routledge.

Firth, Katherine. 2024. *Writing Well and Being Well for Your PhD and Beyond: How to Cultivate a Strong and Sustainable Writing Practice for Life*. Routledge.

Kamler, Barbara, and Pat Thomson. 2014b. *Helping Doctoral Students Write*, 2nd ed. Routledge. (See chap. 5, "Reconsidering the Personal.")

Kara, Helen. 2020. *Creative Research Methods: A Practical Guide*, 2nd. ed. Bristol University Press. (See chap. 10, "Arts-based and Embodied Research Reporting.")

Krauth, Nigel. 2018. "Exegesis and Artefact as a Woven Work: Problems of Examination." *TEXT* 22 (1): 1–12. https://doi.org/10.52086/001c.25111

Lamott, Anne. (1994) 2020. *Bird by Bird: Instructions on Writing and Life*. Canongate Books. (See part 1, "Writing.")

Lemon, Narelle. 2023. "Poetic Inquiry: Transformational Representations of Wellbeing and Self-care in Higher Education." In *Creative Expression and Wellbeing in Higher Education: Making and Movement as Mindful Moments of Self-care*, edited by Narelle Lemon. Routledge.

Phillips, Estelle M., and Colin G. Johnson. 2022. *Phillips and Pugh's How to Get a PhD: A Handbook for Students and their Supervisors*, 7th ed. McGraw Hill Open University Press. (See chap. 7, "Writing your PhD.")

Sword, Helen. 2012. *Stylish Academic Writing*. Harvard University Press. (See chap. 4, "Voice and Echo.")

Sword, Helen. 2017. *Air & Light & Time & Space: How Successful Academics Write*. Harvard University Press.

Thomas, Desmond. 2016. *The PhD Writing Handbook*. Bloomsbury Academic.

Vincs, Robert. 2014. "Deleuze's Hammer: Intertextual Tools for Doctoral Writing Within Practice-Led Research Projects." In *Doctoral Writing in the Creative and Performing Arts*, edited by Louise Ravelli, Brian Paltridge, and Sue Starfield. Libri Publishing.

image, movement, sound
X

# Decalogue X

## TEN ARTEFACT THINGS

Throughout this book, I've discussed the creative artefact, but what exactly constitutes an artefact? How do you develop your practice and artistic work as research? This decalogue continues the discussion from the previous writing decalogue, which examined the written thesis and exegesis; here, I focus on the creative work itself and how it functions as research.[1]

As established earlier, the creative artefact thesis encompasses doctoral research that combines artistic work and exegesis, including practice-led, practice-based, and related approaches. The correlation between making and research varies as practice may guide research, research may guide practice, or both may develop in dialogue. This decalogue addresses what makes artefact research rather than art, how it relates to your exegesis, how you determine what to make, and when it's complete. The creative artefact is not simply a conveyor of research findings but the site where knowledge is generated. Understanding this distinction shapes everything that follows.

Prior to beginning your thesis, investigate how your examiners are likely to approach the artefact. Some assess the creative work as they would a standalone artwork: on aesthetic merit, originality, and technical accomplishment. Others, as I believe is the appropriate approach, assess it on its effectiveness in contributing to your research question and to knowledge. Understanding which approach your examiners are likely to take is essential preparation for the examination. Ensure your exegesis makes the research contribution of your artefact explicit, regardless of the assessment framework.

Let's explore three dimensions: the artefact's nature (definition, relationship to artist, modes, and form), making as research (voice, process, and reflexivity), and engaging others (evaluation and collaboration).

DOI: 10.4324/9781003584209-11

## 1 The nature of the creative artefact

In creative arts research, the artefact is an artistic work produced within and through an academic research process, generating knowledge through making.[2]

Why do creative artefacts matter as research? Brad Buckley and John Conomos offer one answer: "Artists are concerned with making the rest of society able to see, feel, and interact with vivid new uncharted domains of experience, knowledge, and perception" (2012, 180). Through making, research advances artistic knowledge and practice, challenging societal assumptions or revealing new dimensions of human experience.

The artefact embodies this knowledge-generation. It combines established expertise with new knowledge and forms you aim to discover. The artefact is not merely an artwork but a site where research happens through making: a vessel for learning.

I return to Umberto Eco's guidance noted earlier: "You must write a thesis that you are able to write" ([1977] 2015, 8). The same principle applies here: You must make an artefact that you are able to make. This maxim doesn't mean you must create the same type of work you've already made. Your artefact may be something you haven't yet considered, discovered through research, as the form your question requires. Instead, this statement means choosing a form of making that genuinely supports your inquiry.

## 2 The artefact remains art

As creative practitioners, you already know the meaning and significance of art, design, and expressive experiences to you and to others. Through your own making practice, you see, hear, feel, and experience its affect. As an artist, you embody your work, feeling its impact personally. Most creative endeavours reach out to an audience. The definition and effect of art need no elaboration here. What matters is that you don't forget these notions when art becomes research.

When your art acts as a path through research, it fulfills your research aims, but it also remains art, engaging both you and an audience. Juhani Pallasmaa describes a similar experience as an unconscious conversation between two people. This quality points to a characteristic of art that doesn't disappear through its application to research: "A curious exchange takes place; we lend the work our emotions, whereas the work lends us its authority, aura and enigma. Eventually, we meet ourselves in the work" (2024, 56). No matter the form and outcome of your creative artefact, it remains your expression of imagination, the senses, aesthetics, and life.

Art integrates craft. Richard Sennett explains that within "practice, there is no art without craft; the idea for a painting is not a painting" (2008, 65). This acknowledgement is critical for artefact research, as both ideas and practice can be explored in your thesis. The timeline of your PhD affords your work what Sennett refers to as "slow craft time" (295). He explains that this natural process "enables the work of reflection and imagination—which the push for quick results cannot" (295). Recognise the craft in your work; it is a key to research.

Ricardo Falcinelli also recognises this essential side of working with materials and experimentation that "feeds directly into technique, thought and invention" (2022, 410). Creative artefact research allows more deliberate engagement with process than everyday artistic practice does. This opportunity lets your artefact become a vehicle for exploring artistic technique. Falcinelli explains the significance of process: "Ideas—whether they are artistic, to do with design, or stylistic—are not born in the abstract but in the process of confronting real problems" (410). He describes this practice as providing a critical "mental tool" in exploring concepts, materials, and affect.

The research you pursue by way of a creative artefact can focus on questions concerning conceptual, technical, material, sensorial, or any other artistic factor. As elements and characteristics of creative work are limitless, the direction of your research question is also boundless. You are creating art as part of academic research; however, it remains your unique, embodied expression.

## 3 The artefact as a knowledge site

When creating artwork as academic research, you occupy a dual position: simultaneously maker and analyst, insider and observer. Christopher Frayling describes this position as "standing outside the artefact at the same time as standing within it" (1993, 5), a foundational principle of creative artefact research. However, understanding what distinguishes research-making from art-making requires more than acknowledging that duality.

The critical difference lies in how failure, iteration, and process function. As an artist, you might complete a work, judge it unsuccessful, set it aside, and start again. In research, however, the rejected work remains part of your inquiry. It provides evidence, reveals dead ends, and demonstrates the artefact's evolution. This developmental process itself generates knowledge.

Consider what happens when your research question pushes against the boundaries of your established practice. A painter researching object agency through still life may discover their question requires a temporal dimension: moving image, not static painting. Initially, this realisation may feel like failure, as if it highlights an inability to answer the research question within familiar methods. But the recognition that the question demands a different form is itself a research finding. It reveals something about the nature of agency, about what static and temporal forms can and cannot communicate, about the relationship between medium and meaning. The unfolding of research, rather than assumptions about continuing current practice, determines artefact form, propelling the investigation forward.

This development is the artefact operating as an epistemic site: a location where knowledge is generated through making. The painter's resistance to abandoning habitual practice, their experiments with hybrid forms combining painting and video, and their eventual commitment to moving image all constitute research. The final artefact embodies the findings, but the process of arriving there produced knowledge that writing alone could not have uncovered.

As established, your artefact differs from a standalone artwork because it must respond to your research question, not only your creative vision. This distinction doesn't diminish artistic quality or creative freedom. Rather, it channels both towards a specific inquiry. In research contexts, this capacity to reveal uncharted realms becomes systematic and defensible rather than purely intuitive.

Tara Brabazon's pebble metaphor, introduced in the writing decalogue to describe the role of the exegesis in connecting knowledge to process, illustrates the artefact as a pebble, operating as a "loop ahead of the research", moving the exploration forward (2020, 44–46). While the exegesis contextualises and analyses, the artefact propels the inquiry forward into territory that writing cannot access. When you encounter unexpected results through trials of methods, materials, or forms, the artefact shifts. This movement, a capacity to surprise even the maker, is what distinguishes research-making from following an expected vision.

As an artist-researcher, you hold dual passions: for making and for understanding. Ideally, you shift fluidly between these positions. The passion for your artefact and the making process sustains you through the PhD's extended timeline, but passion alone isn't sufficient. You must also cultivate genuine curiosity about what your making reveals, what it resists revealing, and why.

The artefact you create for research purposes need not be a masterpiece. It must effectively answer your research question. However, the distinction between artwork and research artefact lies not in quality but in function and accountability to inquiry.

## 4 Choosing your mode

Once you understand the artefact as an epistemic site, the question of mode becomes practical: what form will best advance your inquiry? Your artefact's mode is typically shaped by your existing practice. However, the framework described in this section, considering audience engagement and research function, may also prompt work in a new medium. As you propose, explore, and make your artefact, remember Frances Whitehead's observation: "Artists do not think outside the box: there is no box" (Elkins 2012, 48; Dahlgren 2012, 140). While scholarly research requires academic parameters, it also opens space for experimentation.[3]

Creative artefacts take many forms: physical, performative, textual, interactive, or hybrid.[4] These categories are not rigid. What matters is how your artefact operates in experience, time, language, or participation, and how those qualities align with your research inquiry. Also consider medium, scale, duration, and materiality when articulating your artefact's research role. Your artefact may blend, shift, or resist categorisation entirely. Expect the artefact to evolve as your understanding deepens.

To understand these artefact characteristics, consider Karin Knorr Cetina's exploration of objects of knowledge, or "epistemic objects", that "are characteristically open, question generating and complex" (2001, 223). Gray and Burnett apply Knorr Cetina's term to artistic work to describe artefacts that are "stable in the sense that they comprise what the artist/maker currently knows so far; and mutable in the sense that they are incomplete and 'open'" (2014, 213). It is this openness that drives the knowledge-generating process of research.

This framework identifies broadly across creative artefact research, validating the idea that artefact form may legitimately change through inquiry. Knorr Cetina explains that epistemic objects

> appear to have the capacity to unfold indefinitely. They are more like open drawers filled with folders extending indefinitely into the depth of a dark closet. Since epistemic objects are always in the process of being materially defined, they continually acquire new properties and change the ones they have.
>
> *(2001, 223–224)*

Begin with your current artistic knowledge and allow the artefact to develop through this process: stable forms based on what you know, mutations responding to the research, and eventual settlement when artefact and research question meet.

This framework has practical implications for how you approach your artefact. Rather than determining your final form at the outset, begin with a mode that your existing practice and research question suggest, and allow it to remain open. Document the transformations: the moments when your artefact resists your original intentions, generates unexpected questions, or demands a different form. These are not problems to solve but evidence of the epistemic process at work. The modes listed here, physical, performative, textual, interactive, and hybrid, are not fixed destinations but starting points. Your artefact will tell you what it needs to become.[5]

## 5 Collaborative artefact-making

Collaboration in PhD research also occurs in artefact-making, as you may work with performers, musicians, fabricators, or technicians. Collaboration raises challenges around hierarchy, intent, voice, timelines, authorship, finances, and acknowledgement, among others. While these issues exist in all collaborative art-making, academic research presents a critical difference: the work is driven by your investigation, not only creative vision.

### *Creative aspects*

As the PhD requires demonstration of individual scholarly contribution, truly collaborative projects with flattened hierarchies are not feasible within this context.[6] The project is driven by the student, much as a film is driven by the director, a dance work by a choreographer, or a building design by an architect. Your collaborators have an unusual guide alongside creative vision: your research question. While collaboration incorporates interpretation, input, and expertise from creative practitioners and performers, choices and direction must answer your academic inquiry.

Collaboration requires deliberate planning. Jennie Morgan and Shelley Castle describe creative collaborative relationships not as research "of" people (or of creative art) but as "being with" people (or with creative art) (2024, 294). As a researcher, you are not observing your collaborators any more than you're observing yourself; you're practising alongside them. Consider the intent of your collaborations: Why are particular roles and specific practitioners critical to your artefact? How do they help fulfil your thesis aims? If unsure, return to your proposal and evolving research question for guidance.

Articulate your artistic voice clearly to collaborators. Ensure they understand your belief system, research framework, and how their contribution supports your inquiry. Brief them not only on the creative project, but also on your academic research question and aims.

### *Process factors*

To effectively manage artefact collaborations, the timeline you establish must be practicable for you, your university, and those working with you. Research schedules may have different priorities from artistic approaches, affecting the creative practice timeline. The relationship between the researcher, collaborators, and process requires careful coordination. For instance, as with all collaborations, balance your first-choice team with their availability, and also with their flexibility within your research timeline. Build contingency into your timeline for delays in collaborative input.

### *Practical concerns*

Key questions for artefact collaboration: How are practitioners compensated? Who owns the work? How are they acknowledged?

Ethical collaboration requires fair recognition and, where appropriate, financial compensation. If you plan to collaborate with practitioners, seek internal and external funding and grants early. Within academic research, treat partnerships ethically by providing fair financial compensation for a practitioner's time and expertise.[7]

Communicate the parameters of collaborative contributions clearly to practitioners, supervisors, and examiners (in your submission). Ensure all parties agree on a practitioner's contributions, how their input will be acknowledged (creative collaboration and technical assistance), and where they will be credited. You may require permissions or releases if using performers' likenesses or third-party material. The collaborative process should be documented both for reference in writing your exegesis and as verification of your practice.

## 6 Creative voice

Your artefact communicates a voice alongside your writer's voice. Ideally, your creative and scholarly voices inform each other. What is artistic voice, and how does it differ from style? Voice expresses your underlying values and perspective. Style is how you realise them formally.[8] Your artistic voice is usually already shaped through practice. Research may refine it, but you are rarely inventing it from scratch.

How do you achieve the balance between personal expression and scholarly contribution? Artists' reflections on practice can be instructive. Corey Mwamba, who describes his work as "Jazz+" (the plus indicating his personal sense of improvisation), points out that "although the musician voice and the researcher voice have slightly different concerns, there are points of dialogue, honesty about mistakes (and what improvising does with those mistakes), and a sharing of the musician's terminology (*thin; full; scream*)" (2022, 702–705, emphasis in original). His approach to research demonstrates how artistic voice can translate into scholarly voice.

Research may refine your voice by revealing dimensions you hadn't consciously accessed. A painter whose voice centres on intimacy through small-scale work may discover through research into public art that their voice adapts to monumental scale without losing its essential character. The research doesn't change who you are as an artist, but it can reveal new registers that your voice adapts to and embraces. This development should feel like an expansion rather than a transformation: your voice is deepening and extending, not being replaced.

Some practitioners worry that academic requirements will flatten their artistic voice into something generic or overly explanatory. This fear is understandable but largely unfounded. Academic research doesn't demand that your artefact be legible or accessible in conventional ways. Instead, it demands that you are able to articulate *why* your voice takes the form it does and *how* it suits your research question. Your voice through the artefact can be oblique, challenging, or experimental. The artefact is where you present your voice; the exegesis is where you make that voice intelligible to examiners.

Research requires you to articulate what was previously intuitive. This process gives language to intuition, and that articulation supports the dialogue between artefact and exegesis. This awareness informs your exegesis, which makes visible the invisible: the "why" beneath the "what" of your artefact.

## 7 Artefact and exegesis relationship

The relationship between artefact and exegesis varies. The creative artefact may drive research, provide a method of research, or become the outcome itself. The artefact is research. Regardless of which relationship you develop, making and analysis intertwine. In this research spiral, the artefact is informed by research, and research is informed by the artefact.[9]

While all these approaches exist in practice, effective creative research requires a genuine interchange between making and writing. Returning to Caroline Durré's observation that the connection between artefact and exegesis is allegorical, she notes that there is an "intriguing symbiosis that occurs when one text is doubled by another and each one points to, comments on and decodes the other" (2014, 195). Neither artefact nor exegesis should be able to stand entirely alone. If they can be completely separated, you have either an art object or an academic essay, but not research.

The artefact embodies content; the exegesis contextualises and analyses it. Neither element alone can fully communicate what artistic research generates. Henk Borgdorff explains that "artistic research seeks to convey and communicate content that is enclosed in aesthetic experiences, enacted in creative practices and embodied in artistic products" (2011, 45). The artefact communicates what writing cannot evoke; writing uncovers what the artefact cannot articulate.

Again, the relationship between artefact and exegesis should be shaped by your research question. Avoid hierarchy: the artefact should not be subsidiary to the writing, nor should writing be an afterthought. When both elements work in genuine dialogue, the thesis "illuminates the context and trajectory of the research, and can, hence, frame our perceptions of the artefact" (Candy and Edmonds 2011, 136). Both deserve your full commitment.

## 8 Revising through iteration

This commitment to both artefact and exegesis develops through an iterative process. Your thesis proposal outlines your intended artefact form, but as with your research question, these plans may shift significantly as you respond to discoveries and unexpected directions. Creative practice unfolds through intuition and imagination, but it develops through responsive and informed decisions. This dynamism is part of any research: embrace it rather than resisting it.

The evolution of your creative artefact means that, like your exegesis, your work will require revision. Methods parallel those discussed for thesis writing: observing, evaluating, and refining. This process allows you to assess whether the work continues to support your aims and research question. The three-step drafting logic also applies to creative work: address technical issues, consider conceptual development, then assess the work as a whole.

Artefact-making generates its own form of reflection, one that deepens into self-evaluation. Linda Candy describes how this process of generating insight into personal and artistic practice can be applied to approaches to revision (2020, 249).[10] Documenting your making process methodically enables clearer, more effective decisions when revising.

Reflection is also an effective tool when receiving supervisor feedback on your creative artefact. Incorporating these notes can be more affecting than feedback on your exegesis, as your creative work may feel more personal. If you've already made your own reflections on the work and its process, you'll be better positioned to constructively evaluate external feedback. Remember: your supervisor's assessment considers your work in relation to your research question, not in isolation.

As with your exegesis, consider all feedback. Seemingly peripheral comments may indicate issues in what you're exploring or how you're communicating. Reflection helps you to determine the next steps.

In his "Practice PhD toolkit", Sunil Manghani advises candidates to "keep making, re-making. The engaged, iterative process of art is a deeply held part of your method" (2021, 394). This spiral process is also central to research through making. A similar idea is articulated through artist Isamu Noguchi's recollection of his mentor Constantin Brâncuși's advice not to treat work as disposable studies. Brâncuși told Noguchi: "That which you do is the thing" (as interviewed by Kuh [1962] 2000, 173). This idea reframes revision. You're not "fixing" failed work but evolving the artefact through successive iterations. Each version has value; remaking isn't correction but discovery.

As one of Robin Nelson's "ten steps to the perfect PhD", he advises candidates to plan their documentation strategy from the outset by identifying what evidence will be needed at the examination stage and editing material as they go, rather than facing an overwhelming archive at the end. As Nelson puts it, the goal is "to focus on the evidence of insights" throughout (2022, 123). This record-keeping advice reflects that of Brâncuși: all work can be significant. Particularly within the process of academic research, all steps and iterations of work articulate your findings.

## 9 First questions

Throughout this recursive process, two broad questions frame your decision-making, bookending the artefact-making journey. First, how do you decide what to create as your artefact? Second, how do you know when your work is complete? In academic research, the artefact must fulfil your research objectives, therefore, the aims of your thesis shape how you answer these two questions.

Throughout this decalogue, I have explored creative artefact modes and characteristics, expressing the breadth of possibilities. Now, the first question: What artefact will enable research to explore your question and generate findings that answer it? How do you determine your artefact?

### Five factors:

1 **Inspiration and passion**: What drives your work?
2 **Technical mastery**: If new skills are required, plan to develop them or collaborate.
3 **Conceptual depth**: Your proposed artefact must have sufficient complexity to explore the depth of your question.

4 **Scale and scope**: Your proposed artefact should be scaled appropriately to address your question fully without overwhelming the research.
5 **The artefact as argument**: Your proposed artefact makes claims and generates knowledge—it is argument, not supplement.

To evaluate these factors, place your proposed artefact and research question side by side. Does your work serve your inquiry? Does your inquiry serve your work? If the answer to both is yes, you've found your artefact.[11]

Also, remember, your seemingly static proposal document will require revision to reflect research development. Have a plan, but also allow it to change. This flexibility doesn't compromise rigour; rather, responding to discoveries as they arise is itself a rigorous research practice.

## 10 Final questions

Now that you've determined what to make, how to make it, and you are nearing the final stage of your research, one question remains: When is the artefact finished?

To answer that question, you need to determine when the artefact has fulfilled its role and successfully communicated your findings in dialogue with the exegesis, and then how you let go.

### Five Signs:

1 **Alignment:** It communicates what your exegesis analyses.
2 **Relevance:** It addresses your research question meaningfully.
3 **Diminishing returns:** Any further refinement would be incremental, not transformative.
4 **Supervisor sign-off:** Your supervisor confirms it meets examination standards and your research aims.
5 **Timeline:** You are approaching or have reached institutional deadlines.

This challenge is universal: artistically (when is art complete?), academically (you have a research question to satisfy), and practically (you have a submission deadline). Artist and arts professor Ivan Toulouse offers one perspective on artistic completion: "a work is 'finished enough' when something material and perceptible has embodied something that is intelligible" (2018, 48). Applied to research, your artefact is "finished enough" when making and meaning have genuinely met. The work is not necessarily finished in the usual sense, but in terms of its contribution to the research question.

Completing an artwork is always challenging: there is always "one more thing". Perfectionism often delays completion. The thesis deadline is a gift: it limits the drift of perfectionism and establishes a necessary point of closure. As noted earlier, your artefact doesn't need to be a masterpiece or even a perfect articulation of ideas, but it must effectively drive your investigation forward and answer your research question. As Brabazon argues: "Art is not a doctorate. It can create a new way to think about evidence. It can be the basis of research. It is not *the* research" (2020, 40, emphasis in original). As the "basis of research", your artefact is finished when it demonstrates the knowledge you claim to have generated and engages meaningfully with your research question.

Remember that your thesis is not your final artistic statement. You will continue making post-PhD. Trust that you've done enough.

## Notes

1 As in the previous chapter, for strategies addressing creative block, see the well-being decalogue and Appendix H.
2 See Linda Candy and Ernest Edmonds (2011).
3 See Anders Dahlgren (2012, 141–142) for his exploration of free space.
4 See Appendix G for an expanded list of artefact mode categories.
5 In a lecture, architect Louis I. Kahn told his students: "You say to a brick, 'What do you want, brick?' Brick says to you, 'I like an arch'" (John Lobell 1979, 40). He also pronounced: "I want to give to the wall a consciousness [...] It wants to be a wall. It's proud to be a wall" (Richard Saul Wurman 1986, 127). Listen to your artefact.
6 Unless, for instance, a flattened hierarchy within creative collaboration is a characteristic of the research question.
7 For an example of challenges within collaboration, see Marcus B. Weaver-Hightower (2025, 412–415).
8 This description of voice draws on the research framework hierarchy outlined in the introduction to the methodology decalogue.
9 For a wider discussion on this aspect of creative artefact research, see Louise Ravelli et al. (2014).
10 For further discussion, see Candy (2020, 251–265).
11 See Judith Mottram for her perspective on framing "practice-based research in the visual arts" (2022, 359–361).

## References

### *Cited works*

Borgdorff, Henk. 2011. "The Production of Knowledge in Artistic Research." In *The Routledge Companion to Research in the Arts*, edited by Michael Biggs and Henrik Karlsson. Routledge.

Brabazon, Tara. 2020. "The Specificity of Creative-led Theses." In *The Creative PhD: Challenges, Opportunities, Reflection*, edited by Tara Brabazon, Tiffany Lyndall-Knight, and Natalie Hills. Emerald Publishing.

Buckley, Brad, and John Conomos. 2012. "What is the Current State of Thinking on the PhD by Art Practice?" In *What do Artists Know?*, edited by James Elkins. The Pennsylvania State University Press.

Candy, Linda. 2020. *The Creative Reflective Practitioner*. Routledge.

Candy, Linda, and Ernest Edmonds. 2011. "The Role of the Artefact and Frameworks for Practice-Based Research." In *The Routledge Companion to Research in the Arts*, edited by Michael Biggs and Henrik Karlsson. Routledge.

Dahlgren, Anders. 2012. "The Common Denominator." In *What do Artists Know?*, edited by James Elkins. The Pennsylvania State University Press.

Durré, Caroline. 2014. "Poetics of the Studio: The Allegorical Impulse." In *Doctoral Writing in the Creative and Performing Arts*, edited by Louise Ravelli, Brian Paltridge, and Sue Starfield. Libri Publishing.

Eco, Umberto. (1977) 2015. *How to Write a Thesis*. Translated by Caterina Mongiat Farina and Geoff Farina. MIT Press.

Elkins, James. 2012. "Artistic Knowledge, Part 2." In *What do Artists Know?*, edited by James Elkins. The Pennsylvania State University Press.

Falcinelli, Riccardo. 2022. *Chromorama: How Colour Changed Our Way of Seeing*. Translated by Simon Carnell and Erica Segre. Penguin Books.

Frayling, Christopher. 1993. "Research in Art and Design." *Royal College of Art Research Papers* 1(1): 1–5. https://researchonline.rca.ac.uk/384/

Gray, Carol, and Gordon Burnett. 2014. "Making Sense: Exploring Materialist Pedagogies Through Imagination, Collaboration and Criticality." In *Material Inventions: Applying Creative Arts Research*, edited by Estelle Barrett and Barbara Bolt. I. B. Taurus. https://doi.org/10.5040/9780755603695

Knorr Cetina, Karin. 2001. "Objectual Practice." In *The Practice Turn in Contemporary Theory*, edited by Theodore R. Schatzki, Karin Knorr Cetina, and Eike von Savigny. Routledge.

Kuh, Katharine. (1960) 2000. *The Artist's Voice: Talks with Seventeen Artists*. Harper and Row.

Lobell, John. 1979. *Between Silence and Light: Spirit in the Architecture of Louis I. Kahn*. Shambhala Publications.

Manghani, Sunil. 2021. "Practice PhD Toolkit." *Journal of Visual Art Practice*, 20(4): 373–398. https://doi.org/10.1080/14702029.2021.1988276

Morgan, Jennie, and Shelley Castle. 2024. "Arts–Research Collaboration: Reflections on Collaboration as Creative Method." *Qualitative Inquiry*, 30(3–4): 291–300. https://doi.org/10.1177/10778004231176280

Mottram, Judith. 2022. "Practice-based Research in the Visual Arts". In *The Routledge International Handbook of Practice-Based Research*, edited by Craig Vear. Routledge.

Mwamba, Corey. 2022. "Improvising as Practice/Research Method." In *The Routledge International Handbook of Practice-Based Research*, edited by Craig Vear. Routledge.

Nelson, Robin. 2022. *Practice as Research in the Arts and Beyond: Principles, Processes, Context, Achievements*, 2nd ed. Palgrave Macmillan.

Pallasmaa, Juhani. 2024. *The Eyes of the Skin: Architecture and the Senses*, 4th ed. John Wiley and Sons.

Ravelli, Louise, Brian Paltridge and Sue Starfield. 2014. "Diversity in Creative and Performing Arts Doctoral Writing: A Way Forward." In *Doctoral Writing in the Creative and Performing Arts*, edited by Louise Ravelli, Brian Paltridge, and Sue Starfield. Libri Publishing.

Sennett, Richard. 2008. *The Craftsman*. Yale University Press.

Toulouse, Ivan. 2018. "How Do they Do It? The Importance of Being… eArNe(ARTI)ST." In *The Creative Process: Perspectives form Multiple Domains*, edited by Todd Lubart. Palgrave Macmillan.

Weaver-Hightower, Marcus B., Nick Sousanis, and Paul J. Kuttner. 2025. "How to Draw Comics the Scholarly Way: Creating Comics-Based Research in the Academy." In *Handbook of Arts-Based Research*, 2nd ed., edited by Patricia Leavy. Guilford Publications.

Wurman, Richard Saul. 1986. *What Will Be Has Always Been: The Words of Louis I. Kahn*. Access Press and Rizzoli.

## *Suggested reading*

Barker, Tim. 2013. "Experimental Research in the Digital Media Arts." In *Handbook of Research on Creativity*, edited by Kerry Thomas and Janet Chan: Edward Elgar Publishing.

Barrett, Estelle. 2007. "Experiential Learning in Practice as Research: Context, Method, Knowledge." *Journal of Visual Art practice* 6 (2): 115–124. https://doi.org/10.1386/jvap.6.2.115_1

Batty, Craig. 2013. "Unpacking Critical Theories to Enhance Creative Practice: A PhD in Screenwriting Case Study" *Media Education Research Journal* 4 (1): 12–26. https://hdl.handle.net/11541.2/145552

Bell, Desmond. 2019. *Research in the Creative and Media Arts: Challenging Practice*. Routledge. (See part 1, "Critical Parameters.")

Bolt, Barbara. 2004. *Art Beyond Representation: The Performative Power of the Image*. I. B. Tauris and Company.

Bourgeois-Bougrine, Samira, and Vlad Petre Glăveanu. 2018. "Collaborative Scriptwriting: Social and Psychological Factors." In *The Creative Process: Perspectives form Multiple Domains*, edited by Todd Lubart. Palgrave Macmillan.

Brabazon, Tara, Narelle Hunter, and Jamie Quinton. 2022. "The Scientist, the Artefact, and the Exegesis: Challenging the Parameters of the PhD." *International Journal of Creative and Arts Studies*, 9 (1): 47–68. https://doi.org/10.24821/ijcas.v9i1.6409

Buckley, Brad. 2014. "Rethinking the Contemporary Art School, or What Artists Know that Others Don't." In *Doctoral Writing in the Creative and Performing Arts*, edited by Louise Ravelli, Brian Paltridge, and Sue Starfield. Libri Publishing.

Candy, Linda, Ernest Edmonds, and Fabrizio Poltronieri. 2018. "Theme: Collaboration." In *Explorations in Art and Technology*, 2nd ed., edited by Linda Candy, Ernest Edmonds, and Fabrizio Poltronieri. Springer-Verlag.

Eco, Umberto. 2011. *Confessions of a Young Novelist*. Harvard University Press.

Freeman, John. 2010. *Blood, Sweat and Theory*. Libri Publishing. (See sec. 4, "Certainties and Institutional Bias: Research for, Into and through Practice; Research Criteria and Creative Intelligence.")

Hughes, Jenny, Jenny Kidd, and Catherine McNamara. 2011. "The Usefulness of Mess: Artistry, Improvisation and Decomposition in the Practice of Research in Applied Theatre." In *Research Methods in Theatre and Performance*, edited by Baz Kershaw and Helen Nichoson. Edinburgh University Press.

Jeffery, Ella, Alex Philp and Emily O'Grady. 2020. "Blueprints: Constructing the Creative Writing PhD." *New Writing* 17(4): 391–401. https://doi.org/10.1080/14790726.2019.1660373

Krauth, Nigel, and Peter Nash. 2018. "Creative Work as Scholarly Work." *New Writing* 16 (3): 281–302. https://doi.org/10.1080/14790726.2018.1545791

Mackh, Bruce. 2022. "The PhD in Visual Arts Practice in the USA: Beyond Elkin's Artists with PhDs." In *The Routledge International Handbook of Practice-Based Research*, edited by Craig Vear. Routledge.

Mäkelä, Anna Maarit, and Nithikul Nimkulrat. 2011. "Reflection and Documentation in Practice-led Design Research." *Nordes–Making Design Matter*, 4. https://doi.org/10.21606/nordes.2011.009

Mann, Sally. 2025. *Art Work: On the Creative Life*. Penguin Books.

Manning, Erin. 2016. "Ten Propositions for Research-Creation." In *Collaboration in Performance Practice*, edited by Colin Noyale and Stefanie Sachsenmaier. Palgrave Macmillan. https://doi.org/10.1057/9781137462466_7

Masson, Sophie. 2018. "Imagination's Afterlife: Influences on and Transformations of Literary Creative Process within a Creative Practice PhD." *New Writing* 15 (1): 31–37. https://doi.org/10.1080/14790726.2017.1334803

Ranković, Katarina 2023. "Scripting for Agency." PhD diss., Goldsmiths, University of London. https://bit.ly/sfa-pdf

Reading, Christina. 2024. "Real and Imagined Explorations of Self: A Conversation with Katarina Ranković." In *Conversations on Creative Process, Methods, Research and Practice: Feminist Approaches to Nurturing the Creative Self*, edited by Christina Reading and Jess Moriarty. Routledge.

Ruhsam, Martina. 2016. "I WANT TO WORK WITTH YOU BECAUSE I CAN SPEAK FOR MYSELF: The Potential of Postconsensual Collaboration in Choreographic Practice." In *Collaboration in Performance Practice: Premises, Workings and Failures*, edited by Noyale Colin and Stefanie Sachsenmaier. Palgrave Macmillan.

Schwarzenbach, Jessica B., and Paul M. W. Hackett. 2016. *Transatlantic Reflections on the Practice-Based PhD in Fine Art*. Routledge.

Steinback, Kenneth. 2018. *Creative Practices for Visual Artists: Time, Space, Process*. Routledge. (See chap. 7, "Creative Practices.")

Stévance, Sophie and Serge Lacasse. 2013. *Research-Creation in Music and the Arts: Towards a Collaborative Interdiscipline*. Routledge.

Stock, Cheryl. 2014. "Writing Embodied Practice from the Inside: Outside the Exegesis." In *Doctoral Writing in the Creative and Performing Arts*, edited by Louise Ravelli, Brian Paltridge, and Sue Starfield. Libri Publishing.

Vaughan, Laurene. 2024. *The Impact of a PhD on Design Practice: International Perspectives*. Bloomsbury Visual Arts.

Vaughan, Sian. 2022. "Understanding Doctoral Communities in Practice-Based Research." In *The Routledge International Handbook of Practice-Based Research*, edited by Craig Vear. Routledge.

Vear, Craig. 2022. "Practitioner Voices." In *The Routledge International Handbook of Practice-Based Research*, edited by Craig Vear. Routledge.

# XI

# Decalogue XI

## TEN WELLBEING THINGS

This eleventh decalogue addresses common emotional challenges in doctoral research, from everyday stress and self-doubt to more serious concerns, including discrimination, bullying, creative stasis, and thoughts of quitting. I offer perspective and strategies for managing mental health, essential tools that are often neglected in doctoral studies. By acknowledging that these experiences are common and not signs of weakness or an indication that you don't belong here, you can take the first step towards seeking support and developing coping strategies.

The following sections address both systemic challenges (discrimination, unsafe environments, and bullying) and internal struggles (imposter syndrome, creative blocks, and burnout). I also consider physical wellbeing, the role of family and friends, and the often-difficult transition after PhD completion. Throughout, the emphasis remains on recognising warning signs early, seeking appropriate support, and understanding that struggling doesn't mean failing.

This decalogue is not clinical advice. If you experience serious mental health concerns, seek professional support through your university's counselling services or healthcare provider. What follows offers perspective drawn from doctoral experience, practical strategies, and reassurance that you're not alone.

### 1 Balancing family, friends, and your PhD

Doctoral study inevitably affects your relationships. Communicating your constraints to family and friends helps manage expectations. Paradoxically, I am suggesting that you not neglect your family and friends, yet prepare them for the times you inevitably will.

Make sure those important to you know your basic timetable and commitments. Build time into your schedule to spend with family and friends. The support of those close to you can be pivotal in completing your PhD.

DOI: 10.4324/9781003584209-12

Protect time for the people who matter to you. Time will be limited, so intentional time matters.

Even if you follow these suggestions, you may still find yourself neglecting family and friends. This drift is natural. Your focus, passion, and time are being consumed by one thing: your thesis. Even if you are studying part-time while working or caring for family, you are still thinking full-time. If you are successfully engaged with your research, you won't have much energy for others: let them know. They are on this journey with you and deserve to know what to expect (that is, as much as you know).

## 2 When supervisor feedback hurts

Every supervisor, like every human, has a different manner of communication. In doctoral study, your supervisor isn't there to teach you directly. They guide you through your research process and, along the way, point out elements that are not serving your research question effectively.

Supervisors typically do acknowledge what is working, ensuring you remain encouraged and focused on moving forward. However, due to their own demanding schedule, they often get to the point quickly, skip the affirmation, and communicate a considerable list of tasks. Your supervisor may more often point out what isn't working, rather than what is working.

Do not take their sometimes demanding or abrupt tone personally. Their job is to direct you towards completion. Honest feedback, even when it stings, is a positive part of your learning and research process.

However, if a supervisor's tone and demands veer towards bullying, this behaviour is never healthy and cannot be tolerated. Unfortunately, there can be a fine line between constructive criticism and insidious bullying. More overt bullying is less complicated to recognise. You may feel pressure to endure it, but you shouldn't have to tough it out. Be aware of your responses to your supervisor's actions and, if their behaviour is immobilising and hurtful, seek help. You may reach out to a co-supervisor, your research department, or another department of your university for practical or emotional support.

## 3 Discrimination, bullying, and unsafe environments

Bullying exists in academia beyond the supervisor-student relationship. It can come from colleagues, administrators, staff, or other students across any part of the university.

Discrimination takes many forms: institutional, interpersonal, and seemingly "casual" prejudice. The impact of all bias can be hurtful, destructive, and ruinous. Students may face discrimination based on age, caste, class, disability, ethnicity, gender, nationality, race, religion, sexual orientation, or other aspects of identity. These systemic issues create unsafe research environments that threaten students' wellbeing and academic success.

The challenge is recognising these behaviours as unacceptable, not normal, and not part of "academic culture". Once you recognise that these actions are wrong, seek support to address the situation. The responsibility for ensuring a safe environment lies with your institution.

Fortunately, attitudes are changing. The old acceptance of bullying and discrimination as "just how academia works", stemming from outdated hierarchies and entitlement, is declining. Universities increasingly provide mechanisms to speak out, and society increasingly supports those who do.

If you are experiencing any type of bullying or discrimination, or feel unsafe in any way, my advice is clear: speak to someone in authority at your university. If you fear retaliation for reporting, seek confidential advice from student support services or external advocacy organisations. Document incidents and seek formal support where needed. Know that you have the right to a safe and positive research environment.

## 4 Stress and anxiety

Many candidates experience periods of distress, doubt, and emotional strain. You will wonder why you are doing this programme. You may feel isolated, overwhelmed, and worried.

Stress and anxiety during a PhD can manifest as depression, insomnia, irritability, or difficulty concentrating, among other effects. You may receive advice to "build resilience" or "be flexible", but anyone who has experienced severe stress or anxiety knows that you cannot control these reactions through willpower alone.

During my PhD, I was a remote student, holding virtual meetings with my supervisor while researching as part of my full-time academic role. When I moved to casual lecturing (sessional or part-time teaching), I continued my research at home. At home, I sat at my desk in a bubble, working long days and keeping distractions to a minimum.

What I didn't realise was that I was getting lost in isolation and depression. I started doubting the validity of my research, my own expertise, and, most damaging of all, myself. I hadn't considered the emotional consequences of this change. I had lost a dedicated research space, a physical library, and the presence of colleagues. I gained household distractions and loneliness. In my tunnel vision, I focused only on my aim: completing the thesis.

I neglected to assess the effects of my new environment or put practices in place to support my research. Had I recognised the potential for academic and emotional isolation, I might have established coping mechanisms: working in a library periodically, maintaining relationships with former colleagues virtually, or setting up my desk in a separate, dedicated area of the house. These simple measures could have helped me separate research work from family time and structure my day with breaks and variation. A workplace with some connection to the academic community would have reduced isolation while allowing regular family time.

Identifying sources of stress allows targeted adjustments. Even small environmental or social changes can make a significant difference.

## 5 Imposter syndrome and self-doubt

During my period of isolation, I also experienced a loss of faith; I questioned whether I was intelligent enough to write on my topic. Who was I to think I could produce significant research or comprehend the work of incredible thinkers? I was experiencing imposter syndrome, and many accomplished researchers will likely feel a similar self-doubt at some point.

Imposter syndrome is characterised by personal or professional success coupled with feelings of inadequacy and undeserved attention. Maddie Breeze explains that suspicion plays a key role: not only about your own accolades, but about those bestowing them upon you. The experience "conveys a particular felt-as inauthentic or fraudulent relationship to indicators of belonging and achievement" (2018, 195). Those experiencing imposter syndrome project confidence and knowledge while floundering inside, believing they are fooling everyone around them.

Pat Thomson and Barbara Kamler point out the destructive force of this condition: it "infects and inflects doctoral writing" (2016, 108). You feel constantly at risk of being exposed as inadequate.

For creative practitioners, imposter syndrome has another layer. You may question whether academic research negates your identity as an artist: As a researcher, am I still an artist? In a field still establishing its academic standing in conventional circles, this self-doubt extends beyond yourself to your thesis as a valid mode of doctoral research.[1]

Self-doubt also arises unrelated to imposter syndrome. You may question your research's value, thinking it's useless, a waste of time. When these thoughts invade, think about your research and its potential impact in your field, on creative practice, and on other artists' research. Your answer will remind you why your research is significant.

At my lowest point, I met with my supervisor in near tears, questioning the value of my work and whether I, as a practitioner and mature student, belonged in this space. My supervisor assured me I was producing new knowledge that would greatly add to my field. He spoke of the valuable contribution of practitioner research and complimented my writing approach. His genuine manner, words, and positive feedback dried my tears and helped me move forward.

When you feel like this, tell someone. Your supervisor, like mine, may know exactly what to say. If not, reach out to your research department, other teaching staff, or anyone you trust. Don't hold these feelings inside. They are real and serious, with enormous impact on both your wellbeing and your research.

## 6 The person, not the researcher

Previous sections address wellbeing challenges that arise from doctoral research itself, such as discrimination, stress, self-doubt, and emotional struggles. This section shifts focus: caring for yourself as a person, not a researcher.

You are not only a PhD student, but you are a human being with a body that needs sleep, food, movement, and physical care. These basic needs don't disappear during a PhD, though they're often the first things sacrificed when research intensifies. Sleep, nutrition, and workplace conditions aren't thesis-specific issues, but they form the foundation that everything else depends on.

It is easy to take shortcuts with basic human needs. Prioritising sleep and addressing insomnia if it arises are critical to concentration. A balanced diet supports good sleep and general health. Physical exercise in whatever form you enjoy and can make time for keeps you fit to cope with long nights, stress, and sedentary work. If your artefact is performance-based or physically demanding, such as creating a large-scale sculpture, your physical health becomes a research requirement.

In addition to the above basic bodily needs, ensure you have time to meditate, embrace stillness, and maintain connection with the people and relationships that ground you. Don't forget who you are.

Make a plan for physical wellbeing and self-care from the outset and incorporate it into your timetable. If you wait until you are busy, these activities will take a back seat to research. Your physical workspace affects your cognitive and creative capacity.

Ergonomic guidelines support human capabilities in devising safe, effective, and appropriate work environments (McKeown 2019, xiii). The disciplines of ergonomics (physical focus) and human factors (cognitive focus) work together to create productive and safe environments, sustaining research and practice. Consider your desk environment and your practice environment (workshop, studio, rehearsal space). If you are neurodivergent or a person with disability, you may have specific requirements. Meet early with your research department to discuss what you require. All students can request training related to specific needs.

Early planning matters. With self-care in place, you're more likely to recognise warning signs in your health, seek help, and reassess needs as they change. This circle of care—signs, awareness, and action—supports you through your process.

## 7 When research meets trauma

Your PhD research may engender trauma through content, personal experience, or creative practice. Ayhan Alman defines trauma as "a deeply embodied experience [that] arises from stress so overpowering that it exceeds our capacity to cope or process the associated emotions" (2025, 8). He uses the term "trauma-sensitive" research to denote awareness of trauma's effects (2). Cultivating this awareness will help you navigate traumatic experiences throughout your PhD journey.

Your research topic may address emotionally challenging issues, including cultural trauma, loss, or conflict. Your own experience, including life circumstances, identity, culture, mental health, or relationships, may inform content or methodology. Disturbing events, personal or global, may occur throughout your PhD. In creative artefact research, the making process can trigger unexpected traumatic responses.

Incorporating traumatic themes into doctoral research requires careful methodological planning. If your research draws on personal cultural experience, autoethnography, as discussed, may be an appropriate methodology. When you recognise that trauma will be central to your research, whether by design through your topic or through personal experience or creative practice, take time to select methodologies that can approach trauma content rigorously and ethically.

Working with trauma-based content requires the establishment of boundaries and support structures. For instance, avoid researching or creating trauma-related work late at night when alone or tired. Exposure to traumatic material, including your own, is cumulative and can manifest in vicarious trauma[2] or re-traumatisation. To help combat these effects, create transition rituals: meditation, walking, or other practices that separate research from personal life.

Current events, whether cultural, political, or local, may cause indirect trauma that can affect you profoundly. Vicarious trauma can have an insidious effect, as the severity of such feelings is not always acknowledged. When personal events occur, such as the death of a family member, coping with bereavement must be prioritised. Grief may necessitate applying for a submission extension or leave of absence. Alexandra Ridgway's experience shows another path: when her father died while she was completing her PhD, her grief informed her methodology. She explains this active process: "namely dialoguing with the dead, which I personally used to transform my grief into an energetic force" (Ridgway 2023, 232). Through continued "dialogue" with her father while remembering his "words of wisdom", Ridgway was able to productively complete her thesis (2023).

In creative artefact research, practice can surface unexpected trauma. Emerging themes may evoke memories, performances may trigger embodied trauma, and techniques may reveal painful patterns. Artistic creation prompts emotional and somatic knowledge, sometimes disturbingly. If these feelings arise, pause. Document your reflections as a personal record and for your exegesis.

Resources for trauma-informed research include your supervisor, institutional counselling services, trauma-focused therapists, and peer support groups. If your topic or methodology involves trauma research, plan ahead: put parameters and support systems in place, and ensure adequate time, as progress may be slower and more deliberate breaks may be necessary. Some students work with therapists concurrently throughout trauma-focused PhDs as part of their research process.

Personal trauma may be too close, too recent, or too unprocessed to research. If traumatic responses feel distressing and immobilising, consider whether now is the right time. Postponing or pivoting isn't failure; it shows self-awareness and protects your wellbeing. If research triggers flashbacks, nightmares, dissociation, or panic attacks, seek professional mental health support immediately.

## 8 Writer's block and creative stasis

Writer's block and creative blocks affect nearly all PhD students at some point. These experiences can feel debilitating, but understanding them as signals rather than failures can transform how you respond to them.

Kate Evans suggests that "[a]llowing the possibility that our writing block may be a useful tool for insight could already lessen its capacity to hinder us" (2013, 2). Experiencing a block may indicate something isn't right with your topic, your mental health, or your approach. Rather than forcing through, a block provides an opportunity to pause, self-assess, and identify what's hampering your progress.

Blocks manifest differently for different people. You may spend hours perfecting a single sentence. You may find yourself deep in tangential research, endlessly reading rather than writing or making. You may simply stop, staring at blank pages or unused materials, unable to restart. These aren't character flaws; they're your psyche signalling that something needs attention.

Creative blocks can occur alongside or separately from writer's block. If your PhD includes a creative artefact, you may experience stasis in making as well as academic writing. A creative block can stem from multiple sources: inaccurate self-assessment (similar to imposter syndrome), disinterest in your topic, fear of failure, perfectionism, or simply loving research more than making. In creative practice, blocks can also arise from the body: physical exhaustion, poor workspace ergonomics, or disconnection from embodied knowledge can impede making.

Brief blocks are normal; prolonged stasis requires intervention. If you've been unable to write or create for weeks despite trying various strategies, this reaction may signal deeper issues such as depression, burnout, anxiety, or fundamental problems with your research direction. These signs indicate a block shifting from a productivity issue to a wellbeing concern.

Don't suffer in silence. Your supervisor may adjust expectations, suggest timeline modifications, or help you identify the underlying issue. Effective writing practices can motivate progress and break through blocks. If the block is connected to mental or physical health, by addressing the wellbeing issue, you may resolve the block. Your research may require a shift in direction, or you may need to change your research approach.

Many practical strategies exist to work through blocks: community practices, structured techniques, environmental changes, and generative exercises. Simple approaches can be surprisingly effective: changing your physical location, setting a fifteen-minute timer for "freewriting" that you may delete later, or beginning with the section that most inspires you rather than forcing linear progression. Experiment to find what works for you; some students thrive in community writing sessions, while others need solitary focus.[3]

If you've tried multiple strategies and remain blocked, consider that the block may be telling you something important. Perhaps your research question needs refinement. Perhaps your methodology doesn't suit your inquiry. Perhaps you need a rest, not more productivity techniques. Listen to what the block is communicating, rather than simply trying to overcome it.

## 9 When you consider quitting

In this decalogue, I have often referred to strategies of reaching out to friends, family, colleagues, academic staff, and mental health professionals for support. I have also highlighted approaches in prioritising yourself by putting healthy practices into place. Self-care, as Zoë J. Ayres explains, is "the shoring up of our foundations so that we increase our chance of success" (2022, 41). By putting self-care plans into place, the likelihood of burnout, characterised by exhaustion, negativity, and loss of productivity, decreases. A focus on self "is not selfish, it is self-preservation" (55). But what if you do reach a critical point in your research progress where you can go no further? What if burnout leads to thoughts of quitting?

Few guides to completing a PhD explore the possibility of quitting. Literature tends to focus on how to reach completion, not whether to continue. Yet sometimes the right decision is to stop. This choice may be due to other obligations, financial constraints, poor fit with your university or supervisor, or loss of interest in your topic. Perhaps you'd like to begin afresh in a different direction.

Pressure may come from multiple sources: academic (institutional and supervisor expectations, funding obligations), family (their goals imposed on you, viewing quitting as failure), and internal (your own expectations, an identity tied to PhD, and fear of judgement). Yet Ayres points to the etymology of the word quit: to be "set free". She reassures: "It is okay to leave if you need to" (2022, 193). Rather than fearing this decision, see it as a form of care for yourself and a way of moving forward. This extremely challenging decision is sometimes the right one.

Please understand: This is not failure. Deciding not to complete a thesis, particularly when you have other significant commitments, is not a collapse. By making this choice, you may be preventing significant harm in another area of your life. Katherine Firth et al. remind you that even if you decide not to submit your PhD thesis, "the skills, ideas, and insights you gained during the process will always be yours" (2021, 190). The experience and knowledge you've gained remain with you, permanently.

## 10 Life after PhD

What is life like after the PhD? Firth et al. suggest that the immediate halt of energy directed towards your thesis can feel uplifting. However, they also explore the downsides of losing that focus, that part of your identity, your academic community, and practical resources like library access (2021, 191–192). As the initial relief fades, you might find yourself experiencing elation (celebrating completion and letting go) or depression (feeling immobilised and undirected). If you feel sustained elation, enjoy it. If not, actively seek a new focus.

If you aren't already employed at a university, applying for jobs may be your first task. Everyone's timeline is different, and the process takes longer than you expect. You're still attached to your computer, but now you're receiving rejections that often begin "Unfortunately…"

You may also be re-establishing family life, thinking about book proposals, and questioning the purpose of it all. This inevitable return to other things in your life is why celebrating your submission, acceptance, and graduation is crucial. These moments affirm the significance of your achievement and provide necessary closure.

As a remote student, I decided to make the 4000-kilometre trip to my university for my graduation ceremony. It seemed like a luxury to travel there for a few days just to receive my piece of paper. However, the celebration not only provided positive closure, but it also gave me the opportunity to chat with my supervisor as a colleague and a friend. I often remember moments at graduation: hearing my name read, toasting with my thesis chair and supervisor, standing among the small cohort of PhD graduates, and wearing the crimson and black gown and floppy hat. It was a proud moment, made more so by sharing it with my husband, who had supported me throughout the seven years. One I often recall.

Yet after the ceremony ended and I returned home, I faced the question many graduates ask: What now?

Following submission, establish a plan. It doesn't matter what it is or whether it changes. By creating structure, you prevent yourself from floundering. Proceed day to day following a schedule that may include job applications, writing projects, and personal activities that you value and enjoy. A timetable similar to your PhD routine eases you into the next stage, allowing you to move forward with intention and purpose.

## Notes

1 For further discussion of imposter syndrome within a public context, see Breeze (2018), and Pearl John's personal experience within a socio-political context (2022, 672–673).
2 Vicarious trauma is also termed secondary or indirect trauma, referring to distress arising from exposure to the traumatic experiences of others, whether encountered through research, news events, or discussion.
3 These approaches and further strategies for both academic writing and creative blocks are detailed in Appendix H.

## References

### *Cited works*

Alman, Ayhan. 2025. *A Practical Guide to Trauma-Sensitive Research: Integrating Trauma-Informed Frameworks into the Qualitative Research Lifecycle*. Routledge.

Ayres, Zöe J. 2022. *Managing your Mental Health During Your PhD: A Survival Guide*. Springer.

Breeze, Maddie. 2018. "Imposter Syndrome as a Public Feeling." In *Feeling Academic in the Neoliberal University: Feminist Flights, Fights and Failures*, edited by Yvette Taylor and Kinneret Lahad. Palgrave Macmillan.

Evans, Kate. 2013. *Pathways Through Writing Blocks in the Academic Environment*. Sense Publishers.

Firth, Katherine, Liam Connell, and Peta Freestone. 2021. *Your PhD Survival Guide: Planning, Writing and Succeeding in Your Final Year*. Routledge.

John, Pearl. 2022. "The Impact of Public Engagement with Research on a Holographic Practice-based Study." In *The Routledge International Handbook of Practice-Based Research*, edited by Craig Vear. Routledge.

McKeown, Céline. 2019. *Office Ergonomics and Human Factors*, 2nd ed. CRC Press.

Ridgway, Alexandra. 2023. "Love, Loss and a Doctorate: An Autoethnography of Grieving While Writing a PhD." *Higher Education Research and Development*, 42(1): 230–243. https://doi.org/10.1080/07294360.2021.2019202

Thomson, Pat, and Barbara Kamler. 2016. *Detox Your Writing: Strategies for Doctoral Researchers*. Routledge.

## *Suggested reading*

Cahusac de Caux, Basil. 2019. "Wax On, Wax Off: Maintaining Confidence and Overcoming Anxiety." In *Wellbeing in Doctoral Education: Insights and Guidance from the Student Experience*, edited by Lynette Pretorius, Luke Macaulay, and Basil Cahusac de Caux. Springer Nature. https://doi.org/10.1007/978-981-13-9302-0_11

Chave, Sarah. 2024. "On Bewilderment, Education and Opening Spaces for Creativity and Emergent Educational Futures." In *Creative Ruptions for Emergent Educational Futures*, edited by Kerry Chappell, Chris Turner, and Heather Wren. Palgrave Macmillan.

Dickinson, Summer. 2018. "Writing Sensation: Critical Autoethnography in Posthumanism." In *Creative Selves/Creative Cultures: Critical Autoethnography, Performance, and Pedagogy*, edited by Stacy Holman Jones, and Marc Pruyn. Springer.

Eco, Umberto. (1977) 2015. "How to Avoid Being Exploited by Your Advisor." In *How to Write a Thesis*. Translated by Caterina Mongiat Farina and Geoff Farina. MIT Press.

Forest, David, ed. 2017. *Doctoral Research in Art*. Australian Scholarly Publishing.

Galvin, Kathleen T., and Les Todres. 2018. "Eighteen Kinds of Well-Being Although There May Be Many More: A Conceptual Framework Illustrated with Practical Direction for Caring." In *Routledge Handbook of Well-Being*, edited by Kathleen T. Galvin. Routledge.

Goodall, Suskya, Joanna Higgins, and Cherie Chu-Fuluifaga. 2022. "An Appreciative Circling Approach to Promoting Doctoral Wellbeing and Growth." In *Creating a Place for Self-Care and Wellbeing in Higher Education: Finding Meaning Across Academia*, edited by Narelle Lemon. Routledge. https://doi.org/10.4324/9781003144397-10

Griffiths, Morwenna. 2011. "Research and the Self." In *The Routledge Companion to Research in the Arts*, edited by Michael Biggs and Henrik Karlsson. Routledge.

Humble, Darryl. 2012. "'This Isn't Getting Easier': Valuing Emotion in Development Research." *Emotion, Space and Society* 5(2): 78–85. https://doi.org/10.1016/j.emospa.2011.04.001

McChesney, Katrina, James Burford, Liezel Frick, and Tseen Khoo. 2024. *Doing Doctoral Research at a Distance: Flourishing in Off-Campus, Hybrid, and Remote Pathways*. Routledge. (See chap. 8, "Unexpected Work: Coping with Changes and Challenges on the Distance Journey.")

McPherson, Megan. 2023. "The Feeling of Doing*thinking* and Thinking*doing* of Making Processes." In *Creative Expression and Wellbeing in Higher Education: Making and Movement as Mindful Moments of Self-care*, edited by Narelle Lemon. Routledge.

Newport, Cal. 2024. *Slow Productivity: The Lost Art of Accomplishment Without Burnout*. Penguin Random House.

Nonterah, Gertrude. 2025. *Navigating the P.I.V.O.T.: A Handbook for PhDs and Academics Looking to Thrive in Careers Beyond the Ivory Tower*. Gertrude Nonterah. https://theboldphd.com/

Noori, Abdul Qawi. 2025. "Does Belonging Affect Wellbeing? A Researcher's Experiences of Transition from a Conflict-affected Country to Australia." In *Prioritising Wellbeing and Self-care in Higher Education: How We can Do Things Differently to Disrupt Silence*, edited by Narelle Lemon. Routledge.

Pihama, Leonie, and Linda Tuhiwai Smith. 2023. *Ora: Healing Ourselves – Indigenous Knowledge, Healing and Wellbeing*. Huia Publishers.

Sprague, Ann, Rowena L. Briones, Nicole Rishel Elias et al. 2017. "Surviving and Thriving in Academia: Obtaining Balance, Health, and Clarity." In *Reflections on Academic Lives: Identities, Struggles, and Triumphs in Graduate School and Beyond*, edited by Staci M. Zavattaro and Shannon K. Orr. Palgrave Macmillan. https://doi.org/10.1057/978-1-137-60009-7_7

Vaughan, Sian. 2022. "Understanding Doctoral Communities in Practice-Based Research." In *The Routledge International Handbook of Practice-Based Research*, edited by Craig Vear. Routledge.

Woolston, Chris. 2019. "PhDs: The Tortuous Truth." *Nature* 575(7782): 403–406. https://doi.org/10.1038/d41586-019-03459-7

# CONCLUSIONS

> First, writing a thesis should be fun. Second, writing a thesis is like cooking a pig: nothing goes to waste.
>
> Umberto Eco, *How to Write a Thesis*

This conclusion is a tribute to the magical: all things spontaneous, accidental, impromptu, or intuitive, and the unimagined significance of randomness in research and creation. It is also a tribute to the magic found in a piece of music, in our natural surroundings, and in the intangible spirit within us.

Books are not only useful sources of information and ideas; both their *thingness* and their words motivate and stimulate thought. The physicality of their cover, weight, and pages enchants me. My favourite method of discovering seemingly unrelated and surprisingly significant authors is unsystematic: old-fashioned browsing. When stuck with my thesis, I went straight to a bookshop, library, friend's bookcase, my own shelves of forgotten books, or "browsed" online, though algorithms sometimes got in the way. I would find myself turning around to discover a book gazing right at me, its title having nothing at all to do with my research. Reflexively, I would reach for it, open it, read it, and at that moment, my direction would be altered.

I had a sensation of "becoming friends" with author Susan Stewart. Early in my research, I found *On Longing: Narratives of the Miniature, the Gigantic, the Souvenir, the Collection* (1993), which became a support *thing*, an anchor that gave me energy to move forward. Stewart's linking of object to narrative to being human is written in such beautiful language; it impelled me to hug the book. It was later that I discovered that she is a poet. She laid the stones for my path.

In a similar vein, at times of self-doubt, a song would magically play at the right moment. One in particular, Elbow's "One Day Like This" (Garvey 2008), often lifted me out of my inertia. It isn't solely a positive song; it has a quality of melancholic nostalgia. A cheerful song would not

DOI: 10.4324/9781003584209-13

have spoken to me in the same way as the poetry of those chords. The lyrics, repeated many times as if in conversation with the emotional strings, saw me right.

Nature is also a friend. I discovered a tree, a towering mahogany, at the bottom of our garden. A gigantic limb had fallen, lying high up but parallel to the ground. I would sometimes walk to this tree, climb onto its branch, and smell its musk, feel the scratch of its bark, and gaze at the colours of its leaves. The tree encouraged me to simply be.

A thesis is not only a scholarly endeavour but a personal and transformative one. I had moved from practitioner to scholar-practitioner. My research has contributed to my own knowledge and to that of my field. Sometimes I think about how proud my father would have been. I like to think he does know. At that simple moment, all the hardship, self-doubts, and tears disappear, and a great sense of achievement, pride, and calm move over me.

I referred to Umberto Eco's 1985 introduction to *How to Write a Thesis* in the preface of this book. In his concluding lines, he reflects on the beauty of the twist in his story with this hope: "I aspire to become someone else's abbot Vallet" (Eco [1977] 2015, xxvi). Eco has become my abbot Vallet, and my hope is that in turn, this book will help you to find your "magic key".

## References

### *Cited works*

Eco, Umberto. (1977) 2015. *How to Write a Thesis*. Translated by Caterina Mongiat Farina and Geoff Farina. MIT Press.

Elbow. "One Day Like This" Written by Guy Garvey. Produced by Craig Potter. Fiction Records. Released June 2, 2008.

Stewart, Susan. 1993. *On Longing: Narratives of the Miniature, the Gigantic, the Souvenir, the Collection*. Duke University Press.

### *Suggested reading*

Although I encountered many significant resources throughout my thesis, the following unreferenced works were found accidentally, prompting a change in direction or serving as an invitation to dive more deeply. You may find in my reading journey something that leads you to your own productive randomness.

Barker, Jennifer M. 2009. *The Tactile Eye: Touch and the Cinematic Experience*. University of California Press.

Garcia, Tristan. 2014. *Form and Object: A Treatise on Things*. Translated by Mark Allan Ohm and Jon Cogburn. Edinburgh University Press.

Gee, Felicity. 2021. *Magic Realism, World Cinema, and the Avant-Garde*. Routledge.
Lee, Christina, ed. 2012. *Violating Time: History, Memory, and Nostalgia in Cinema*. Continuum International Publishing Group.
Morin, Edgar. (1956) 2005. *The Cinema or the Imaginary Man*. Translated by Lorraine Mortimer. University of Minnesota Press.
Pallasmaa, Juhani. 2024. *The Eyes of the Skin: Architecture and the Senses*, 4th ed. John Wiley and Sons.
Schwenger, Peter. 2006. *The Tears of Things: Melancholy and Physical Objects*. University of Minneapolis Press.
Skrodzka, Aga. 2014. *Magic Realist Cinema in East Central Europe*. Edinburgh University Press.
Stern, Lesley. 2004. "'Paths that Wind through the Thicket of Things.'" In *Things*, edited by Bill Brown. The University of Chicago Press.
Trigg, Dylan. 2012. *The Memory of Place: A Phenomenology of the Uncanny*. Ohio University Press.
Weerasethakul, Apichatpong, dir. *Uncle Boonmee Who Can Recall His Past Lives*. 2010. Kick the Machine Films. DVD.

# GLOSSARY

While not exhaustive, this glossary defines key terms as used throughout *CAPC*, both technical and theory-based, that are essential for creative arts doctoral research. It covers foundational concepts that are often misunderstood or used ambiguously within creative arts research environments, though commonly understood terms such as supervisor or field have not been defined here.

Please note that to include every method listed in *Appendix B: Methods Reference Guide* falls outside the scope of this glossary, as the range is too broad for a comprehensive definition. For deeper engagement with any particular method, consult the reference lists accompanying each decalogue.

**a/r/tography** An arts-based methodology of living inquiry that integrates the overlapping identities and practices of the artist, researcher, and teacher.

**action research** A methodology in which researchers and participants work collaboratively through iterative cycles of action and reflection, oriented towards practical transformation in applied and practice-based research contexts.

**agential realism** A philosophical and methodological framework, developed by Karen Barad, positing a reality constituted through dynamic exchanges and entanglements between human and non-human entities rather than their independent actions. It foregrounds the relationship between maker and material, between objects and meaning, and between practice and knowledge. See also: *diffraction, intra-action.*

**applied research** A process of inquiry aimed at developing practical solutions to real-life problems.

**approach** A researcher's overall orientation to inquiry, reflecting their worldview, aims, and assumptions about knowledge, and informing their choice of methods.

**artefact** An object, or thing, that is made or manipulated by a human being.

**artistic research** Any mode of inquiry in which creative practice is both the primary means and the site of generating new knowledge.

**arts-based research (ABR)** A methodology that employs artistic processes as tools for investigation, and for recording, developing, and communicating research findings, regardless of the field of study.

**autoethnography** A method of inquiry and analysis in which a researcher reflects on their own life experience in relation to broader cultural or social contexts to generate and inform their process and findings.

**axiology** A branch of philosophy that examines what is considered valuable: ethically, aesthetically, and spiritually.

**backward mapping** A planning tool that creates a research schedule by working backwards from a final submission date, plotting each milestone to ensure realistic time allocation.

**basic research** A theoretical or empirical study that aims to develop new knowledge without a specified practical application.

**concept** An abstract idea or notion expressed through language or representation.

**conceptual framework** A broad analytical structure that acts as an organising device and as a guide to method, more flexible and wide-ranging than a theoretical framework. See also: *theoretical framework, theoretical perspective.*

**constructivism** A research paradigm in which reality is actively constructed through social interaction rather than existing independently.

**creative artefact** An original artistic or design work realised through practice as part of doctoral research.

**creative arts** A field of study that investigates the creation, presentation, and analysis of works across artistic, design, and other creative practices and disciplines.

**creativity** The capacity to generate original ideas, concepts, connections, or objects through imaginative thinking and practice.

**critical realism** A research paradigm that posits a stratified reality comprising the real, the actual, and the empirical domains, existing independently of human perception while acknowledging that knowledge of reality is always partial and fallible.

**critical theory** A research paradigm that examines and challenges existing social structures, power relations, and linguistic and ideological systems with the aim of promoting emancipation, breaking down hegemony, and enacting social change.

**cross-disciplinary** A mode of inquiry that draws on methodologies, theories, and perspectives from one academic discipline to view another through its lens. See also: *interdisciplinary, multidisciplinary*, and *transdisciplinary*.

**cultural analysis** A methodology, developed by Mieke Bal, that applies principles of interdisciplinary, non-binary thinking, and social relevance to the analysis of cultural objects and texts, maintaining that objects have agency and that meaning emerges non-linearly.

**decalogue** A set of ten principles or propositions, used in *CAPC* to structure each chapter around key ideas for creative arts doctoral researchers.

**decolonising methodology** A range of methodologies based in First Nations worldviews and knowledge processes, including those of storytelling, learning circles, and relationality. Rather than an alternative to Western methodology, these varied methodologies, developed by Linda Tuhiwai Smith and other First Nations scholars globally, establish holistic, complete approaches while resolutely repudiating the hegemony of Western research traditions. See also: *relational accountability, storywork*.

**diffraction** A concept within agential realism that attends to difference and change, examining what happens when ideas, forces, or materials come together and move apart to make new patterns. See also: *agential realism, intra-action*.

**discourse analysis** A method of inquiry that examines how meaning, knowledge, and social understanding are constructed and shaped through language, communicative practices, and experiences.

**dissertation** A substantial work presenting the findings and outcomes of academic research. Commonly used in the US. See also: *thesis*.

**embodied research** A methodology that positions the body as an active site of knowledge and reflection, integrating bodily experience, sensation, and perception into the research process.

**epistemology** A branch of philosophy that considers theories of knowledge and how humans know what they know.

**ethico-onto-epistemological** A term coined by Karen Barad describing a philosophical framework in which being (ontology), knowing (epistemology), and ethics (axiology) are mutually constitutive and inextricable rather than distinct spheres. See also: *agential realism, onto-epistemological*.

**ethnography** A research methodology that engages with cultures, communities, and societies through sustained immersion, observation, and participation in their everyday practices.

**exegesis** The written scholarly work that develops alongside the creative artefact, together presenting the findings and outcomes of a creative arts thesis.

**First Nations** A term used internationally to describe peoples with original and ongoing connections to a particular land, acknowledging cultural and historical diversity amongst a range of peoples and communities. See also: *Indigenous*.

**generative AI** A subset of artificial intelligence (AI) that originates new content that may include image, text, sound, code, or video. See also *large language models*.

**grounded theory** A methodology and method as both a strategy and a set of tools that generates theory inductively and systematically from data, rather than testing existing theoretical frameworks against it.

**Indigeneity** A quality experienced by First Nations peoples of having a deep and ongoing connection to place, land, and community.

**Indigenous** A term used internationally to describe people with original and ongoing connections to a particular land. In Australia, this term encompasses both Aboriginal peoples (nations and custodians of mainland Australia and most of its islands) and Torres Strait Islander peoples (nations and custodians of islands between Queensland, Australia, and Papua New Guinea). See *First Nations*.

**intellectual property** Creative works, inventions, designs, and symbols over which a creator or rights holder may seek legal protection through copyright, patents, or trademarks.

**interdisciplinary** A mode of inquiry that integrates methodologies, theories, and perspectives from two or more academic disciplines to investigate questions or problems that exceed the boundaries of any single field. See also: *cross-disciplinary, multidisciplinary*, and *transdisciplinary*.

**interpretivism** A research paradigm that recognises multiple valid interpretations of an existing reality, focusing on how individuals understand and make meaning from their experiences.

**intra-action** A concept within agential realism, coined by Karen Barad, that posits that agency emerges through entanglement rather than residing in pre-existing entities, in contrast to interaction, where distinct entities act upon each other. See also: *agential realism; diffraction*.

**knowledge** Understanding that may be propositional, procedural, or tacit, acquired through inquiry, experience, and practice.

**large language models (LLMs)** A type of artificial intelligence (AI) used to analyse, edit, and generate text through instruction and prompts. See also: *generative AI*.

**literature review** A critical analysis and synthesis of existing scholarship that locates a project within a field of study, identifies gaps in current knowledge, and establishes the theoretical and conceptual context for the research.

**method** The tools, techniques, and procedures used to gather and generate research material, enact making, and yield findings through analysis.

**methodology** An overarching framework and strategy that bridges philosophical assumptions and the selection and application of methods within a research project.

**mixed methods research (MMR)** Research that combines qualitative and quantitative approaches that function together to investigate a question or problem.

**monograph** A book-length scholarly work focusing on a single topic, typically by one author.

**multidisciplinary** A mode of inquiry that connects methodologies, theories, and perspectives from two or more academic disciplines, each contributing independently to the investigation of a question or problem. See also: *cross-disciplinary, interdisciplinary*, and *transdisciplinary*.

**multimodal research** Research that combines multiple modes of representation and meaning-making to investigate complex phenomena.

**new materialism** A philosophical and methodological framework associated with scholars Rosi Braidotti and Manuel DeLanda that challenges binary thinking and the primacy of human agency, recognising matter and non-human entities as active participants in the production of knowledge and meaning. See also: *agential realism*.

**non-representational theory** A theoretical framework, associated with Nigel Thrift, that holds that not everything can be captured through language or representation, privileging immediate engagement with action, movement, bodily experience, and atmosphere over the interpretation of meanings and symbols.

**object** A material entity defined by its physical properties and function. See also: *thing, thingness*.

**onto-epistemological** A philosophical and methodological framework in which being (ontology) and knowing (epistemology) are mutually constitutive and inextricable rather than distinct spheres. See also: *ethico-onto-epistemological*.

**ontology** A branch of philosophy that examines the nature of reality and what is said to exist.

**participatory action research (PAR)** A collaborative methodology in which participants act as co-researchers, working alongside the researcher through iterative cycles of engagement and reflection towards social change.

**peer-reviewed** A scholarly work that has been rigorously assessed by experts in the field, ensuring quality, accuracy, and originality prior to publication.

**performative research** Research that uses live, embodied, or enacted practice as the primary means of communicating findings and addressing a research question, rather than conventional written or numerical forms.

**phenomenology** A branch of philosophy that examines the meaning and structure of lived experience from the perspective of the experiencing subject.

**poetic inquiry** A method of inquiry that uses the writing and reading of poetry as a means of generating and communicating research knowledge.

**positivism** A research paradigm that holds that reality exists independently of the observer and that all knowledge can be objectively measured through empirical methods.

**post-qualitative inquiry (PQI)** A mode of inquiry, associated with Elizabeth Adams St. Pierre, that moves away not only from conventional methods but from the construct of methodology itself, with each project structured uniquely according to its own logic and commitments.

**Post-positivism** A research paradigm that retains a commitment to empirical inquiry and objective reality while acknowledging that complete independence is unattainable and that knowledge is always partial and subject to revision.

**practice as research (PaR)** A methodology in which creative practice is the research method itself, with new knowledge arising directly from the process of making. In short, practice is research.

**practice-based** A methodology in which creative practice provides the context for research, with the creative artefact analysed through conventional academic methods. In short, the research is about practice.

**practice-enabled knowledge** Umbrella term covering all methodological approaches in which the creative artefact serves as a vehicle for generating research.

**practice-led** A methodology in which the process of making the artefact leads and forms the research question and methods. In short, practice generates research.

**practice** The tools, techniques, and procedures that constitute the ways of doing, whether within a creative project or a research context.

**practitioner** A person engaged in a creative discipline who has developed a level of expertise, professional practice, and an expressive voice.

**pragmatism** A philosophical approach and research paradigm that holds that meaning, truth, and knowledge are determined by their practical consequences and usefulness rather than abstract principles.

**qualitative data** Information collected that concerns words, images, sounds, meaning, and experience.

**qualitative research** A mode of inquiry describing both methodology and method, grounded in the humanities and interpretive traditions, concerned with understanding meaning, experience, and context through the collection and analysis of non-numerical data such as words, images, and sounds. Typically inductive and reflexive in orientation.

**quantitative data** Information collected that is numerical, measurable, and statistical.

**quantitative research** A mode of inquiry describing both methodology and method, grounded in the sciences, concerned with measuring, testing, and generalising through the collection and analysis of numerical data. Typically deductive in orientation, prioritising objectivity, replicability, and statistical validity.

**reference style** A set of rules governing citation order, punctuation, placement, and formatting choices. Also referred to as *citation format, referencing system*, or *bibliographic style*.

**reflective practice** A process of ongoing analysis, associated with Donald Schön, in which a researcher examines past and current experiences to connect theory and practice and inform future decisions. Schön introduces the terms *reflection-in-action* and *reflection-on-action* to differentiate between reflecting in the midst of experience and reflecting upon it afterward.

**relational accountability** An ethical framework in research, associated with Shawn Wilson, that promotes respectful, responsible, and reciprocal practice, attending to the emotional impact of the research process on both researcher and participants. See also: *decolonising methodology, storywork*.

**research paradigm** A framework of fundamental assumptions that describes a researcher's worldview and their position within knowledge and reality. Research paradigms commonly include constructivism, critical theory, interpretivism, positivism, and post-positivism.

**research question** A specifically formulated line of inquiry that guides a research investigation as a focused, bounded, and actionable study.

**research-creation** A methodology that integrates creative and academic research practices to generate knowledge that may exceed conventional disciplinary boundaries and forms of inquiry. Used primarily in Canada.

**research-enabled practice** Umbrella term covering all methodological approaches in which the creative artefact emerges as an outcome of research.

**research-led practice** A methodology in which the research drives the process of making the artefact. In short, research generates the making.

**research** A structured investigation of a formulated question that generates new knowledge and contributes to scholarly discussion, whether through written inquiry or through the creation of a creative artefact.

**snowballing** A technique for discovering new resources through the bibliographies of key or foundational publications in a field.

**storywork** A research methodology that uses First Nations traditions of storytelling as a method of inquiry, guided by Jo-ann Archibald Q'um Q'um Xiiem's seven relational principles that empower stories responsibly and holistically to guide research. See also: *decolonising methodology, relational accountability*.

**tacit knowledge** Internalised understanding acquired through experience, practice, and intuition that resists full articulation in language.

**theoretical framework** A foundational structure that uses a set of theories as a blueprint for the research process. See also: *conceptual framework, theoretical perspective*.

**theoretical perspective** An orienting structural framework of conceptual lenses from which to observe, consider, analyse, and reflect on research phenomena. See also: *conceptual framework, theoretical framework*.

**theory** A set of ideas or hypotheses that offers a systematic way of thinking, explaining, interpreting, or predicting phenomena within an area of knowledge or a field of study.

**thesis statement** A concise claim or argument that defines the central position of a research project and guides its inquiry and conclusions.

**thesis** A substantial work presenting the findings and outcomes of academic research. Commonly used in the UK and Australia. See also: *dissertation*.

**thing** That which exists in a given place and time, and through which meaning and presence may emerge beyond its given function. See also: *thingness, object*.

**thingness** The quality by which an object exceeds its given function to assert its own presence through its emergent agency, drawing on Martin Heidegger's conception of thing and Bill Brown's thing theory. See also: *thing, object*.

**transdisciplinary** A mode of inquiry that transcends the perspectives of individual academic disciplines, often incorporating those from non-academic knowledge bases, to generate new frameworks beyond disciplinary boundaries. See also: *cross-disciplinary, interdisciplinary, multidisciplinary*.

**transformative research** A research paradigm that not only identifies issues of social injustice but actively develops strategies for change.

**triangulation** A research approach that employs multiple methods to investigate a single question or phenomenon, strengthening the credibility and validity of findings.

**vicarious trauma** A psychological phenomenon in which a researcher develops a secondary traumatic response through significant exposure to deeply distressing experiences recounted by others.

***viva voce*** An oral academic examination conducted following the submission of a doctoral thesis. Also referred to as dissertation defence, oral examination, and thesis defence.

**voice** The distinct personality, style, and perspective through which knowledge is communicated and scholarly and creative identity is expressed.

**worldview** A fundamental framework of beliefs, attitudes, and values through which a person understands and interprets the world and their place within it.

# APPENDICES

# APPENDIX A

## Creative Artefact Research Terms

A range of methodological terms currently describe artistic practice-inclusive doctoral research. Specific names are often used generically and interchangeably. These terms include artistic research, arts-based research (ABR), practice as research (PaR), practice-based, practice-led, research-creation, and research-led practice. Recently introduced terms, *research-enabled* (outcome-based) and *practice-enabled* (method-based), further distinguish this research by focusing on the process of discovery (Batty and Zalipour 2025, 469).

The following table provides side-by-side definitions from the *CAPC Glossary*, alongside suggested principal sources for each term. All methodological approaches fit under the overarching term used in this book: creative artefact.

*Creative Artefact Research Terms*

| *Term* | *Definition* | *Principle sources* |
|---|---|---|
| **Artistic Research** | Any mode of inquiry in which creative practice is both the primary means and the site of generating new knowledge. | Henk Borgdorff (2011)<br>Christopher Frayling (1993)<br>Falk Hübner (2024) |
| **Arts-based Research (ABR)** | A methodology that employs artistic processes as tools for investigation, and for recording, developing, or communicating research findings, regardless of the field of study. | Patricia Leavy (2020)<br>Shaun McNiff (2013)<br>Graham Sullivan (2010) |

*Creative Artefact Research Terms*

| *Term* | *Definition* | *Principle sources* |
|---|---|---|
| **Practice as Research (PaR)** | A methodology in which creative practice is the research method itself, with new knowledge arising directly from the process of making. In short, practice is research. | Estelle Barrett and Barbara Bolt (2007)<br>Robin Nelson (2022) |
| **Practice-based** | A methodology in which creative practice provides the context for research, with the creative artefact analysed through conventional academic methods. In short, the research is about practice. | Linda Candy (2006, 2011)<br>Estelle Barrett and Barbara Bolt (2007)<br>Candy, Ernest Edmonds, and Craig Vear (2026) |
| **Practice-led** | A methodology in which the process of making the artefact leads and forms the research question and methods. In short, practice generates research. | Candy (2006, 2011)<br>Barrett and Bolt (2007) |
| **Practice-enabled knowledge** | Umbrella term covering all methodological approaches in which the creative artefact serves as a vehicle for generating research. | Batty and Zalipour (2025) |
| **Research-creation** | A methodology that integrates creative and academic research practices to generate knowledge that may exceed conventional disciplinary boundaries and forms of inquiry. Used primarily in Canada. | Owen Chapman and KimSawchuk (2012) Erin Manning (2016)<br>Natalie Loveless (2020) |
| **Research-enabled practice** | Umbrella term covering all methodological approaches in which the creative artefact emerges as an outcome of research. | Craig Batty and Arezou Zalipour (2025) |
| **Research-led practice** | A methodology in which the research drives the process of making the artefact. In short, research generates the making. | Hazel Smith and Roger T. Dean (2009) |

## References


Barrett, Estelle and Barbara Bolt. 2007. *Practice as Research: Approaches to Creative Arts*. I. B. Tauris.

Batty, Craig, and Arezou Zalipour. 2025. "Research, Practice, Knowledge: Introducing the Creative Knowledges Enabling Framework." *Media Practice and Education* 26 (4): 461–477. https://doi.org/10.1080/25741136.2024.2384686

Borgdorff, Henk. 2011. "The Production of Knowledge in Artistic Research." In *The Routledge Companion to Research in the Arts*, edited by Michael Biggs and Henrik Karlsson. Routledge.

Candy, Linda. 2006. *Practice Based Research: A Guide*. Sydney-Gadigal, AU: Creative and Cognition Studios. https://www.creativityandcognition.com/wp-content/uploads/2011/04/PBR-Guide-1.1-2006.pdf

Candy, Linda. 2011. "Research and Creative Practice." In *Interacting: Art, Research and the Creative Practitioner*, edited by Linda Candy and Ernest Edmonds. Libri Publishing Ltd.

Candy, Linda, Ernest Edmonds, and Craig Vear. 2026. *Practice-Based Research: Foundations and Frameworks*. Routledge.

Chapman, Owen, and Kim Sawchuk. 2012. "Research-Creation: Intervention, Analysis and 'Family Resemblances'." *Canadian Journal of Communication*, 37 (1): 5–26. https://doi.org/10.22230/cjc.2012v37n1a2489

Frayling, Christopher. 1993. "Research in Art and Design". *Royal College of Art Research Papers*, 1 (1): 1–5. https://researchonline.rca.ac.uk/384/

Hübner, Falk. 2024. *Method, Methodology and Research Design in Artistic Research: Between Solid Routes and Emergent Pathways*. Routledge.

Leavy, Patricia. 2020. *Method Meets Art: Arts-based Research Practice*, 3rd ed. The Guilford Press.

Loveless, Natalie. 2020. *Knowings and Knots: Methodologies and Ecologies in Research-Creation*, edited by Natalie Loveless. University of Alberta Press.

Manning, Erin. 2016. "Ten Propositions for Research-Creation." In *Collaboration in Performance Practice*, edited by Colin Noyale and Stefanie Sachsenmaier. *Palgrave Macmillan*. https://doi.org/10.1057/9781137462466_7

McNiff, Shaun, ed. 2013. *Art as Research: Opportunities and Challenges*. Intellect.

Nelson, Robin. 2022. *Practice as Research in the Arts and Beyond: Principles, Processes, Context, Achievements*, 2nd ed. Palgrave Macmillan.

Smith, Hazel, and Roger T. Dean, eds. 2009. *Practice-led Research, Research-led Practice in the Creative Arts*. Edinburgh University Press.

Sullivan, Graeme. 2010. *Art Practice as Research: Inquiry in the Visual Arts*, 2nd ed. Sage Publications.

# APPENDIX B

## Method Reference Guide

### A list of lists

This method appendix is the second part of a two-tiered list. The first list, in the method decalogue, introduces a range of method categories: "quantitative and qualitative", "mixed methods", "performative", and "emergent and emerging". This second list presents specific methods for each group.

These methods provide starting points for further exploration. Unlike terms that appear in the main text of the decalogue, the specific methods listed here are not necessarily included in the *CAPC Glossary*, as the range is too broad for comprehensive definition. For deeper engagement with any particular method, consult the bibliography accompanying the method decalogue. Use these lists as prompts for your own investigation. And remember, as Mieke Bal points out: no one can "escape the task of doing research" (2013, 69). No one.

**1. Examples of quantitative methods**

- Coding
- Computational modelling
- Correlational studies
- Cross-sectional studies
- Data analysis
- Experimental research (pre-experiment, true experiment, and quasi-experiment)
- Longitudinal studies
- Meta-analyses
- Prediction studies
- Probability sampling (simple random, systematic, and cluster)
- Questionnaires
- Randomisation (random assignment)

- Statistical analysis
- Survey research

This list has been compiled with information from Daniela Aidley (2019) and Laura M. O'Dwyer and James A. Bernauer (2014).

**2. Examples of qualitative methods**

**Interpretive**: analyse and interpret artistic texts (written, visual, sonic, and performative)

- Autoethnography
- Comparative analysis (across texts, cases, or contexts)
- Creative work as primary source material
- Critical analysis
- Discourse analysis
- Interviews (artists, audiences, collaborators)
- Literature review/synthesis
- Narrative inquiry
- Phenomenological
- Reflective writing, including personal narratives, memory work, and journaling
- Thematic analysis
- Visual analysis

**Contextual**: context as an integral element of research

- Archival research
- Biographical research
- Case study analysis
- Grounded theory
- Historical/cultural research
- Historiography (how history is written/recorded)
- Literature review and theoretical analysis
- Narrative analysis
- Oral history
- Primary source analysis
- Secondary source synthesis

**Participatory**: conducted with people, not on them

- Action research
- Case studies
- Content analysis
- Document analysis

- Ethnographic
- Field research
- Focus groups
- Immersive fieldwork
- Interviewing (highly structured, semi-structured, and unstructured)
- Life stories and life histories
- Participant observation
- Participatory action research (PAR)
- Photo-elicitation interviews

This list has been compiled with information from Norman K. Denzin and Yvonna S. Lincoln (2018), Lisa M. Given (2008), and Patricia Leavy (2014).

3. **Examples of mixed methods**

- Concurrent triangulation
- Data transformation
- Embedded design
- Explanatory sequential design
- Exploratory sequential design
- Joint display (presenting mixed data visually for comparison)
- Merging data sets
- Multiphase design
- "Quantising and qualitising" (Tashakkori and Teddlie 1998, 126-133)
- Research-question dependent designs

This list has been compiled with information from R. Burke Johnson, Anthony J. Onwuegbuzie, and Lisa A. Turner (2007), Patricia Leavy (2014, 2017), Donna M. Mertens (2023), Abbas Tashakkori and Charles Teddlie (1998), and Charles Teddlie and Abbas Tashakkori (2011).

4. **Examples of performative methods**

**Engagement**: audience/community response, evidence-based

- Action research
- Audience research and response studies
- Community engagement and participatory approaches
- Enacted, generative, and embodied (doing, making, and experiencing)
- Embodied exploration
- Participant observation (in studios, performances, and exhibitions)
- Reflexive interviews (Denzin 2001)
- Workshop/teaching as research

**Creative practice**

- "embodied reflexive retrospection" (Gilbertson 2015)
- "listening" (Gallagher et al. 2020)
- Collaborative creation processes
- Exploring material, technique, and form
- Iterative development and critique
- Reflective documentation (journals, video, and audio)
- Reflective practice: reflection-in-action (at time of practice) and reflection-on-action (after practice)
- Studio practice/developing processes

**Data collection**

- Audio/video recording
- Discussion
- Experience workshop: a method enabling "participants to consider their own experiences in relation to those of others in relation to the same artworks" (Candy et al. 2022, 313)
- Field diaries
- Field notes
- Multiview perspective (data from multiple viewpoints)
- Personal logbooks
- Photography as documentation
- Primary data
- Questionnaires
- Sampling strategies
- Semi-structured interviews (with participants, including members of the general public)
- Still and moving images
- Structured interviews
- Structured observation
- Transcripts from sound files, notes, or questionnaires
- Unstructured observation
- Verbatim reports
- Video-cues recall: "a method for closely investigating the detail of individual experiences" (Candy et al. 2022, 313)
- Written data

This list has been compiled with information from Linda Candy et al. (2022), Norman K. Denzin (2001), Kathleen Gallagher (2022), Brad Haseman (2006), Falk Hübner (2024), Rae Johnson et al. (2021), and Baz Kershaw and Helen Nicholson (2011).

5. **Examples of decolonising methods**:

    - **Action research**, including community-based interviews and appreciative inquiry: adapted with participant as "coresearcher", "participatory transformative", and "healing participatory" (Chilisa 2020, 267–292)
    - **Chronology**: history as "a time of 'discovery'" (Tuhiwai Smith 2021, 33–34)
    - **Collective accountability**: responsibility and protocol (Kovach 2005, 30–31)
    - **Critical place inquiry-six methods**: "Indigenous storywork", "Mapping Place-worlds and Place-making", "(Re)mapping", "Eating the Landscape", "Urban Indigenous Land-Based Pedagogies and Community-Based Design Research", "Shellmounds" (Tuck and McKenzie 2015, 130–149)
    - **Cyclical methods**: "circular ontology" (González 2000)
    - **Learning circle** (Absolon and Willett 2005, 116, Nabigon et al. 1999)
    - **Oral traditions**: storywork and storytelling through "sharing of stories to strengthen relationships, such as yarning, storywork" (Windchief and San Pedro 2019, half title page; also see Archibald Q'um Q'um Xiiem and Parent Nox Ayaaẃilt 2019)
    - **Philosophic sagacity**: a reflective system of thought based on the wisdom and the traditions of people (Chilisa 2020, 254–255)
    - **Relational accountability**: "Respect, relevance, reciprocity, responsibility" (Wilson 2008; Kirkness and Rarnhardt 1991)
    - **Relational principles**: activating responsibility between nature, objects, and human beings (Tuhiwai Smith 2021, 192–193)
    - **Songlines**: "An all-encompassing worldview where all parts are indivisible from all other parts and functions" (Neale and Kelly 2020, 42)
    - **Storywork**: "we transcend time and space, connecting on deeper levels of understanding with each other, with all living beings, with the earth and the multiverse" (Archibald Q'um Q'um Xiiem et al. 2022)

This list has been compiled with information from Kathy Absolon and Cam Willett (2005), Begele Chilisa (2020), Antonia Darder (2019), Maria Cristina González (2000), Margaret Kovach (2005, 2015, 2021), Linda Tuhiwai Smith (2021), Eve Tuck and Marcia McKenzie (2015), Tiina Seppälä et al. (2021), Shawn Wilson (2008), and Sweeney Windchief and Timothy San Pedro (2019).

6. **Examples of arts-based methods (including art-based and research-creation)**:

    - **A/r/tography**: "living inquiry" through practice/artist/teacher relationship
    - **Body mapping**: participatory sensory and psychological experience

- **Choreographic inquiry**: dance and movement communication
- **Poetic inquiry**: method for data exploration and representation
- **Videography**: spatial knowledge and documentation/documentary

This list has been compiled with information from Tom Barone and Eliot W. Eisner (2012), M. Katherine Boydell (2021), Lisa M. Given (2008), Anna Juliane Heinrich et al. (2024), Patricia Leavy (2016, 2020), Natalie Loveless (2019, 2020), Shaun McNiff (2013), Tiina Seppälä et al. (2021), and Graeme Sullivan (2010).

7. **Examples of non-representational process-based methods**

- **Deep mapping**: a tracing and observing relationships from micro to macro (Edwardes 2026)
- **Diarising**: documenting daily practice without refining, through any medium
- **Experimentation and play**: for instance, to track bodily and affective response, including surprises and "mistakes"
- **Inefficient mapping**: gives primacy to raw data as a "chaosgraph", which maintains research information in the potentially random, dead-end, disordered form as originally recorded (Knight 2021)
- **Integral ethics**: "part of the fabric of the world" of the research (Murris and Zhao 2022, 93)
- **Response-ability**: listening, speaking back, and responding to humans and matter equally

This list has been compiled with information from Christian Edwardes (2026), Beth Greenhough et al. (2025), Linda Knight (2021), Karin Murris and Weili Zhao (2022), and Phillip Vannini (2015, 2025).

8. **Examples of agential realism (more broadly, new materialism) methods**

- **Apparatus analysis**: research tools such as cameras used to record events are not neutral; they are equal phenomena that actively intra-act with the researcher, other humans, and objects
- **Diffractive analysis**: focused on difference, observing one event or element through another, and while they come into contact. Look for "agential cuts" created through the research process (see Bozalek and Murris, 2022; Taguchi, 2012)
- **Entanglement**: traces inseparable relationships between, for instance, performance, audience, space, performer, and researcher, where physicality and processes are entangled rather than analysed as separate entities

- **Intra-action**: different elements (bodies, space, sound, light, and memory) become mutually constituted; this event does not recognise individual beings prior to their coming together. These actions are "cut together apart at the same time, which means that they are differentiated and entangled simultaneously" (Murris and Bozalek 2023, 71)
- **Intra-active interviewing**: interviewer and interviewee co-create knowledge and the interview space, questions, and the presence of all matter and humans shapes analysis

This list has been compiled with information from Karen Barad (2007), Annouchka Bayley (2023), Karin Murris (2022), and Karin Murris and Vivienne Bozalek (2023).

9. **Examples of cultural analysis methods**

- **Concept-based analysis**: "the temporal encounter" (Bal 2025, 26)
- **Concepts as tools**: facilitate conversations between disciplinary fields (33)
- **Dialogue with the object**: "an attitude of responsiveness" (26)
- **Differentiation**: process of flexibility "to avoid rigidity" (32)
- **Listening**: overcoming the "loudness of the world" (35)

This list has been compiled with information from Mieke Bal (2007, 2013, 2025).

## References


Absolon, Kathy, and Cam Willett. 2005. "Putting Ourselves Forward: Location in Aboriginal Research." In *Research As Resistance: Critical, Indigenous, and Anti-oppressive Approaches*, edited by Leslie Brown and Susan Strega. Canadian Scholars' Press.

Aidley, Daniela. 2019. *Introducing Quantitative Methods: A Practical Guide*. Red Globe Press.

Archibald Q'um Q'um Xiiem, Jo-ann, and Amy Parent Nox Ayaaŵilt. 2019. "Hands Back, Hands Forward for Indigenous Storywork as Methodology." In *Applying Indigenous Research Methods: Storying with Peoples and Communities*, edited by Sweeney Windchief and Timothy San Pedro. Taylor and Francis.

Archibald Q'um Q'um Xiiem, Jo-ann, Jo-ann, Jenny Bol Lee-Morgan, and Jason De Santolo, eds. 2022. *Decolonizing Research: Indigenous Storywork as Methodology*. Bloomsbury Academy.

Bal, Mieke. 2007. "Working with Concepts" In *Conceptual Odysseys: Passages to Cultural Analysis*, edited by Griselda Pollock. I. B. Tauris

Bal, Mieke. 2013. "Lexicon for Cultural Analysis." In *Die Lust an der Kultur/Theorie. Transdisziplinäre Interventionen Für Wolfgang Müller-Funk*, edited by Anna Babka, Daniela Finzi, and Clemens Ruthner. Turia + Kant Verlag.

Bal, Mieke. 2025. "Cultural Analysis: Critical Encounters in Time, Space, and Thought." In *The Future of Cultural Analysis: A Critical Inquiry*, edited by Murat Ayemir, Noa Roei, and Aylin Kuryel. Routledge. https://doi.org/10.5117/9789048559794

Barad, Karin. 2007. *Meeting the Universe Halfway: Quantum Physics and the Entanglement of Matter and Meaning*. Duke University Press.

Barone, Tom, and Elliot W. Eisner. 2012. *Arts Based Research*. SAGE Academic Books. https://doi.org/10.4135/9781452230627

Bayley, Annouchka. 2023. "Entanglements and the Many-Worlded Doing of Research-Based Practice, Practice-Based Research, Practice-as-Research, and Postqualitative Inquiry in the Academy." In *Diffracting New Materialisms: Emerging Methods in Artistic Research and Higher Education*, edited by Annouchka Bayley and J. J. Chan. Palgrave Macmillan. https://doi.org/10.1007/978-3-031-18607-3

Boydell, Katherine M. 2021. "Introduction." In *Applying Body Mapping in Research: An Arts-Based Method*, edited by Katherine M. Boydell. Routledge.

Bozalek, Vivienne, and Karin Murris. 2022. "Diffraction." In *A Glossary for Doing Postqualitative, New Materialist and Critical Posthumanist Research Across Disciplines*, edited by Karin Murris. Routledge.

Candy, Linda, Ernest Edmonds, and Craig Vear. 2022. "Method." In *The Routledge International Handbook of Practice-Based Research*, edited by Craig Vear. Routledge.

Chilisa, Bagele. 2020. *Indigenous Research Methodologies*, 2nd ed. SAGE Publications.

Darder, Antonia. 2019. "Decolonizing Interpretive Research." In *Decolonizing Interpretive Research: A Subaltern Methodology for Social Change*, edited by Antonia Darder. Routledge.

Denzin, Norman K. 2001. "The Reflexive Interview." *Qualitative Research* 1 (1): 23–46. https://doi.org/10.1177/146879410100100102

Denzin, Norman K., and Yvonna S. Lincoln, eds. 2018. *The Sage Handbook of Qualitative Research*, 5th ed. Sage Publications.

Edwardes, Christian. 2026. "On Becoming Intimate with Scorched Earth: Research-Creation and Infrathin Data." In *Non-Representational and More-Than-Human Research: Vitalist Methodologies for the End of Data*, edited by Phillip Vannini. Routledge.

Gallagher, Kathleen. 2022. *Hope in A Collapsing World: Youth, Theatre, and Listening as a Political Alternative*. University of Toronto Press.

Gallagher, Kathleen, Dirk J. Rodricks, and Kelsey Jacobson, eds. 2020. *Global Youth Citizenry and Radical Hope: Enacting Community-Engaged Research through Performative Methodologies*. Springer Nature.

Gilbertson, Simon. 2015. "In Visible Hands: The Matter and Making of Music Therapy." *Journal of Music Therapy* 52 (4): 487–514. https://doi.org/10.1093/jmt/thv014

Given, Lisa M., ed. 2008. *The SAGE Encyclopedia of Qualitative Research Methods*, vols. 1 and 2. SAGE Publications.

González, Maria Cristina. 2000. "The Four Seasons of Ethnography: A Creation-centered Ontology for Ethnography." *International Journal of Intercultural Relations* 24 (5): 623–650. https://doi.org/10.1016/S0147-1767(00)00020-1

Greenhough, Beth, Jamie Lorimer, Joshua Evans, and Oscar Hartman Davies. 2025. "More-than-representational Methods for Encountering Viruses, Bacteria, and Other Microbes." In *Non-Representational and More-Than-Human research: Vitalist Methodologies for the End of Data*, edited by Phillip Vannini. Routledge.

Haseman, Brad. 2006. "A Manifesto for Performative Research." *Media International Australia, Incorporating Culture and Policy* 118 (1): 98–106. https://doi.org/10.1177/1329878X0611800113

Heinrich, Anna Juliane, Séverine Marguin, Angela Million, and Jörg Stollmann. 2024. "Introduction: Spatial Research from an Interdisciplinary Perspective." In *Handbook of Qualitative and Visual Methods in Spatial Research*, edited by Anna Juliane Heinrich, Séverine Marguin, Angela Million, and Jörg Stollmann. transcript Verlag. https://doi.org/10.14361/9783839467343

Hübner, Falk. 2024. *Method, Methodology and Research Design in Artistic Research: Between Solid Routes and Emergent Pathways*. Routledge. (See chap. 3, "In the Centre of the Orbits – Crafting Methods.")

Johnson, R. Burke, Anthony J. Onwuegbuzie, and Lisa A. Turner. 2007. "Towards a Definition of Mixed Methods Research." *Journal of Mixed Methods Research* 1 (2): 112–113. https://doi.org/10.1177/1558689806298224

Johnson, Rae, with Rebecca Morgan, Jessica Pink, and Masha Mikulinsky. 2021. "Body Stories: Researching and Performing the Embodied Experience of Oppression." In *The Art and Science of Embodied Research Design: Concepts, Methods and Cases*, edited by Jennifer Frank Tantia. Routledge.

Kershaw, Baz, and Helen Nicholson. 2011. "Introduction: Doing Methods Creatively." In *Research Methods in Theatre and Performance*, edited by Baz Kershaw and Helen Nichoson. Edinburgh University Press.

Kirkness, Verna J., and Ray Rarnhardt 1991. "First Nations and Higher Education: The Four R's – Respect, Relevance, Reciprocity, Responsibility." *Journal of American Indian Education*, 30 (3): 1–15. https://www.jstor.org/stable/24397980

Knight, Linda. 2021. *Inefficient Mapping: A Protocol for Attuning to Phenomena*. Punctum Books. (See chap. 2, "Chaosgraphics.")

Kovach, Margaret. 2005. "Emerging From the Margins: Indigenous Methodologies." In *Research As Resistance: Critical, Indigenous, and Anti-oppressive Approaches*, edited by Leslie Brown and Susan Strega. Canadian Scholars' Press.

Kovach, Margaret. 2015. "Emerging From the Margins: Indigenous Methodologies." In *Research As Resistance: Revisiting Critical, Indigenous, and Anti-oppressive Approaches*, 2nd ed., edited by Susan Strega and Leslie Brown. Canadian Scholars' Press.

Kovach, Margaret. 2021. *Indigenous Methodologies: Characteristics, Conversations, and Contexts*, 2nd ed. University of Toronto Press.
Leavy, Patricia, ed. 2014. *The Oxford Handbook of Qualitative Research*. Oxford University Press.
Leavy, Patricia. 2016. *Essentials of Transdisciplinary Research: Using Problem-Centered Methodologies*. Routledge. (See chap. 5, "Arts-Based Research Practices: Designing Research that Is Useful for the Public.")
Leavy, Patricia. 2017. *Research Design: Quantitative, Qualitative, Mixed Methods, Arts-Based, and Community-Based Participatory Research Approaches*. The Guilford Press.
Leavy, Patricia. 2020. *Method Meets Art: Arts-based Research Practice*, 3rd ed. The Guilford Press.
Loveless, Natalie. 2019. *How to Make Art at the End of the World: A Manifesto for Research-Creation*. Duke University Press. (See Introduction, "Art in the Expanded Field.")
Loveless, Natalie. 2020. "Research-Creation Interdisciplinary Praxis: Natalie Loveless in Conversation with Erin Manning." In *Knowings and Knots: Methodologies and Ecologies in Research-Creation*, edited by Natalie Loveless. University of Alberta Press.
McNiff, Shaun, ed. 2013. *Art as Research: Opportunities and Challenges*. Intellect.
Mertens, Donna M. 2023. *Mixed Methods Research: Research Methods*. Bloomsbury Academic. (See chap. 1, "Definition of Mixed Methods and its Emergence as a Methodological Approach.")
Murris, Karin, ed. 2022. *A Glossary for Doing Postqualitative, New Materialist and Critical Posthumanist Research Across Disciplines*. Routledge.
Murris, Karin and Vivienne Bozalek, eds. 2023. *In Conversation with Karen Barad: Doings of Agential Realism*. Routledge.
Murris, Karin and Weili Zhao. 2022. "Non/representational." In *A Glossary for Doing Postqualitative, New Materialist and Critical Posthumanist Research Across Disciplines*, edited by Karin Murris, 92–93. Routledge.
Nabigon, Herb, Rebecca Hagey, Schuyler Webster, and Robert Mackay. 1999. "The Learning Circle as a Research Method: The Trickster and Windigo in Research." *Native Social Work Journal* 2 (1): 113–137. https://laurentian.scholaris.ca/handle/10219/461
Neale, Margot, and Lynne Kelly. 2020. *Songlines: Power and Promise*. Australia: Thames and Hudson.
O'Dwyer, Laura M., and James A. Bernauer. 2014. *Quantitative Research for the Qualitative Researcher*. SAGE Publications. (See chap. 3, "Research in the Quantitative Tradition.")
Seppälä, Tiina, Melanie Sarantou, and Satu Miettinen, eds. 2021. *Arts-Based Methods for Decolonising Participatory Research*. Routledge.
Sullivan, Graeme. 2010. *Art Practice as Research: Inquiry in Visual Arts*, 2nd ed. SAGE Publications.
Taguchi, Hillevi Lenz. 2012. "A Diffractive and Deleuzian Approach to Analysing Interview Data." *Feminist Theory* 13 (3): 265–281. https://doi.org/10.1177/1464700112456001

Tashakkori, Abbas, and Charles Teddlie. 1998. *Mixed Methodology: Combining Qualitative and Quantitative Approaches*. SAGE Publications.
Teddlie, Charles, and Abbas Tashakkori. 2011. "Mixed Methods: Contemporary Issues in an Emerging Field." In *The SAGE Handbook of Qualitative Research*, 4th ed., edited by Norman K. Denzin and Yvonna S. Lincoln. SAGE Publications.
Tuck, Eve, and Marcia McKenzie. 2015. *Place in Research: Theory, Methodology, and Methods*. Routledge. (See chap. 6, "Indigenous Methods of Critical Place Inquiry.")
Tuhiwai Smith, Linda. 2021. *Decolonizing Methodologies: Research and Indigenous Peoples*, 3rd ed. Zed Books.
Vannini, Phillip. 2015. "Non-Representational Research Methodologies: An Introduction." In *Non-Representational Methodologies: Re-Envisioning Research*, edited by Phillip Vannini. Routledge.
Vannini, Phillip, ed. 2025. *Non-Representational and More-Than-Human Research: Vitalist Methodologies for the End of Data*. Routledge.
Wilson, Shawn. 2008. *Research is Ceremony: Indigenous Research Methods*. Fernwood Publishing.
Windchief, Sweeney, and Timothy San Pedro, eds. 2019. *Applying Indigenous Research Methods: Storying with Peoples and Communities*. Taylor and Francis.

# APPENDIX C

## Font Selection Guide

A note on fonts. In theses, the most commonly used font is 12-point Times New Roman, as academics consider it easily readable, traditional, and professional. Whatever font is chosen, it should be applied consistently throughout the thesis document.

**Commonly accepted fonts for academic theses include**:

- **Times New Roman** (12 pt): Traditional serif, widely accepted
- **Garamond** (12 pt): Elegant serif alternative
- **Arial** (11–12 pt): Clean sans-serif
- **Calibri** (11–12 pt): Contemporary sans-serif

Note that for all fonts, a smaller size is typically specified for footnotes, endnotes, and captions (9–10 pt).

### Serif vs. Sans-serif

Serif fonts (like Times New Roman and Garamond) have small decorative strokes at the ends of letters and are traditionally preferred for long-form academic writing as they're considered easier to read in print. Sans-serif fonts (like Arial and Calibri) lack these strokes and offer a more contemporary appearance and are generally preferred for on-screen reading.

### Line spacing

Most universities require 1.5 or double line spacing, which supports readability. Check this requirement before formatting your document. Single spacing is often specified for footnotes, endnotes, and captions.

## Discipline-specific considerations

Generally, institutions suggest a few font choices, rather than require a specific one, though particular disciplines may have specific requirements. Check with your research office and supervisor before committing to a choice. If you have a creative preference for a font not on your university's list and a good argument for using it, prepare a rationale for why it serves your thesis and request approval early.

## Monospaced fonts (rare requirement)

Some institutions may require monospaced fonts (also called fixed-width fonts) such as Courier, Monaco, or Consolas. In these fonts, each character occupies the same width, ensuring uniform spacing. Monospaced fonts can appear rigid and less attractive than proportional fonts, but offer consistency in formatting. This requirement is a legacy of typewriter conventions and is increasingly rare but still appears in some current university guidelines. Verify whether this applies to your institution.

# APPENDIX D

## Reference Systems Comparison

If your university or department requires a particular citation style, selecting your reference system can be straightforward. If not, this comparison chart may help make your decision. Selection factors include discipline norms, supervisor or departmental convention, visual layout or grammatical considerations, flexibility with atypical sources such as creative artefacts, and footnoting requirements. This chart indicates basic citation differences only.

**Important reminders**: Commit to your system early to avoid reformatting all references later, verify with your supervisor before finalising your choice, and access the most current version of your chosen citation style guide (style guides do update conventions).

**Commonly used reference systems**:

| *Reference System* | *Common Disciplines* | *In-text format (shortened version used, where relevant)* | *Bibliography format (Please note full title should be used in entries)* | *Key variations: Bibliography entry* |
|---|---|---|---|---|
| **APA** (American Psychological Association) | Psychology, Education, Social Sciences, Business. | (Stollman, 2026, p. 1) | Stollman, S. (2026). *CAPC*. Taylor and Francis. | Parenthetical year; no place of publication; first name initial only; Capitalise only the first word of the title (and subtitle). |
| **Chicago** (Author-Date) | Humanities, Social sciences, Creative arts, Film and media, Sciences. | (Stollman 2026, 1) | Stollman, Sarah. 2026. *CAPC*. Taylor and Francis. | No parenthetical year; no place of publication, and no page number range for individual chapter entry. |

| *Reference System* | *Common Disciplines* | *In-text format (shortened version used, where relevant)* | *Bibliography format (Please note full title should be used in entries)* | *Key variations: Bibliography entry* |
|---|---|---|---|---|
| **Chicago** (Notes and Bibliography) | Humanities, History, Art, Literature, Social sciences, Creative arts, Film and media. | Superscript footnote: 1. Sarah Stollman, *CAPC*, 1. | Stollman, Sarah. *CAPC*. Taylor and Francis. 2026. | Year at the end of entry, no place of publication, and no page number range for the individual chapter entry. |
| **Harvard** | Interdisciplinary, Mixed methods, Creative artefact, Business. | (Stollman, 2026); format varies | Stollman, S. (2026). *CAPC*. Abingdon, Oxon, UK: Taylor and Francis. | Parenthetical year; includes place of publication; first initial only; varies by institution. |
| **MLA** (Modern Language Association) | Humanities, Languages, Creative writing, Film, Literature. | (Stollman 1) | Stollman, Sarah. *CAPC*. Taylor and Francis, 2026. | Year at the end of entry; no year in in-text reference. |
| **MHRA** (Modern Humanities Research Association) | Humanities, literature (UK primarily). | superscript footnote: 1. Sarah Stollman, *CAPC*, p. 1. | Stollman, Sarah, *CAPC* (Abingdon, Oxon, UK: Taylor and Francis, 2026). | Parenthetical place of publication, publisher, year; place of publication not always required. |
| **Oxford** | Humanities (UK primarily) | superscript footnote: 1. Sarah Stollman, *CAPC*, p. 1. | Stollman, Sarah, *CAPC* (Abingdon, Oxon, UK: Taylor and Francis, 2026). | Year at the end of entry; similar to MHRA; varies by institution or discipline. |

# APPENDIX E

## Tense Conventions in Thesis Writing

This appendix outlines tense conventions that are typical but not universal. Many universities do not require prescribed tense expectations, and creative arts theses often have more flexibility than other disciplines.

### Common tense conventions by thesis section:

### Introduction

- **Present tense:** for stating what the thesis does ("This thesis examines…")
- **Future tense:** for outlining what will be discussed ("Chapter 3 will explore…")
- **Example:** "This research investigates the relationship between material and meaning. Chapter Two reviews relevant literature, while Chapter Three will present the methodological framework."

### Body Chapters

- **Present tense:** for discussing your artefact, analysing texts, or presenting arguments ("The installation creates…", "This approach reveals…")
- **Past tense:** for describing what you did in your research ("I conducted three interviews…", "I created five prototypes…")
- **Future tense:** occasionally for signposting ("The next section will demonstrate…")
- **Example:** "The documentary explores themes of memory through layered imagery. I filmed across three locations and edited the footage to create temporal disruption."

### Conclusion

- **Past tense:** for summarising what the research has shown ("This thesis has demonstrated…", "The artefact revealed…")
- **Past perfect:** for referring to earlier stages ("Having established the theoretical framework, the practice-based work then explored…")

- **Example:** "This research has examined the intersection of sound and space. Having established that acoustic environments shape embodied experience, the installation work demonstrated how spatial design can amplify this relationship."

## Tense review:

- **Present:** Happens now or is generally true ("The artwork challenges…", "Creative artefact research offers…")
- **Past:** Happened at a specific time ("I created…", "The exhibition opened…")
- **Future:** Will happen ("Chapter Five will discuss…")
- **Past perfect:** Happened before another past event ("Having completed the initial prototypes, I then refined…"). Past perfect is relatively rare in thesis writing, though students often overuse it. It is most useful when the sequence of past events needs clarification. If the order is already clear from context or connective words, the simple past is sufficient and less cumbersome.

When in doubt, consider the present tense to discuss ideas and arguments, and the past tense to describe your specific research activities. Tense conventions will become clearer when you receive feedback on your first draft. In the meantime, here is a tense refresher chart:

## Twelve English Verb Tenses

| | *Past* | *Present* | *Future* |
|---|---|---|---|
| Simple | I worked on my thesis yesterday. | I work on my thesis every day. | I will work on my thesis tomorrow. |
| Continuous | I was working on my thesis when you called. | I am working on my thesis right now. | I will be working on my thesis when you call. |
| Perfect | I had worked on my thesis introduction when you called. | I have worked on my thesis introduction. | I will have worked on my thesis introduction by the time you call. |
| Perfect Continuous | I had been working on my thesis all morning when you called. | I have been working on my thesis all morning. | I will have been working on my thesis all morning when you call. |

# APPENDIX F

## Presentation Design Checklist

Simplicity equals clarity. As Garr Reynolds observes in *Presentation Zen: Simple Presentation Design and Delivery*, simplicity is "essentially synonymous with clarity, directness, subtlety" (2020, 117). Slides support your spoken content and delivery, adding depth to your presentation, while reminding you of key points as you present. The most common error in slide design is overcomplication. Visuals should exemplify your points without distracting from what you're saying. Don't allow your slides to force your audience to choose between listening to you and reading them. As Eelko K. R. E. Huizingh (2023) advocates, preparation is everything.

**Common mistakes in slide design**:

- **Text overload:** Too much text (often in too small a font size for readability).
- **Duplication:** Text on slides that repeats verbatim what you're saying verbally.
- **Bullet overload:** Too many bullet points per slide.
- **Visual clutter:** Too many visual elements per slide, which compete for attention.
- **Diagram density:** Overly complex diagrams or images.

**Presentation design principles**:

- **One discussion point per slide**: Don't try to cover multiple concepts.
- **Limit text**: Maximum 6 lines per slide, 6 words per line (the "6×6 rule" is a rough guide).
- **Readable fonts**: Sans-serif often works best for digital displays; ensure body text is large enough to be read from the back of the room (smaller sizes only acceptable for captions/citations).
- **High-quality images**: Use high-resolution images to avoid pixelation.
- **Single focal point**: One image or cohesive group of related images.
- **White space**: Leave ample space; avoid cluttering with too many elements.

- **High contrast**: Ensure strong contrast between text and background.
- **Accessibility**: Avoid red/green combinations, colour against black, and low-contrast pairings; add alt text descriptions to images.
- **Video material**: Use a high-resolution file, ensure it plays properly, and ensure it is either embedded in the presentation file or linked accurately to an external file.

## References

Huizingh, Eelko K. R. E. 2023. *Unlocking PhD Success: How to Acquire Crucial PhD Skills*. Springer. (See chp. 5, "Presentation Skills.")

Reynolds, Garr. 2020. *Presentation Zen: Simple Ideas on Presentation Design and Delivery*, 3rd ed. New Riders. (See chap. 5, "Simplicity: Why it Matters.")

# APPENDIX G

## Artefact Mode Categories

The following list details four main artefact modes as identified in *Decalogue X: Ten Artefact Things*. A fifth category, hybrid, encompasses any combination of the following modes:

- **Physical: spatial or static**
  Physical artefacts include painting, drawing, sculpture, illustration, textiles, and ceramics. These tangible works exist in space and rely primarily on visual (and sometimes tactile) experience. The viewer's interpretation varies based on perception, sensation, and personal relationship to the work.
- **Performative: temporal or time-based**
  Performative artefacts include dance, theatre, sonic work (live sound and music performance), installation, and film. These are experiential and temporal. They unfold over time. While some (like dance) are ephemeral with no object remaining post-performance, others (like film) exist as repeatable digital files, though the work itself remains a time-based audiovisual experience.
- **Textual: language or word-based**
  Textual artefacts include poetry, fiction, creative non-fiction, scripts (theatre and screen), and composed or scored music. While creative arts scholars may refer to films or artworks as "texts", here "textual" specifically refers to language or word-based work.
- **Interactive: audience engagement and participation**
  Interactive artefacts require audience participation, creating varied experiences. These include installations (physical or virtual), games, and participatory performances. Interactive work may be ephemeral or tangible and often incorporates sonic, filmic, textual, or digital elements. Engagement can range from physical environments to virtual reality (VR).

# APPENDIX H

## Writing and Creative Block Strategies

This appendix offers unblocking strategies for writing and creative arts practices to motivate progress, overcome blocks, and generate new directions. Familiarise yourself with these approaches at the beginning of your process and return to them whenever you encounter a block.

### Writing Block Strategies

The following strategies, drawn from academic and creative writing practice, are divided into community and individual approaches.

**Community approaches**:

- **"Shut Up and Write!"**: Sessions that bring scholars together to meet weekly for focused one-hour writing sessions, creating accountability, focus, and momentum.[1]
- **Thesis Boot Camp**: This intensive program is aimed at students in the final stages, focused on writing strategies that lead to significant progress.[2]
- **Writing Circle**: A monthly meeting allowing students to share work and exchange feedback. Annalea Beattie's development of the Writing Circle "encourages art students to treat their writing as a conceptual project that investigates writing as form and idea" while connecting to their creative practice (2014, 180).

**Individual approaches**:

- **Freewriting** creates open space to explore thoughts without any feedback from others or yourself. The intent of freewriting is, basically, to have no intent or predetermined agenda. Write continuously for 10–20 minutes without pausing to edit, organise, or censor. Joan Bolker calls freewriting inclusive and messy (1998, 43). This process moves you closer to knowing what your thesis is about.[3]

- **Poetic inquiry** as defined by Sandra L. Faulkner, is a technique of articulating any type of data or findings into a poetic form (2020, 13). By using a different written form for the expression of research, concepts, and findings, a researcher can shift perspective, which may reveal patterns and connections less visible in conventional prose. Poetic inquiry can also be a technique for prompting the writing process. Through poetry, personal experience is often merged with cultural, social, or historical concepts, providing a powerful way to see your research afresh. To try this approach, take a section of your thesis and rewrite it as a poem, whether free verse, haiku, or another form. Don't be concerned with poetic quality; focus on distilling core ideas. You may discover metaphors, connections, or framings that clarify your scholarly writing.[4]
- **Time-based strategies**: The Pomodoro Technique uses timed writing intervals (typically 25 minutes) to build momentum and overcome procrastination. Daily word count goals prioritise consistency over volume, helping you build sustainable writing habits.[5]
- **The Writing Cycle**: Katherine Firth's model depicts writing as cyclical: "Read and Think", "Plan", "Write", "Edit", "Polish", "Review and Re-write", with breaks between each stage (2024, 7–9). Writing is iterative, not linear: you return to earlier stages repeatedly, refining with each cycle.
- **Zero first draft and Lamott's "shitty" first draft**: The "zero-draft" is a preliminary draft from which you don't expect much: a safe space to begin articulating ideas. Although much of the content may not make it into your first draft, the process gets you there. Bolker describes this moment of possibility: "to imagine, or discern, a shape to your material, to see the method in your madness" (1998, 50). This writing can be an outline, a list of aims, or a fully written start to your first draft (1998, 50).[6]

  Elements of freewriting and the zero draft operate together to create what Anne Lamott calls the "shitty" first draft. She describes this opportunity as a time to write without over-monitoring or performing for imagined readers such as supervisors and examiners (1994/2020, 49–56). Pour out all your ideas without filter. Sometimes this process simply gets you writing, reveals your research core, or provides a draft (no matter how rough) to move forward from.

These are just a few established approaches. Experiment to find what works for you. Some students thrive in community writing sessions, while others need solitary focus; some need structure, others need freedom.

## Creative Block Strategies

As with creative stasis in writing, blocks in creative practice can also be addressed through targeted strategies. Some writing approaches listed above transfer to creative work, for instance, community practices such as Writing Circles. However, depending on your mode, it may not be feasible to share work-in-progress or create while in a group setting. The following approaches address individual creative practice:

- **"Character switching"**
  Artist Katarina Ranković developed this approach during her PhD: inhabiting different characters or perspectives while creating work to gain new insight (Ranković 2023, 287; Christina Reading 2024, 47). She suggests that "character switching" can function "as a creative engine in the crafting of stories and artworks" (Ranković 2023, 287). For example, approach your work from the perspective of a critic, a child, or a sceptic. Each "character" may reveal new directions or different motivations.
- **Free-making**
  This method is modelled on the notion of freewriting. Step away from your research project and make something else, anything else, without considering its relation to your artefact or research question or having any plan. This method provides space to explore without concern for feedback, aim, or agendas. The goal is play, not product.
- **Mode-switching**
  Take the essence or intent of your artefact and recreate it in another mode. For instance, if you are painting an image, create a sculptural work or a dance movement that explores similar ideas. This cross-modal translation may reveal aspects of your concept you hadn't recognised.[7]
- **Planned spontaneity**
  Sculptor Jacques Lipchitz describes his approach to overcoming a block in his sculpture practice:

  > I decided to take my creative temperature. I determined to go to the foundry each morning and every day to make a spontaneous sculpture from one of the leftover wax chisels. In twenty-six working days I made twenty-six sculptures. It was a cure. After that I was ready to go on—to go on to more planned work.
  >
  > *(as interviewed by Kuh (1962) 2000, 156)*

  This strategy, committing to regular spontaneous making within constraints, can break perfectionism and restore creative flow.

- **Unrelated activity**
  It is often the case that "idea generation and problem-solving occur frequently during unrelated tasks" (Bourgeois-Bougrine and Glăveanu 2018, 139). This strategy seems obvious, but when blocked, it's easy to forget simple solutions. Let your work rest and do anything else. Often, while vacuuming, walking, or shopping, your conscious mind is distracted, but your unconscious mind may still work on solving your problem.

There are many other practical approaches worth exploring, including documenting and reviewing work, applying artificial constraints to spark creativity, or changing your work environment. Experiment to discover what works for you.

## Notes

1 See Inger Mewburn et al. (2019, 9), Katherine Firth et al. (2021, 125-126), Thomson and Kamler (2016, 166), and Shut Up and Write (2026).
2 See Firth et al. (2021, 2-4; 111-127) and Peta Freestone (2025).
3 See also Mewburn et al. (2019, 76-79).
4 See Narelle Lemon (2023), Helen Kara (2020), and Heidi van Rooyan and Raphael d'Abdon (2025).
5 See Firth et al. (2021, 39-42) and Francesco Cirillo (2025-2026).
6 See also Firth et al. (2021, 116-117).
7 Kenneth Steinbach also presents this strategy in the context of visual art education (2018, 89). He also lists other methods that may prove supportive for your particular work.

## References

Beattie, Annalea. 2014. "How Artists Write in a Doctoral Writing Circle." In *Doctoral Writing in the Creative and Performing Arts*, edited by Louise Ravelli, Brian Paltridge, and Sue Starfield. Libri Publishing.
Bolker, Joan. 1998. *Writing your Dissertation in Fifteen Minutes a Day: A Guide to Starting, Revising, and Finishing your Doctoral Thesis*. Holt Paperbacks.
Bourgeois-Bougrine, Samira, and Vlad Petre Glăveanu. 2018. "Collaborative Scriptwriting: Social and Psychological Factors." In *The Creative Process: Perspectives form Multiple Domains*, edited by Todd Lubart. Palgrave Macmillan.
Cirillo, Francesco. "Pomodoro Technique." Updated 2025–2026. https://www.pomodorotechnique.com/
Faulkner, Sandra L. 2020. *Poetic Inquiry: Craft, Method and Practice*, 2nd ed. Routledge.

Firth, Katherine. 2024. *Writing Well and Being Well for Your PhD and Beyond: How to Cultivate a Strong and Sustainable Writing Practice for Life*. Routledge.

Firth, Katherine, Liam Connell, and Peta Freestone. 2021. *Your PhD Survival Guide: Planning, Writing, and Succeeding in Your Final Year*. Routledge. (See part III, "Focusing on the Text.")

Freestone, Peta. "Thesis Boot Camp." Dr. Peta Freestone, updated 2025. https://www.petafreestone.com/thesis-boot-camp

Kara, Helen. 2020. *Creative Research Methods: A Practical Guide*, 2nd ed. Bristol University Press.

Kuh, Katharine. (1960) 2000. *The Artist's Voice: Talks with Seventeen Artists*. Harper and Row.

Lamott, Anne. 1994/2020. *Bird by Bird: Instructions on Writing and Life*. Canongate Books. (See part 1, "Writing.")

Lemon, Narelle. 2023. "Poetic Inquiry: Transformational Representations of Wellbeing and Self-care in Higher Education." In *Creative Expression and Wellbeing in Higher Education: Making and Movement as Mindful Moments of Self-care*, edited by Narelle Lemon. Routledge.

Mewburn, Inger, Katherine Firth, and Shaun Lehmann. 2019. *How to Fix your Academic Writing Trouble: A Practical Guide*. McGraw-Hill Education. (See chap. 4, "Your Writing doesn't Flow: Making Your Text Coherent and Fluent.")

Ranković, Katarina 2023. "Scripting for Agency." PhD diss., Goldsmiths, University of London. https://bit.ly/sfa-pdf

Reading, Christina. 2024. "Real and Imagined Explorations of Self: A Conversation with Katarina Ranković." In *Conversations on Creative Process, Methods, Research and Practice: Feminist Approaches to Nurturing the Creative Self*, edited by Christina Reading and Jess Moriarty. Routledge.

Shut Up and Write, updated 2026. https://www.shutupwrite.com/

Steinback, Kenneth. 2018. *Creative Practices for Visual Artists: Time, Space, Process*. Routledge. (See chap. 7, "Creative Practices.")

Thomson, Pat, and Barbara Kamler. 2016. *Detox Your Writing: Strategies for Doctoral Researchers*. Oxfordshire: Routledge. (See chap. 7, "Structuring the Thesis.")

van Rooyan, Heidi, and Raphael d'Abdon, eds. 2025. *Poetic Inquiry as Research: A Decolonial Guide*. Bristol University Press.

# INDEX

Pages in **bold** refer to tables, and pages followed by "n" refer to notes.

For Product Safety Concerns and Information please contact our EU
representative GPSR@taylorandfrancis.com
Taylor & Francis Verlag GmbH, Kaufingerstraße 24, 80331 München, Germany

www.ingramcontent.com/pod-product-compliance
Lightning Source LLC
LaVergne TN
LVHW011246220926
848584LV00027B/290
*9781032953076*